graphis annual   84|85

84|85 graphis annual

The International Annual of Advertising and
Editorial Graphics

Das internationale Jahrbuch der Werbe-
graphik und der redaktionellen Graphik

Le répertoire international de l'art graphique
publicitaire et rédactionnel

Edited by / Herausgegeben von / Réalisé par:

Walter Herdeg

Graphis Press Corp., Zurich (Switzerland)

GRAPHIS PUBLICATIONS

GRAPHIS, International bi-monthly journal of graphic art and applied art
PHOTOGRAPHIS, The international annual of advertising and editorial photography
GRAPHIS POSTERS, The international annual of poster art
GRAPHIS PACKAGING VOL. 4, An international survey of package design
CHILDREN'S BOOK ILLUSTRATION VOL. 3, VOL. 4, An international survey of children's book illustration
GRAPHIS DIAGRAMS, The graphic visualization of abstract data
FILM + TV GRAPHICS 2, An international survey of the art of film animation
ARCHIGRAPHIA, Architectural and environmental graphics
GRAPHIS EPHEMERA, Artists' Self-Promotion

GRAPHIS-PUBLIKATIONEN

GRAPHIS, Die internationale Zweimonatsschrift für Graphik und angewandte Kunst
PHOTOGRAPHIS, Das internationale Jahrbuch der Werbephotographie und der redaktionellen Photographie
GRAPHIS POSTERS, Das internationale Jahrbuch der Plakatkunst
GRAPHIS PACKUNGEN BAND 4, Internationales Handbuch der Packungsgestaltung
KINDERBUCH-ILLUSTRATION BAND 3, BAND 4, Eine internationale Übersicht über die Kinderbuch-Illustration
GRAPHIS DIAGRAMS, Die graphische Visualisierung abstrakter Gegebenheiten
FILM + TV GRAPHICS 2, Ein internationaler Überblick über die Kunst des Animationsfilms
ARCHIGRAPHIA, Architektur- und Umweltgraphik
GRAPHIS EPHEMERA, Künstler-Eigenwerbung

PUBLICATIONS GRAPHIS

GRAPHIS, La revue bimestrielle internationale d'arts graphiques et d'arts appliqués
PHOTOGRAPHIS, Le répertoire international de la photographie publicitaire et rédactionnelle
GRAPHIS POSTERS, Le répertoire international de l'art de l'affiche
GRAPHIS EMBALLAGES VOL. 4, Répertoire international des formes de l'emballage
ILLUSTRATIONS DE LIVRES D'ENFANTS VOL. 3, VOL. 4, Un aperçu international des illustrations de livres d'enfants
GRAPHIS DIAGRAMS, La visualisation graphique de données abstraites
FILM + TV GRAPHICS 2, Un panorama international de l'art du film d'animation
ARCHIGRAPHIA, La création graphique appliquée à l'architecture et à l'environnement
GRAPHIS EPHEMERA, Autopromotion des artistes

Distributors / Auslieferung / Distribution:

USA: WATSON-GUPTILL PUBLICATIONS, INC., 1515 Broadway, New York, N.Y. 10036 – **(ISBN: 0-8230-2156-4)**
CANADA: HURTIG PUBLISHERS, 10560-105 Street, Edmonton, Alberta T5H 2W7, tel. (403) 426-2469
FRANCE: GRAPHIS DISTRIBUTION, Milon-la-Chapelle, F-78470 St-Rémy-lès-Chevreuse, tél. 052-13-26
ITALIA: INTER-ORBIS, Via Lorenteggio, 31/1, I-20146 Milano, tel. 422 57 46
SPAIN: COMERCIAL ATHENEUM, S.A., Consejo de Ciento, 130-136, Barcelona 15, tel. 223 14 51-3
AMERICA LATINA, AUSTRALIA, JAPAN AND OTHER ASIAN COUNTRIES, AFRICA:
FLEETBOOKS S.A., c/o Feffer & Simons, Inc., 100 Park Avenue, New York, N.Y. 10017, tel. (212) 686-0888

All other countries / Alle anderen Länder / Tout autres pays:

GRAPHIS PRESS CORP., 107 Dufourstrasse, CH-8008 Zurich (Switzerland)

PUBLICATION No. 176 (ISBN 3-85709-184-3)

Contents   Inhalt   Sommaire

Abbreviations Abkürzungen Abréviations

Argentina	ARG	Argentinien	ARG	Afrique du Sud	SAF
Australia	AUS	Australien	AUS	Allemagne occidentale	GER
Austria	AUT	Belgien	BEL	Argentine	ARG
Belgium	BEL	Brasilien	BRA	Australie	AUS
Brazil	BRA	Bulgarien	BUL	Autriche	AUT
Bulgaria	BUL	Dänemark	DEN	Belgique	BEL
Canada	CAN	Deutschland (BRD)	GER	Brésil	BRA
Columbia	COL	Finnland	FIN	Bulgarie	BUL
Cuba	CUB	Frankreich	FRA	Canada	CAN
Czechoslovakia	CSR	Grossbritannien	GBR	Colombie	COL
Denmark	DEN	Hongkong	HKG	Cuba	CUB
Finland	FIN	Indien	IND	Danemark	DEN
France	FRA	Iran	IRN	Espagne	SPA
Germany (West)	GER	Irland	IRL	Etats-Unis	USA
Great Britain	GBR	Island	ICE	Finlande	FIN
Hong Kong	HKG	Israel	ISR	France	FRA
Iceland	ICE	Italien	ITA	Grande-Bretagne	GBR
India	IND	Japan	JPN	Hongkong	HKG
Iran	IRN	Kanada	CAN	Inde	IND
Ireland	IRL	Kolumbien	COL	Indes-Occidentales	WIN
Israel	ISR	Korea	KOR	Iran	IRN
Italy	ITA	Kuba	CUB	Irlande	IRL
Japan	JPN	Mexiko	MEX	Islande	ICE
Korea	KOR	Niederlande	NLD	Israël	ISR
Mexico	MEX	Norwegen	NOR	Italie	ITA
Netherlands	NLD	Österreich	AUT	Japon	JPN
Norway	NOR	Peru	PER	Korea	KOR
Peru	PER	Polen	POL	Mexique	MEX
Poland	POL	Portugal	POR	Norvège	NOR
Portugal	POR	Schweden	SWE	Pays-Bas	NLD
South Africa	SAF	Schweiz	SWI	Peru	PER
Spain	SPA	Spanien	SPA	Pologne	POL
Sweden	SWE	Südafrika	SAF	Portugal	POR
Switzerland	SWI	Tschechoslowakei	CSR	Suède	SWE
USA	USA	USA	USA	Suisse	SWI
West Indies	WIN	Westindien	WIN	Tchécoslovaquie	CSR

COVER / UMSCHLAG / COUVERTURE
Design / Entwurf / Maquette: Milton Glaser
Photograph / Aufnahme / Photo: Matthew Klein

At this point we should like once again to heartily thank our friends and co-workers throughout the world. Their untiring support has made it possible for us to compile this comprehensive, versatile and in an artistic respect, fascinating selection.

An dieser Stelle möchten wir wiederum unseren Freunden und Mitarbeitern in aller Welt herzlich danken. Ihre unermüdliche Unterstützung hat es uns ermöglicht, diese umfassende, vielseitige und in künstlerischer Hinsicht faszinierende Auswahl zusammenzustellen.

Nous aimerions une fois de plus remercier chaleureusement nos amis et collaborateurs dans le monde entier, dont l'appui jamais démenti nous a permis de procéder à cette sélection exhaustive, aux facettes multiples, fascinante par son caractère artistique. Qu'ils trouvent ici l'expression de notre vive reconnaissance!

MILTON GLASER, the designer of our cover, is so well-known in the profession that we will limit ourselves here to a few highlights in his career. His work has been appreciated not only in numerous publications, but also in one-man shows including the Museum of Modern Art, the Royal Museum of Fine Arts in Brussels the Pompidou Centre and the Lincoln Center Gallery. His latest work is to be seen in a two-year touring exhibition in Japan. His new book *The Conversation* (Harmony Books), produced in collaboration with Jean Michel Folon, is now on the international book market.

MILTON GLASER, der Gestalter des Umschlags, ist in der Fachwelt so bekannt, dass wir uns hier auf einige Höhepunkte seiner Karriere beschränken wollen. Seine Arbeiten wurden nicht nur in zahlreichen Publikationen gewürdigt, sondern auch in Einzelausstellungen, u. a. im Museum of Modern Art, im Musée Royal des Beaux-Arts in Brüssel, im Centre Pompidou und in der Lincoln Center Gallery. In einer zwei Jahre dauernden Wanderausstellung sind gegenwärtig seine neuesten Arbeiten in Japan zu sehen. Neu auf dem internationalen Buchmarkt ist *The Conversation* (Harmony Books, Crown Publishers), ein Buch, das in Zusammenarbeit mit Jean Michel Folon entstanden ist.

MILTON GLASER, qui a réalisé notre couverture, est une telle vedette de sa spécialité que nous nous bornerons ici à évoquer quelques points culminants de sa carrière. Ses travaux n'ont pas seulement eu les honneurs de nombreuses publications, mais aussi d'expositions individuelles, entre autres au Museum of Modern Art, au Musée royal des beaux-arts de Bruxelles, au Centre Georges-Pompidou et à la Lincoln Center Gallery. Une exposition itinérante sur deux ans fait actuellement connaître ses derniers travaux au Japon. Il vient de publier un ouvrage réalisé en collaboration avec Jean Michel Folon, *The Conversation* (Harmony Books, Crown Publishers).

Philip B. Meggs

Preface

The author of our introduction, Philip B. Meggs, is a graphic designer, author, and educator. He serves as Chairman of the Communication Arts and Design Department of Virginia Commonwealth University in Richmond, Virginia, where he teaches design and lectures on design history. His books include *A History of Graphic Design* and *Typographic Design: Form and Communication*, co-authored with Rob Carter and Ben Day.

The philosopher Marshall McLuhan spoke of the world as being "recreated in the image of a global village". Phenomenal advances in communication and transportation have made his observation a reality, and we find ourselves on a shrinking globe where time and place are increasingly compressed. In 1620 the sailing vessel "Mayflower" required sixty-six days to transport its passengers from Europe to North America; by contrast, the Concorde supersonic jetliner reduces travel time between Paris and New York to a mere three hours. Today, we find that voices, data, and images are projected around the globe by instantaneous satellite transmission.

A vast international dialogue now takes place, influencing all aspects of human activity. Visual communications has become an international profession, for concepts and innovations spread beyond national boundaries to become part of a worldwide language of forms and images. Major design periodicals with globe-girding circulations rapidly disseminate contemporary work. The formal vocabulary of European constructivism can be found in Japan, where it combines with more traditional, oriental ways of organizing space. Likewise, paraphrases of popular culture from the United States, such as the ubiquitous comic book iconography and product marketing strategies, can be found in the emerging graphic arts of developing nations.

During the postwar period, innovation in graphics has been associated with specific cities, including Basel, Zurich, New York and Tokyo. The broad influence of design ideas from these centres has led to cries of cultural imperialism, the imposition of one society's values and lifestyles upon another society. But design from these centres has not been a steamroller overturning the culture of other nations; rather, the concepts developed in these centres have flourished and expanded in the hands of sensitive designers who are working in countries throughout the world.

Because visual communications is an applied *art* form, with cultural and aesthetic values—as well as a major communications vehicle, with significant social and economic importance, this internationalism raises important philosophical questions for the graphic designer. Should the designer have a responsibility to his or her own national culture, and attempt to develop forms and images that express the experience of that nation? Or does the designer's responsibility now extend beyond national boundaries, relating to the inhabitants of the "global village"? Strong arguments can be made on both sides of this issue. On the one hand, the international role of graphic design becomes inescapable in an era of multinational corporations that operate in over one hundred countries. It might be said that the sun never sets on the logotypes of large corporations whose activities span the globe. International airports and events, such as the Olympics and world expositions, require objective graphics that transcend language and speak with universal symbols to the global family.

This objective approach to graphic design goes beyond the functional communication of information. It must delve deeply into the nature of the problem, which must be fully comprehended by the designer before and during the design process. The needs and aspirations of the audience become a major concern of the responsible designer.

The problem of internationalism versus nationalism might be comprehended by defining the global village concept. A village is a unit of compact settlement, a community. The lives of all the inhabitants interlace with, and influence, the lives of one another. Extending this concept to a global scale, one finds that individuals and nations cannot exist in isolation from the sweep of world events. Happenings in the Middle East and Central America profoundly affect life in Europe and North America. A world view becomes important for the graphic designer, for human understanding and communications no longer know any national boundaries.

Ultimately, discussion about international and national design poses a perplexing dilemma. The human family is united by common needs and dreams, yet it possesses great diversity and cultural plurality. If graphic design is to speak to and for the human community, a similar plurality of expression is needed. One exciting occurrence of recent times has been the unfolding of significant design in Middle Eastern, Latin American, and other developing nations. It is hoped that designers in these nations will learn from the global dialogue, while maintaining and developing unique heritages within their national cultures.

As we struggle with the problems and challenges raised by a shrinking globe and multinational communications, we must not forget that the language of design has often been extended by those individuals who stubbornly follow their own vision, ignoring accepted professional standards and contemporary styles. Individual intuition, poetic expression, and the unexpected viewpoint must never be discarded. Indeed, our experience is enriched by folk art and ethnic expressions as surely as it is expanded by objective, universal visual communications.

Philip B. Meggs

Vorwort

Der Autor dieser Einführung, Philip B. Meggs, ist Graphik-Designer, Autor und Lehrer. Als Leiter der Fakultät für Kommunikations-Graphik und Design an der Virginia Commonwealth University, Richmond, Virginia, unterrichtet er Design und hält Vorlesungen über Design-Geschichte. In diesem Zusammenhang seien zwei der von ihm veröffentlichten Bücher erwähnt: *A History of Graphic Design* und *Typographic Design: Form and Communication* (das letztere entstand in Zusammenarbeit mit Rob Carter und Ben Day).

Der Philosoph Marshall McLuhan sah die Welt als «Neuschöpfung nach dem Bild eines globalen Dorfes». Phänomenale Fortschritte in Kommunikation und Transportmöglichkeiten liessen diese Behauptung Wirklichkeit werden; wir befinden uns heute in einer immer kleiner werdenden Welt, in der Zeit und Raum zusammenschrumpfen. Anno 1620 benötigte das Segelschiff «Mayflower» für den Transport seiner Passagiere von Europa nach Nordamerika sechsundsechzig Tage, während der Flug von Paris nach New York mit dem Ultraschall-Jet Concorde heute gerade noch drei Stunden dauert. Und Stimmen, Fakten und Bilder werden dank der Satelliten quasi in Direktübertragung in alle Welt ausgestrahlt.

Es findet ein grosser internationaler Dialog statt, der alle Aspekte der menschlichen Tätigkeiten beeinflusst. Visuelle Kommunikation ist zu einem internationalen Beruf geworden, denn Konzepte und Innovationen überschreiten die nationalen Grenzen und werden Teil einer internationalen Sprache der Formen und Bilder. Bedeutende Design-Zeitschriften mit weltweiter Zirkulation verhelfen zeitgenössischen Arbeiten zu rapider Verbreitung. Das formale Vokabular des europäischen Konstruktivismus taucht in Japan auf, wo es mit traditionelleren fernöstlichen Arten der Raumaufteilung kombiniert wird. Ebenso sind Elemente der Populär-Kultur der Vereinigten Staaten, wie z. B. die allgegenwärtige Ikonographie der Komikbücher und die Produkt-Marketing-Strategien, in der heranwachsenden graphischen Kunst der Entwicklungsländer zu finden.

Während der Nachkriegszeit wurde Innovation in der Graphik mit bestimmten Städten assoziiert, wie u.a. Basel, Zürich, New York und Tokio. Der grosse Einfluss der Design-Ideen, der von diesen Zentren ausging, führte zu dem Begriff des «kulturellen Imperialismus»: die Überschüttung einer Gesellschaft mit den Werten und dem Lebensstil einer anderen. Aber Design aus diesen Zentren wirkte durchaus nicht wie eine Dampfwalze, welche die Kulturen anderer Nationen überrollt; die Konzepte, die an solchen Orten entwickelt wurden, blühten und gediehen in den Händen begabter Graphik-Designer, die es überall auf der Welt gibt.

Weil die visuelle Kommunikation eine angewandte Form der *Kunst*, mit kulturellen und ästhetischen Werten ist und gleichzeitig ein wichtiges Kommunikationsmittel von grosser sozialer und wirtschaftlicher Bedeutung darstellt, erwachsen für den Graphik-Designer aus diesem Internationalismus wichtige philosophische Fragen. Sollte er sich seiner nationalen Kultur verpflichtet fühlen und versuchen, Formen und Bilder zu entwickeln, welche die Erfahrungen seiner Nation ausdrücken, oder geht die Verantwortung des Graphik-Designers als Bewohner des «globalen Dorfes» jetzt über die nationalen Grenzen hinaus? Für beide Standpunkte gibt es gute Argumente. Einerseits muss Graphik Design international sein in einer Zeit der multinationalen Gesellschaften, die in über hundert Ländern operieren. Man könnte sagen, dass auf den Firmensymbolen der grossen Gesellschaften, deren Aktivitäten den Globus umspannen, die Sonne nie untergeht. Internationale Flughäfen und Veranstaltungen, wie die Olympiade und Weltausstellungen, verlangen objektive Graphik, die über die Sprache hinausgeht und mittels universaler Symbole zur globalen Familie spricht.

Diese objektive Lösung der Design-Aufgaben geht über die funktionelle Kommunikation hinaus. Sie verlangt vom Designer eine sorgfältige Analyse der Problemstellung, er muss die Aufgabe ganz begreifen und sich ihrer vor und während des Design-Prozesses vollkommen bewusst sein. Die Bedürfnisse und Wünsche des Publikums sind für den verantwortungsbewussten Designer ein Hauptanliegen.

Wenn man sich das Konzept des globalen Dorfes vergegenwärtigt, mag das Problem «Internationalismus versus Nationalismus» verständlicher werden. Ein Dorf bedeutet eine Einheit, eine kompakte Siedlung, eine Gemeinschaft. Das Leben der Einwohner ist miteinander verflochten und der gegenseitigen Beeinflussung ausgesetzt. Wenn man dieses Konzept auf die globale Stufe überträgt, begreift man, dass weder der einzelne noch Nationen sich den Ereignissen in der Welt entziehen können. Das Geschehen im Mittleren Osten und in Mittelamerika beeinflusst das Leben in Europa und Nordamerika entscheidend. Der Graphik-Designer muss dies verarbeiten und umsetzen, weil Verstehen und Kommunikation zwischen den Menschen keine nationalen Grenzen mehr kennen.

Schlussendlich gerät die Diskussion über internationales und nationales Design in ein verwirrendes Dilemma. Gemeinsame Bedürfnisse und Träume vereinen die menschliche Gesellschaft, während sie sich gleichzeitig durch eine immense Vielfalt und kulturelle Pluralität auszeichnet. Wenn Graphik-Design mit und für die menschliche Gesellschaft sprechen soll, ist eine ähnliche Pluralität des Ausdrucks notwendig. Eines der beeindruckendsten Ereignisse der jüngeren Zeit ist das Zutagetreten bedeutenden Designs im Mittleren Osten, in Latein-Amerika und anderen aufstrebenden Regionen der Welt. Es ist zu hoffen, dass Graphik-Designer in diesen Ländern von dem globalen Dialog lernen und gleichzeitig das einzigartige Erbe ihrer nationalen Kulturen beibehalten und entwickeln.

Wenn wir uns mit den Problemen und Aufgaben des zusammenschrumpfenden Globus und der multinationalen Kommunikation befassen, dürfen wir nicht vergessen, dass die Sprache des Designs oft von jenen bereichert wird, die hartnäckig ihrer eigenen Vision folgen, indem sie anerkannte professionelle Normen und zeitgenössische Stilrichtungen ignorieren. Individuelle Intuition, poetische Ausdrucksformen und ungewöhnliche Gesichtspunkte dürfen nicht verlorengehen. Schlussendlich werden unsere Erfahrungen durch Volkskunst und ethnische Ausdrucksarten ebenso bereichert, wie sie durch objektive und universale visuelle Kommunikation erweitert werden.

Philip B. Meggs

Préface

L'auteur de notre préface, Philip B. Meggs, est un graphiste, auteur et enseignant de valeur. Président du Département d'arts de la communication et de design de la Virginia Commonwealth University de Richmond (Virginie, U.S.A.), il enseigne l'art graphique appliqué et l'histoire du design. Citons parmi ses livres *A History of Graphic Design*, ainsi que *Typographic Design: Form and Communication*, écrit en collaboration avec Rob Carter et Ben Day.

Le philosophe des médias Marshall McLuhan voyait le monde où nous vivons «recréé dans l'image d'un village global». Les progrès extraordinaires réalisés dans les communications et les transports ont traduit cette vue dans les faits, de sorte que nous habitons aujourd'hui un globe terrestre en peau de chagrin, où le temps et l'espace sont comprimés de plus en plus. Le voilier «Mayflower» de 1620 mit encore 66 jours à faire la traversée de l'Atlantique, que le Concorde supersonique expédie aujourd'hui en trois heures, reliant Paris à New York. Et les voix, les données et les images sont projetées quasiment sans délai autour du globe grâce à la transmission instantanée par satellite.

Un vaste dialogue international s'est instauré, qui influence tous les aspects de l'activité des hommes. Les communications visuelles ont accédé au stade d'une profession internationale, car les conceptions et les innovations franchissent les frontières nationales pour s'intégrer dans un langage mondial des formes et des images. Les grandes publications périodiques en matière de design, avec leur diffusion circumterrestre, font rapidement connaître les créations contemporaines à l'échelle mondiale. Le vocabulaire formel du constructivisme européen peut se retrouver au Japon, où il se combine avec des manières plus traditionnelles, proprement orientales d'organiser l'espace. De façon analogue, des paraphrases de la culture populaire étatsunienne, telles l'iconographie omniprésente de la bande dessinée et les stratégies de marketing de produits, se retrouvent dans les arts graphiques qui naissent dans les pays en voie de développement.

L'après-guerre avait vu certaines villes prétendre à la primauté en matière d'innovation graphique. L'influence qu'exercèrent ainsi Bâle, Zurich, New York et Tōkyō, pour ne nommer que celles-là, fit hurler un certain temps à l'impérialisme culturel, à la dictature imposant les valeurs et styles de vie d'une société à d'autres sociétés désarmées sur le plan du design. Justice doit toutefois être rendue à ces centres, dont les créations n'ont pas servi de rouleau compresseur nivelant les aspirations culturelles d'autres nations. On constate bien plutôt que les conceptions élaborées dans ces centres urbains se sont épanouies et développées entre les mains de designers doués de sensibilité œuvrant dans tous les pays du monde.

Les communications visuelles représentent une forme d'*art* appliqué porteur de valeurs culturelles et esthétiques, en même temps qu'un véhicule de communication capital. C'est ce caractère international qui suscite des questions philosophiques importantes, que le designer doit résoudre impérativement. Doit-il opter pour sa propre culture nationale et, fort de sa responsabilité à son égard, chercher à développer des formes et des images qui donnent expression à l'expérience particulière de cette nation? Ou est-ce que sa responsabilité s'étend désormais par-delà les frontières, englobant les habitants du «village global»? Des arguments de poids peuvent être invoqués en faveur de l'une ou l'autre de ces conceptions. Il faut bien reconnaître que le rôle international du design est dorénavant ancré dans le fait même que les grandes entreprises multinationales opèrent dans une centaine de pays à la fois. Paraphrasant Charles Quint, on pourrait dire que, de nos jours, le soleil ne se couche jamais sur les logos des groupes dont l'activité s'étend à la planète entière. Tant les aéroports que les manifestations internationales telles que les Jeux Olympiques et les expositions universelles imposent la mise au point de réalisations graphiques qui transcendent les barrières linguistiques et s'adressent en symboles universels à la famille globale.

Cette approche objective de l'art graphique appliqué dépasse la seule fonction de communication inhérente à l'information. Elle nécessite de la part du graphiste l'analyse en profondeur du problème posé qui doit être compris à fond dès avant et tout le long du processus créatif. Les besoins et les aspirations du public visé deviennent la préoccupation majeure du designer responsable.

L'antinomie internationalisme – nationalisme se résout lorsque l'on se donne la peine de définir le concept de village global. Un village est une unité compacte de peuplement, une communauté. La vie de tous ses habitants s'interpénètre, chacune influençant celle des autres. En appliquant ce concept à l'échelle planétaire, on découvre que les nations, pas plus que les individus, ne peuvent vivre hors du courant majeur des événements affectant la communauté mondiale. L'isolation n'est plus possible. Ce qui se produit au Proche-Orient et en Amérique centrale exerce une influence durable sur la vie en Europe et en Amérique du Nord. L'artiste publicitaire doit nécessairement développer une vision intégrée du monde où il vit, étant donné que la compréhension et les communications entre hommes ignorent désormais les frontières nationales.

En fin de compte, le débat sur la dimension internationale ou nationale du design soulève un dilemme de taille. La famille humaine est unie par des besoins et des rêves communs et se caractérise néanmoins par une extrême diversité, ainsi que par un pluralisme culturel. Si le design graphique entend parler à et pour la communauté des hommes, il doit rechercher un pluralisme analogue de l'expression. Un développement récent des plus prometteurs à cet égard est l'avènement d'un design remarquable au sein des nations du Proche-Orient, d'Amérique centrale et d'autres régions du globe en voie de développement. Espérons que les artistes de ces pays s'instruiront par le dialogue global tout en préservant et en développant leur héritage culturel national exceptionnel.

Dans la mesure où nous nous expliquons avec les problèmes et les défis posés par une planète qui va en se rétrécissant et par le réseau grandissant des communications multinationales, nous garderons présente à l'esprit l'action féconde de créateurs individuels obstinément attachés à leur vision personnelle en dépit de toute norme professionnelle reconnue et de tout style contemporain, et qui ont fait beaucoup pour élargir le champ d'action du langage du design. L'intuition individuelle, l'expression poétique et la perspective insolite sont des atouts à ne jamais écarter. En somme, notre expérience s'enrichit autant par le retour aux sources populaires et à l'expression spécifique d'une ethnie qu'elle s'élargit par le fait de communications visuelles objectives et universelles.

Index to Artists
Verzeichnis der Künstler
Index des Artistes

Index to Designers
Verzeichnis der Gestalter
Index des Maquettistes

Index to Art Directors
Verzeichnis der künstlerischen Leiter
Index des Directeurs Artistiques

Index to Publishers
Verzeichnis der Verleger
Index des Editeurs

Index to Agencies, Studios and Producers
Verzeichnis der Agenturen, Studios und Produzenten
Index des Agences, Studios et Producteurs

Index to Advertisers
Verzeichnis der Auftraggeber
Index des Clients

■ Entry instructions may be requested by anyone interested in submitting samples of exceptional graphics or photography for possible inclusion in our annuals. No fees involved. Closing dates for entries:
GRAPHIS ANNUAL (advertising and editorial art and design): 31 January
PHOTOGRAPHIS (advertising and editorial photography): 30 June
GRAPHIS POSTERS (an annual of poster art): 30 June
Write to: Graphis Press Corp., Dufourstrasse 107, 8008 Zurich, Switzerland

■ Einsendebedingungen können von jedermann angefordert werden, der uns Beispiele hervorragender Photographie oder Graphik zur Auswahl für unsere Jahrbücher unterbreiten möchte. Es werden keine Gebühren erhoben.
Einsendetermine:
GRAPHIS ANNUAL (Werbe- und redaktionelle Graphik): 31. Januar
PHOTOGRAPHIS (Werbe- und redaktionelle Photographie): 30. Juni
GRAPHIS POSTERS (ein Jahrbuch der Plakatkunst): 30. Juni
Adresse: Graphis Verlag AG, Dufourstrasse 107, 8008 Zürich, Schweiz

■ Tout intéressé à la soumission de travaux photographiques et graphiques recevra les informations nécessaires sur demande. Sans charge de participation.
Dates limites:
GRAPHIS ANNUAL (art graphique publicitaire et rédactionnel): 31 janvier
PHOTOGRAPHIS (photographie publicitaire et rédactionnelle): 30 juin
GRAPHIS POSTERS (annuaire sur l'art de l'affiche): 30 juin
S'adresser à: Editions Graphis SA, Dufourstrasse 107, 8008 Zurich, Suisse

Editor and Art Director: Walter Herdeg
Assistant Editor: Joan Lüssi
Project Managers: Romy Herzog, Heinke Jenssen
Designers: Marino Bianchera, Martin Byland,
Art Assistants: Peter Wittwer, Walter Zuber

1

Magazine Advertisements

Newspaper Advertisements

Zeitschriften-Inserate

Zeitungs-Inserate

Annonces de revues

Annonces de presse

Unfortunately, most food allergy regimens tend to cut patients down to size.

In a big chunk of the world they'd call that starvation: depriving someone of essential nutrition.

And for that very reason, rice diets or near total abstinence aren't really ideal diagnostic tools.

Malnutrition never is.

But there is a way to eliminate practically *all* possible allergens without seriously compromising nutrition:

STANDARD VIVONEX®

A nutritionally complete and chemically defined

medical alternative to traditional elimination methods, STANDARD VIVONEX enables allergic patients to become symptom-free within days, ready and encouraged to continue the search for offending foods.

And, because STANDARD VIVONEX is the most hypoallergenic medical food available anywhere, diagnosis becomes definitive, not debilitating.

STANDARD VIVONEX.

It's only deficient in allergens.

STANDARD VIVONEX®

the reason some patients do better than others

SELECT SYVA® QST™ TECHNOLOGY FOR 30-DAY CURVE STABILITY

With a 30-day standard curve, the Syva Qst System makes drug testing practical and economical — even for single samples. Premeasured and premixed in single vials, Qst powdered drug assays make it easy for any technologist to get a quantitative result in as little as 50 seconds. Instant access to drug monitoring any day on any shift. What's more, the system also performs qualitative Emit®st™ toxicology assays. The Syva Qst System. Another reason why you should never settle for less than Syva.

SELECT, DON'T SETTLE.   SYVA

The rubber damn.

Our employees have worked for centuries perfecting our product line.

5

ARTIST / KÜNSTLER / ARTISTE:

1 R.O. Blechman
2 Lonni Sue Johnson
3 Bill Mayer
4 Bernard Durin
5, 6 Osterwalder Office

DESIGNER / GESTALTER / MAQUETTISTE:

1 James McFarland
2 Orin Kimball
3, 4 Bill Kumke
5, 6 Ernst Friedel Maischein

ART DIRECTOR / DIRECTEUR ARTISTIQUE:

1 James McFarland
2 Orin Kimball
3, 4 David Bartels
5, 6 Ernst Friedel Maischein

AGENCY / AGENTUR / AGENCE – STUDIO:

1 Lally, McFarland & Pantello
2 Gross Townsend Frank
3, 4 Bartels & Company, Inc.
5, 6 BASF/Werbung

6

Advertisements / Inserate / Annonces

1 Full-page colour ad in a campaign for *Standard Vivonex*, a medical nourishment for patients with food allergies—who must live on a strict diet until a medical search eliminates those foods to which they are allergic. (USA)
2 Trade-magazine advertisement for a drug testing system with a 30-day curve stability, marketed by the *Syva* company. Watercolour, mainly in shades of blue. (USA)
3, 4 From a series of trade-magazine colour ads for rubber and beeswax products used in dental moulding work. (USA)
5, 6 Illustration, in actual size, and the complete trade-magazine ad for BASF vitamin preparations. (GER)

1 Anzeige aus einer Kampagne für *Standard Vivonex*, das für die Ernährung bei Nahrungsmittel-Allergie empfohlen wird. Mehrfarbige Illustration. (USA)
2 Fachzeitschriften-Inserat für ein Nachweissystem für Medikamente mit einer 30-Tage-Kurvenstabilität. (USA)
3, 4 Beispiele aus einer Serie von mehrfarbigen Fachzeitschriften-Anzeigen für zahnmedizinische Produkte. In Abb. 3 geht es um eine Technik, in Abb. 4 um Dental-Wachs, das aus Bienenwachs gewonnen wird. (USA)
5, 6 Illustration in Originalgrösse und vollständige Fachzeitschriften-Anzeige für BASF-Vitamin-Präparate. (GER)

1 Annonce figurant dans une campagne pour *Standard Vivonex*, un produit recommandé pour les personnes souffrant d'allergie alimentaire. Illustration en polychromie. (USA)
2 Annonce de revue spécialisée: détection de médicaments présentant une courbe de stabilité de 30 jours. (USA)
3, 4 Exemples d'une série d'annonces de revues spécialisées, en polychromie, pour des produits dentaires de *Columbus Dental*. La fig. 3 illustre une technique, la fig. 4 une cire dentaire tirée de la cire d'abeilles. (USA)
5, 6 Illustration grandeur nature et annonce complète (revues spécialisées) pour les produits vitaminés BASF. (GER)

Im Grand-Hotel zum Amazonas.

wassers der Erde sind im Amazonasbecken gespeichert. Der Fluß ist 6300 km lang. Davon sind 3700 km für Überseeschiffe befahrbar. Seine Mündung ist 320 km breit, und in ihr liegt eine Insel, so groß wie die Schweiz. Die Wälder ringsum stehen seit über 100 Millionen Jahren. Die Pflanzen- und Tierwelt ist überreich. Es gibt allein 319 Kolibriarten und 1500 verschiedene Fische.

Die neue Europa ist wie ein wunderschönes und perfekt organisiertes Hotel. Mit Rezeption, Restaurant, Salons, Ladenstraße mit Frisiersalon, Juweliergeschäft, Boutique, Musikstudio, Bibliothek, Nachtclub,

FKK-Plätzchen, Fitness Center, Bars, Druckerei, Bäckerei, Sonnendeck, drei Schwimmbädern, verschiedenen Sportmöglichkeiten und vielem mehr.

Auf 600 Gäste kommen rund 300 Mann

(und Frau) Besatzung. Die privaten Räumlichkeiten – sprich Kabinen – sind fast alle 21 qm groß und haben bequeme Betten, ein reichlich bemessenes Bad, eine gemütliche Sitzecke, Telefon, Farbfernseher,

Klimaanlage usw. Alle Außenkabinen (das sind 82% aller Passagierkabinen) verfügen über ein 70 x 130 cm großes Doppelfenster.

Und während Sie endlich Ihr Lieblingsbuch lesen, endlich den

Wolken nachschauen, endlich jeden Tag ein paar Runden schwimmen, endlich mal zum Frühstück Champagner trinken, endlich das tun, wozu Sie zu Hause nie Zeit haben, bringt Sie unser schwimmen-

des Grand-Hotel zu den schönsten Plätzen dieser Welt. Zum Beispiel von der Karibik nach Brasilien und 1600 km den Amazonas hinauf.

Wenn Sie mehr über unser Grand-Hotel Europa und unsere Amazo-

nas-Kreuzfahrten wissen wollen, dann gehen Sie doch mal bei Ihrem Reisebüro vorbei. Dort sagt man Ihnen auch, wohin die Reisen sonst noch gehen (z.B. zur Packeisgrenze oder nach Sansibar, Bombay, Casa-

blanca, San Francisco, Manila, Istanbul, Kirkwall, Ibiza, Heraklion, Leningrad, Dublin... oder woanders hin...).

*Hapag-Lloyd AG
Kreuzfahrten
Postfach 107947
D-2800 Bremen 1*

DAS AMAZONASGEBIET ist 6,5 Mio. qkm groß (Europa ca. 10 Mio.). 2/3 des gesamten Süß-

Die neue Europa ·········· ⫽⫽ Hapag-Lloyd AG

7

ARTIST / KÜNSTLER / ARTISTE:

7 Dieter Ziegenfeuter
8 Wilfried Gebhard
9 Heseler & Heseler
10–12 Guy Billout

7–9 Double spreads in an advertising campaign by the *Hapag-Lloyd* line for cruises aboard its liner "Europa", shown by Fig. 7 in a setting appropriate for this "Grand Hotel to the Amazon" and, by Fig. 8, in cross-section of her thirteen decks. Fig. 9 details German thoroughness: any slight temperature change in the caviar store triggers a warning in the way headlined here, "Caviar Alarm on the Bridge!" (GER)
10–12 Full-colour advertisements using graphic interpretation of ancient Japanese proverbs, in a JAL campaign for the Japanese airline's cargo division. (USA)

7–9 Doppelseitige Inserate aus einer Kampagne für das Kreuzfahrtenschiff «ms Europa» von *Hapag-Lloyd*. Das Hauptthema in allen drei Anzeigen sind die Annehmlichkeiten, die das Schiff bietet. (GER)
10–12 Beispiele aus einer Kampagne für Luftfracht mit der japanischen Fluggesellschaft JAL. Alle Illustrationen interpretieren alte japanische Sprichworte: «Durchquere einen seichten Strom so vorsichtig wie einen tiefen»; «Auch die längste Reise beginnt mit einem einzelnen Schritt»; «Wenn man nicht in die Höhle geht, kann man den Tiger nicht fangen». (USA)

7–9 Annonces double page pour une campagne en faveur des croisières à bord du paquebot «Europa» de la *Hapag-Lloyd*. Ces annonces font ressortir le confort et les agréments qu'offre la vie à bord. (GER)
10–12 Exemples tirés d'une campagne pour le fret transporté par la compagnie aérienne japonaise JAL. Toutes les illustrations interprètent d'antiques proverbes japonais: «traverse un fleuve guéable avec autant de prudence qu'un fleuve profond»; «même le voyage le plus long commence par un seul pas»; et finalement: «si l'on ne pénètre pas dans la caverne où il se terre, on n'aura pas de chance d'attraper le tigre». (USA)

Kaviar-Alarm auf der Kommandobrücke!

Es waren einmal zwei deutsche Reedereien. Die eine hieß »Hamburg-Amerikanische Packetfahrt-Actien-Gesellschaft«, kürzer Hapag. Die andere war der »Norddeutsche Lloyd« in Bremen. Beide taten sich 1970 als Hapag-Lloyd zusammen; doch jede Reederei hatte bereits vorher mit über 1300 Schiffen jede Menge Erfahrung auf den sieben Meeren gesammelt. Und das spüren Sie, wenn Sie auf das Hapag-Lloyd-Kreuzfahrtschiff ms Europa kommen. Hier geht's ganz schön gründlich, pünktlich und perfekt zu.

Beispielsweise die Landausflüge: Sie werden ein Jahr im voraus organisiert. Wenn wir am Mittwoch, dem 26. Dezember 1984, einen Maultier-Ritt zur Zitadelle in Cap Haitien auf Haiti anbieten, dann findet er auch statt.

Oder die Betreuung: Auf 600 Kreuzfahrer kommen 300 Mann und Frau Besatzung, um Sie rundrum zu verwöhnen.

Oder das himmlische Essen: Da fliegen wir zur Spargelzeit gut und gern mal 350 Kilo frischen Schwetzinger Stangenspargel von Frankfurt nach Montego Bay/Jamaika, wenn dort gerade die Europa kreuzt.

Perfekt sind auch die 21 qm großen Kabinen und das Kinoprogramm und die Gymnastiklehrerin und die Liederabende und das Fitness Center und der Nachtclub und der Tango-Unterricht und die Lagerräume...

A propos Lagerräume, nur ein kleines Beispiel: Wir lagern unseren russischen Kaviar in einem besonders gesicherten Kühlraum, der elektronisch bewacht wird. Schwankt die Temperatur im Kaviarraum auch nur um 1,1 Grad C, gibt es Kaviar-Alarm auf der Kommandobrücke!

Daß wir bei all dem Perfektionismus ganz schön gemütlich sein können, möchten wir Ihnen nebenbei auch sagen.

Wollen Sie mehr über die Europa wissen? Dann kreuzen Sie doch mal bei Ihrem Reisebüro auf. Oder schreiben Sie uns: Hapag-Lloyd AG, Kreuzfahrten, Postfach 107947, D-2800 Bremen 1.

ms Europa ·········· ⫽⫽ Hapag-Lloyd AG

9

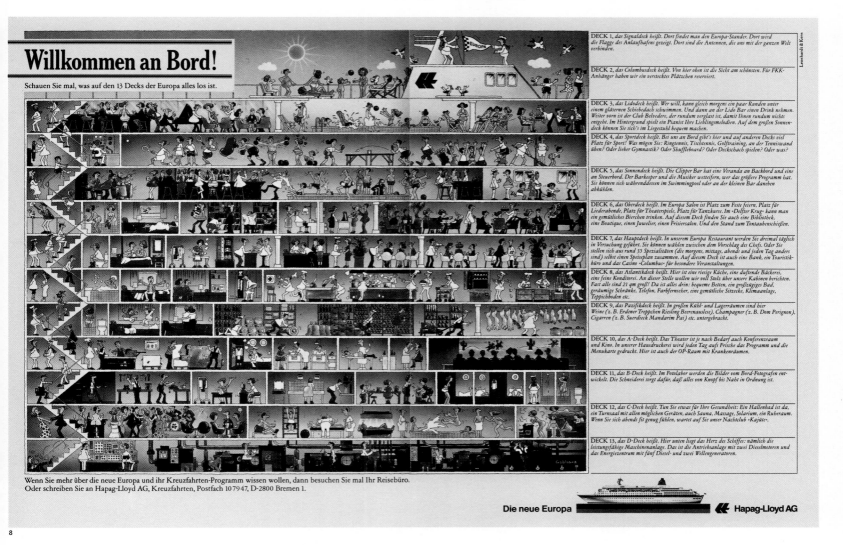

Willkommen an Bord!

Schauen Sie mal, was auf den 13 Decks der Europa alles los ist.

DECK 1, das Signaldeck heißt. Dort findet man den Europa-Stander. Dort wird die Flagge des Anlaufhafens gezeigt. Dort sind die Antennen, die uns mit der ganzen Welt verbinden.

DECK 2, das Columbusdeck heißt. Von hier oben ist die Sicht am schönsten. Für FKK-Anhänger haben wir ein verstecktes Plätzchen reserviert.

DECK 3, das Lidodeck heißt. Wer will, kann gleich morgens ein paar Runden unter einem gläsernen Schiebedach schwimmen. Und dann an der Lido Bar einen Drink nehmen. Weiter vorn ist der Club Belvedere, der rundum verglast ist, damit Ihnen rundum nichts entgeht. Im Hintergrund spielt im Pianist Ihre Lieblingsmelodien. Auf dem großen Sonnendeck können Sie sich's im Liegestuhl bequem machen.

DECK 4, das Sportdeck heißt. Bei uns an Bord gibt's hier und auf anderen Decks viel Platz für Sport! Was mögen Sie: Ringtennis, Tischtennis, Golftraining, an der Tenniswand üben? Oder lieber Gymnastik? Oder Shuffleboard? Oder Deckschach spielen? Oder was?

DECK 5, das Sonnendeck heißt. Die Clipper Bar hat eine Veranda an Backbord und eine an Steuerbord. Der Barkeeper und die Musiker wetteifern, wer das größere Programm hat. Sie können sich währenddessen im Swimmingpool oder an der kleinen Bar daneben abkühlen.

DECK 6, das Oberdeck heißt. Im Europa Salon ist Platz zum Feste feiern, Platz für Liederabende, Platz für Theaterspiele, Platz für Tanzkurse. Im «Delfter Krug» kann man ein gemütliches Bierchen trinken. Auf diesem Deck finden Sie auch eine Bibliothek, eine Boutique, einen Juwelier, einen Friseursalon. Und den Stand zum Tontaubenschießen.

DECK 7, das Hauptdeck heißt. In unserem Europa Restaurant werden Sie dreimal täglich in Versuchung geführt. Sie können wählen zwischen dem Vorschlag des Chefs. Oder Sie stellen sich aus rund 35 Spezialitäten (die morgens, mittags, abends und jeden Tag anders sind) selbst einen Speiseplan zusammen. Auf diesem Deck ist auch eine Bank, ein Touristikbüro und das Casino «Columbus» für besondere Veranstaltungen.

DECK 8, das Atlantikdeck heißt. Hier ist eine riesige Küche, eine duftende Bäckerei, eine feine Konditorei. An dieser Stelle wollen wir voll Stolz über unsere Kabinen berichten. Fast alle sind 21 qm groß! Da ist alles drin: bequeme Betten, ein großzügiges Bad, geräumige Schränke, Telefon, Farbfernseher, eine gemütliche Sitzecke, Klimaanlage, Teppichboden etc.

DECK 9, das Pazifikdeck heißt. In großen Kühl- und Lagerräumen sind hier Weine (z. B. Erdener Treppchen Riesling Beerenauslese), Champagner (z. B. Dom Perignon), Cigarren (z. B. Suerdieck Mandarim Pai) etc. untergebracht.

DECK 10, das A-Deck heißt. Das Theater ist je nach Bedarf auch Konferenzraum und Kino. In unserer Hausdruckerei wird jeden Tag aufs Frische das Programm und die Menukarte gedruckt. Hier ist auch der OP-Raum mit Krankenräumen.

DECK 11, das B-Deck heißt. Im Fotolabor werden die Bilder vom Bord-Fotografen entwickelt. Die Schneiderei sorgt dafür, daß alles von Knopf bis Naht in Ordnung ist.

DECK 12, das C-Deck heißt. Tun Sie etwas für Ihre Gesundheit: Ein Hallenbad ist da, ein Turnsaal mit allen möglichen Geräten, auch Sauna, Massage, Solarium, ein Ruheraum. Wenn Sie sich dann fit genug fühlen, wartet auf Sie unser Nachtclub «Kajüte».

DECK 13, das D-Deck heißt. Hier unten liegt das Herz des Schiffes: nämlich die leistungsfähige Maschinenanlage. Das ist die Antriebsanlage mit zwei Dieselmotoren und das Energiezentrum mit fünf Diesel- und zwei Wellengeneratoren.

Wenn Sie mehr über die neue Europa und ihr Kreuzfahrten-Programm wissen wollen, dann besuchen Sie mal Ihr Reisebüro. Oder schreiben Sie an Hapag-Lloyd AG, Kreuzfahrten, Postfach 107947, D-2800 Bremen 1.

Die neue Europa   ⚓ **Hapag-Lloyd AG**

8

ART DIRECTOR / DIRECTEUR ARTISTIQUE:

7–9 Uli Weber
10–12 Steve Hogand / Max Fujishima

AGENCY / AGENTUR / AGENCE – STUDIO:

7–9 Leonhardt & Kern

Cross a shallow stream as carefully as a deep one.
—ancient Japanese proverb—

At JALCARGO, we're proud of our reputation for successfully handling the most complex, most delicate, most demanding shipments. And we're happy that knowledgeable shippers tend to choose us over other carriers for especially difficult consignments.

But it dismays us that many of those shippers, for reasons we won't mention, entrust their "easy" jobs to other, less reliable carriers.

We think all shippers deserve the special care, the extra service of JALCARGO. And you deserve to know that with JALCARGO, no matter how deep the stream, you'll never take a bath.

✈ JALCARGO
NO ONE TAKES CARGO MORE SERIOUSLY.

10

The longest journey begins with a single step.
—ancient Japanese proverb—

More often than not, the longest cargo journey begins with a single phone call.

Make that call to JALCARGO, and your journey's as good as accomplished. Because no other cargo carrier takes such good care of your cargo. Or goes to such pains to give you service.

Call JALCARGO for all your cargo journeys. And make sure they all end with a single feeling. Satisfaction.

✈ JALCARGO
NO ONE TAKES CARGO MORE SERIOUSLY.

11

If you don't go into the cave, you can't catch the tiger.
—ancient Japanese proverb—

The easy way is not always the way that gets results. JALCARGO has known that for a long time. That's why we take such extraordinary pains to guarantee you total satisfaction.

So don't be fooled by other carriers' discounted rates and superficial service. If you want to catch the tiger, call JALCARGO. We go into the cave for you.

✈ JALCARGO
NO ONE TAKES CARGO MORE SERIOUSLY.

12

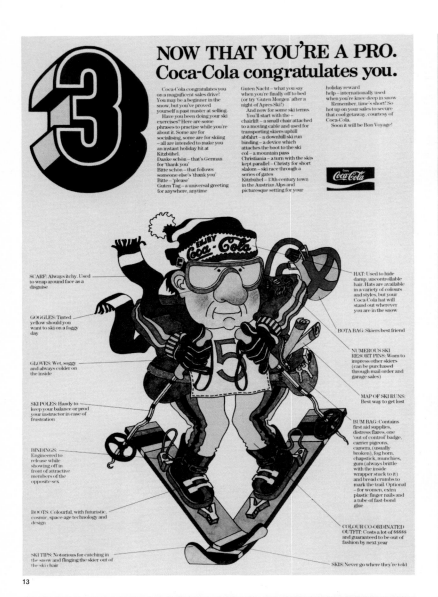

13

14

16

17

13, 14 Examples of advertising to promote a sales competition among *Coca Cola* retailers in South Africa, with a countdown on the start of Austrian ski-ing holidays for winners. (SAF)
15 To advertise a large annual sale of hunting and outdoor-sportswear and accessories at reduced prices, hosted by a manufacturer of sporting goods. (USA)
16–19 Full-colour double spreads from a *Volkswagen* campaign. For low-consumption models: Fig. 16, "The bad news: *Volkswagen's* turbo diesels are here"; Fig. 17, "You usually get farther with a *Volkswagen*". Fig. 18, 19 about *Volkswagen's* inclusive "extras": "No naked cars." (GER)

13, 14 Exemples tirés d'une campagne *Coca Cola* en Afrique du Sud offrant des vacances de ski au détaillant *Coca Cola* qui réalisera le meilleur chiffre d'affaires. (SAF)
15 Annonce pleine page pour les équipements et habits de chasse *Schoellkopf*. On s'y réfère en particulier aux soldes spéciaux. (USA)
16–19 Annonces double page pour une campagne publicitaire en faveur de *Volkswagen*. Fig. 16 et 17: consommation réduite des modèles diesel («mauvaises nouvelles: les VW turbo-diesel sont arrivées»); fig. 18, 19: «pas d'autos nues» – l'accent est mis sur l'équipement. (GER)

13, 14 Beispiele aus einer Kampagne von *Coca Cola*, Südafrika, in der es um einen Wettbewerb für den Einzelhandel geht: der beste *Coca-Cola*-Umsatz wird mit Ski-Ferien belohnt. (SAF)
15 Ganzseitiges Inserat für die Ankündigung eines speziellen Ausverkaufs von Jagd-, Camping und ähnlichen Artikeln der Marke *Schoellkopf*. (USA)
16–19 Doppelseitige Anzeigen aus einer Werbekampagne für *Volkswagen*. In Abb. 16 und 17 geht es um den niedrigen Verbrauch der *Volkswagen* Diesel, in Abb. 18, 19 um die Ausstattung. (GER)

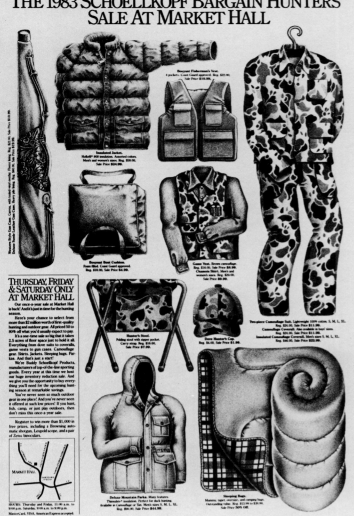

15

ARTIST / KÜNSTLER / ARTISTE:

13, 14 Dirk G. Voorneveld
16–19 Willi Rieser

DESIGNER / GESTALTER / MAQUETTISTE:

13, 14 Clive Gay
15 Gary Gibson

ART DIRECTOR / DIRECTEUR ARTISTIQUE:

13, 14 Clive Gay
15 Tony Diamond
16–19 Boris Eucker

AGENCY / AGENTUR / AGENCE – STUDIO:

13, 14 Pentagraph (Pty) Ltd
15 The Richards Group
16–17 Doyle Dane Bernbach GmbH

19

18

PLUMP FOR CONTINENTAL QUILTS WITH TERYLENE FILLING.

20

Advertisements / Inserate / Annonces

ARTIST / KÜNSTLER / ARTISTE:

20 Tony Meeuwissen
21 Sandra Higashi
22, 23 Jözef Sumichrast
24–26 Woody Pirtle

DESIGNER / GESTALTER / MAQUETTISTE:

21 Marty Neumeier / Sandra Higashi
22, 23 Jözef Sumichrast
24–26 Woody Pirtle

20 Double spread of a newspaper advertisement for quilts with ICI *Terylene* filling. (GBR)
21 Full-page newspaper advertisement announcing the "arrival" of a new TV channel. (USA)
22, 23 Illustration and complete double spread in trade magazines for *Levi's* jeans of corduroy material with fewer but thicker ridges—known in the trade as wales, hence pun. (USA)
24–26 From a series of full-page newspaper ads with full-colour illustrations to advertise a shopping mall of more than 130 sales outlets. (USA)

20 Doppelseitiges Zeitschrifteninserat für Steppdecken mit ICI-*Terylene*-Füllung. (GBR)
21 Ganzseitiges Zeitungsinserat für die Ankündigung eines neuen Fernseh-Senders. (USA)
22, 23 Illustration und vollständiges Fachzeitschriften-Inserat für *Levi's*-Jeans aus Cord. Das englische Wort für Wal ist gleichlautend mit einem webtechnischen Begriff, um den es in der Beschreibung der Stoffqualität geht, die besonders strapazierfähig sein soll. (USA)
24–26 Ganzseitige Zeitungsinserate mit mehrfarbigen Illustrationen aus einer Gemeinschaftskampagne von Kaufhäusern und Geschäften für ein Einkaufszentrum. (USA)

20 Annonce de magazine double page pour les couvertures piquées garnies de *térylène* ICI. (GBR)
21 Annonce de journal pleine page annonçant la mise en service d'un émetteur TV. (USA)
22, 23 Illustration et annonce de revue spécialisée complète pour les jeans *Levi's* en velours côtelé. Un homonyme du mot anglais pour «baleine» désigne la nervure, d'où l'allusion à un tissu particulièrement résistant à l'usage. (USA)
24–26 Annonces de journaux pleine page illustrées en polychromie, pour une campagne collective de grands magasins et de détaillants en faveur d'un centre commercial. (USA)

A CHANNEL IS BORN

KGOX3 SANTA BARBARA

21

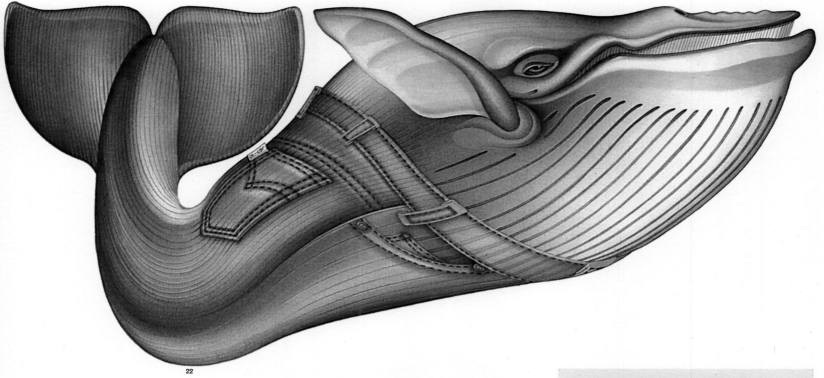

22

23

ART DIRECTOR:

20 Jemmy Gray
21 Marty Neumeier
22, 23 Glen DeCicco
24–26 Woody Pirtle

AGENCY / AGENTUR / AGENCE – STUDIO:

20 The Leagas Delaney Partnership Ltd
21 Neumeier Design Team
22, 23 Foote, Cone & Belding/Honig
24–26 Pirtle Design

24

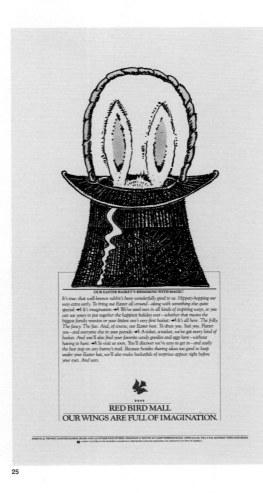

25

26

33

28

29

30

Advertisements
Inserate
Annonces

ARTIST / KÜNSTLER / ARTISTE:

27–30 René Gruau

27 Unpublished study for the advertising of *Van Cleef & Arpels*, jewellers. Ink and watercolour. (FRA)
28 Illustration for an advertisement for *Bemberg* lingerie. Mixed media, 35 × 26 cm. (ITA)
29 For an advertisement for *Bemberg* stockings. Mixed media, 41,5 × 29,5 cm. Yellow dress and shoes, green background. (ITA)
30 Illustration (41 × 30 cm, mixed media) for an advertisement for a *Bemberg* lining. White coat with green lining. (ITA)

27 Studie für die Werbung der Juweliere *Van Cleef & Arpels*. Tusche und Aquarell. (FRA)
28 Illustration aus einem Inserat für *Bemberg*-Wäsche. Mischtechnik, Format 35 × 26 cm. (ITA)
29 Eine weitere Illustration für die *Bemberg*-Werbung, hier für Strümpfe. Mischtechnik, Format 41,5 × 29,5 cm. Schuhe und Kleid gelb, Hintergrund grün. (ITA)
30 Illustration in Mischtechnik, Format 41 × 30 cm, für die *Bemberg*-Futterstoff-Anzeigenwerbung. Weisser Mantel mit grünem Futter. (ITA)

27 Ebauche pour la publicité de *Van Cleef & Arpels*, bijoutiers. Encre et aquarelle. (FRA)
28 Illustration pour une annonce, lingerie *Bemberg*. Techniques mixtes, 35 × 26 cm. (ITA)
29 Pour une annonce pour les bas *Bemberg*. Techniques mixtes, 41,5 × 29,5 cm. Robe et souliers jaunes, fond vert. (ITA)
30 Illustration d'une annonce pour une doublure *Bemberg*. Techniques mixtes, 41 × 30 cm. Cape blanche, doublure verte. (ITA)

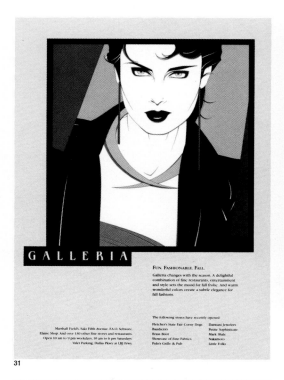

31

32

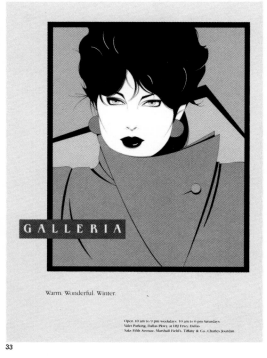

33

34

ARTIST / KÜNSTLER / ARTISTE:

31, 33 Pat Nagel
32 Giovanni Mulazzani
34 Tomi Ungerer
35 Kazumasa Nagai

DESIGNER / GESTALTER / MAQUETTISTE:

31, 33 Woody Pirtle/David Kampa
35 Kazumasa Nagai

ART DIRECTOR / DIRECTEUR ARTISTIQUE:

31, 33 Woody Pirtle
32 Fritz Tschirren
34 Robert Pütz
35 Kazumasa Nagai

AGENCY / AGENTUR / AGENCE – STUDIO:

31, 33 Pirtle Design
32 STZ S.r.l.
34 Robert Pütz GmbH
35 Nippon Design Center

31, 33 Full-colour ads from a magazine series as examples of co-operative advertising for a Dallas shopping mall. (USA)
32 "Light in an interior", illustrated in soft pastels, from a series of magazine double spreads by an Italian company that specializes in lighting equipment. (ITA)
34 A full-colour ad in a campaign for *Nixdorf* computers. (GER)
35 Magazine ad for the Takeo Paper Company, Tokyo. (JPN)

31, 33 Beispiele aus einer Serie von mehrfarbigen Anzeigen als Gemeinschaftswerbung eines Einkaufszentrums. (USA)
32 «Licht in einem Raum.» Zeitschrifteninserat für ein Unternehmen der Beleuchtungsindustrie. In sanften Farbtönen. (ITA)
34 Beispiel aus einer Werbekampagne mit mehrfarbigen Anzeigen für *Nixdorf*-Computer. (GER)
35 Zeitschriftenanzeige für den Papierhersteller *Takeo*. (JPN)

31, 33 Exemples d'annonces polychromes dans une série servant à la publicité collective d'un centre commercial. (USA)
32 «De la lumière dans un espace intérieur.» Annonce de magazine pour une fabrique de lampes. Teintes adoucies. (ITA)
34 Exemple d'annonce polychrome utilisée dans une campagne publicitaire pour les ordinateurs *Nixdorf*. (GER)
35 Annonce de magazine pour le papetier *Takeo*. (JPN)

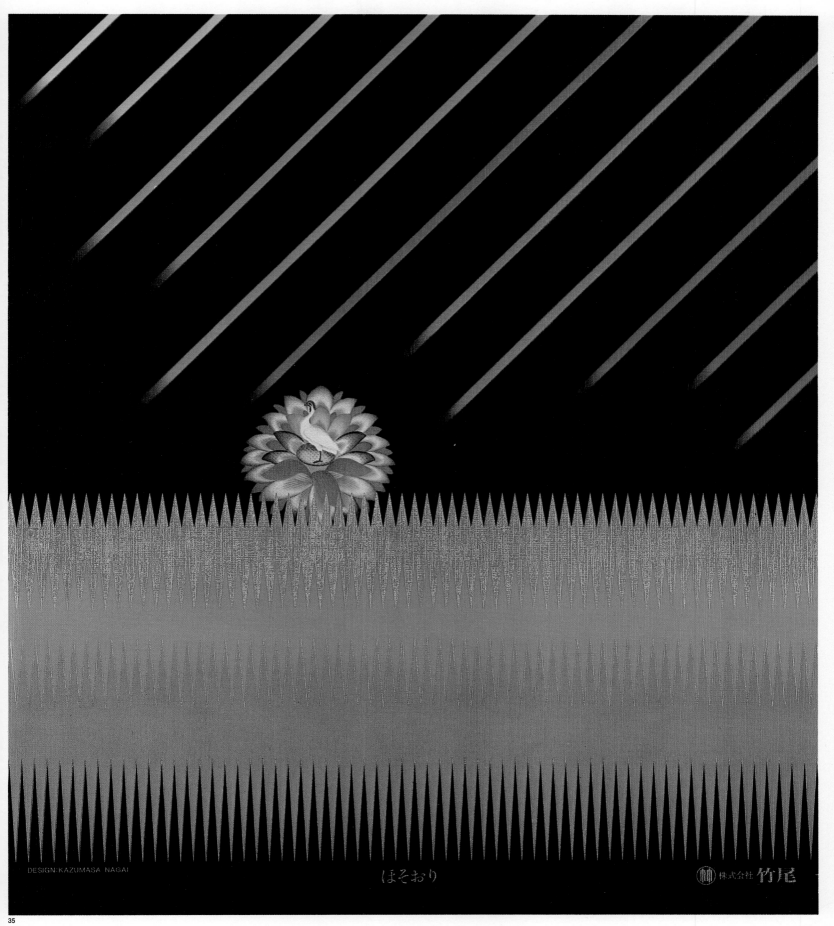

DESIGN:KAZUMASA NAGAI

ほそおり

株式会社 竹尾

36

37

36, 37 Illustration and complete full-page advertisement for *Bontempi* electronic organs. (FRA)
38, 40 Examples from an advertising campaign in full colour for Pils beer brewed by *Spaten*. Fig. 38: "The cultivated taste of drinking a clear Pils"; Fig. 40: "The inspiring experience of drinking a clear Pils." (GER)
39 "We particularly like solving intricate problems." Full-page advertisement published in trade magazines, for a metal trader. (SWI)
41 Full-page advertisement in black and white which appeared in international trade magazines for *Cast* fast-firing floor and wall tiles. (ITA)

36, 37 Illustration und vollständige Konsumenten-Anzeige für *Bontempi*-Orgeln. (FRA)
38, 40 Beispiele aus einer Werbekampagne für *Spaten*-Pils. Die Illustrationen wurden auch für Grossflächenplakate verwendet. (GER)
39 In Fachzeitschriften erschienene ganzseitige Image-Anzeige für einen Metallhändler. (SWI)
41 Für eine internationale Leserschaft von Fachzeitschriften bestimmtes Inserat von *Cast*. Es geht hier um ein neues Brennverfahren für keramische Boden- und Wandkacheln. (ITA)

36, 37 Illustration et annonce consommateurs complète pour les orgues *Bontempi*. (FRA)
38, 40 Exemples d'éléments publicitaires pour une campagne en faveur de la bière *Spaten*-Pils. Fig. 38: «Un plaisir haut de gamme: boire une Pils intelligente»; fig. 40: «Une expérience galvanisante: boire une Pils intelligente». Ces illustrations ont aussi été utilisées sous forme d'affiches au grand format. (GER)
39 Annonce de prestige pleine page pour une quincaillerie. Revues professionnelles. (SWI)
41 Annonce de *Cast* destinée aux lecteurs internationaux des revues professionnelles. Il y est question d'un nouveau procédé de fabrication de carreaux en céramique pour sols et parois. (ITA)

ARTIST / KÜNSTLER / ARTISTE:

36, 37 Folon
38, 40 Mike Knepper
39 Hanspeter Rolly
41 Gianni Bortolotti

DESIGNER / GESTALTER / MAQUETTISTE:

38, 40 Mike Knepper/Lutz Stermann
39 Hanspeter Rolly
41 Gianni Bortolotti

ART DIRECTOR / DIRECTEUR ARTISTIQUE:

36, 37 Horst Blachian
38, 40 Lutz Stermann
41 Maria Santi

AGENCY / AGENTUR / AGENCE – STUDIO:

36, 37 Intermarco-Farner
38, 40 S.T.B.
39 Hanspeter Rolly
41 Gianni Bortolotti

38

39

40

41

In Hessen: Freundlich.

Licher Bier. Aus dem Herzen der Natur.

42

ARTIST / KÜNSTLER / ARTISTE:

42 Harald Schlüter
43 Birney Lettick
44 Milou Hermus
45, 46 Norio Hikone

DESIGNER / GESTALTER / MAQUETTISTE:

42 Harald Schlüter
43 Hans Peter Weiss
45, 46 Mamoru Suzuki

Advertisements / Inserate / Annonces

42 Double spread in a campaign advertising a Pils brewed by *Licher*, forecasting clear skies—and clear, pure beer. Dark green, gold and white labels on green-and-white ground. (GER)
43 What can happen in a summer heat-wave if you don't have *Carrier* air-conditioning. (USA)
44 Double-page spread advertising a Dutch insurance company. The theme of the body copy is the stamp shown here, illustrated in shades of magenta and bluish grey. (NLD)
45, 46 Examples from an advertising campaign for *Suntory* canned beer in which a penguin is the centre-piece. Bluish tones with yellow. (JPN)

42 Doppelseitige Anzeige für *Licher*-Bier, aus einer Werbekampagne, die auf dem Thema Natur aufgebaut ist. Kräftiges Gelbgrün und Weiss. (GER)
43 Die zu erwartende Sommerhitze ist Thema dieses Inserates für *Carrier*-Klimaanlagen. (USA)
44 Doppelseitiges Inserat für eine Versicherungsgesellschaft. Der Stempel ist das zentrale Thema des Werbetextes. Illustration in Magenta und Blaugrau. (NLD)
45, 46 Beispiele aus einer Inseraten-Kampagne für *Suntory*-Dosenbier, deren Mittelpunkt der Pinguin ist. Blautöne und Gelb. (JPN)

42 Annonce double page pour une bière *Licher*. La campagne correspondante a pris la nature pour thème central. Vert jaunâtre vigoureux, blanc. (GER)
43 La chaleur estivale à venir fournit le sujet de cette annonce des climatiseurs *Carrier*. (USA)
44 Annonce double page pour une compagnie d'assurances. Le timbre constitue le motif central du texte publicitaire. Illustration exécutée en magenta et gris bleuté. (NLD)
45, 46 Annonces figurant dans une campagne en faveur de la bière *Suntory* en boîtes, avec un pingouin pour vedette. Divers bleus et jaune. (JPN)

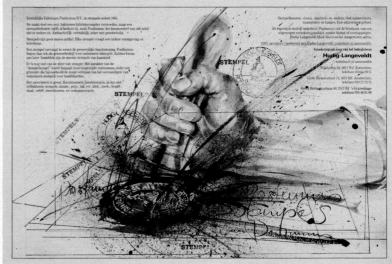

44

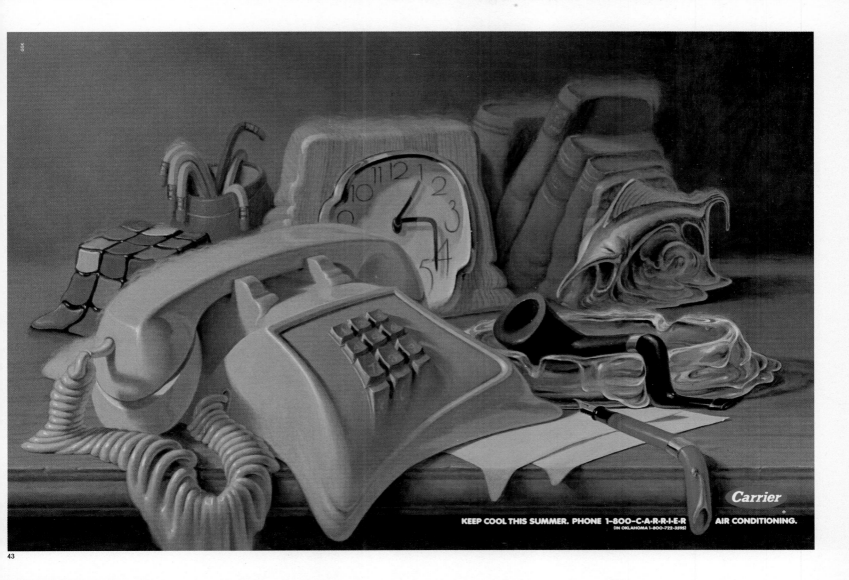

KEEP COOL THIS SUMMER. PHONE 1-800-C·A·R·R·I·E·R
(IN OKLAHOMA 1-800-722-3595)   AIR CONDITIONING.

Carrier

43

ART DIRECTOR / DIRECTEUR ARTISTIQUE:

43 Hans Peter Weiss
44 Etienne Veen Lex v. Droge
45, 46 Masatoshi Toda

AGENCY / AGENTUR / AGENCE – STUDIO:

42 Harald Schlüter Werbeagentur GmbH
43 GGK

45

46

Advertisements / Inserate / Annonces

ARTIST / KÜNSTLER / ARTISTE:

47 Heinz Hefel
48 Jung & Jung
49, 50 Tomi Ungerer
51 Chaval
52 Dennis Mukai

DESIGNER / GESTALTER / MAQUETTISTE:

47 Benedict Fasnacht
48 Mathias Babst
52 Ron Howell

ART DIRECTOR / DIRECTEUR ARTISTIQUE:

47 Benedect Fasnacht
48 Mathias Babst
49, 50 Robert Pütz
51 Thomas Rempen
52 Ron Howell/Steve Beaumont

AGENCY / AGENTUR / AGENCE – STUDIO:

47 Urs Tschan AG
48 Young & Rubicam
49, 50 Robert Pütz GmbH
51 Hildmann, Simon, Rempen & Schmitz/SMS
52 Chickering/Howell

47 Full-page advertisement for *Courvoisier* cognac. (SWI)
48 In a long-term ad campaign for whisky, *Johnnie Walker* got lit up—by an electronic pin-ball machine. (GER)
49, 50 Full-page advertisements in full colour from a campaign for *American Star*, a tobacco shag for roll-your-own cigarettes. (GER)
51 From an image campaign for cigarettes by *British-American Tobacco*: "Smoking unites." (GER)
52 Full-colour advertisement in magazines for *Hang Ten* sportswear and accessories, with its trademark also on the palms. (USA)

47 Ganzseitiges Inserat für *Courvoisier*-Cognac. (SWI)
48 Die bekannte *Johnnie-Walker*-Figur als Mittelpunkt eines Inserats, das zu einer langfristigen Werbekampagne gehört. (GER)
49, 50 Beispiele aus einer Inseraten-Kampagne für *American-Star*-Tabak für Zigaretten. In Farbe. (GER)
51 Inserat aus einer Image-Kampagne für die B.A.T. Cigaretten-Fabriken GmbH. (GER)
52 Zeitschrifteninserat mit mehrfarbiger Illustration für Sportkleidung und Accessoires der Marke *Hang Ten*. Das Markenzeichen, zwei Füsse, ist hier auch in den Palmen wiederzufinden. (USA)

47 Annonce pleine page pour le cognac *Courvoisier*. (SWI)
48 Le personnage de *Johnnie Walker* constitue le thème d'une campagne d'annonces à long terme. (GER)
49, 50 Exemples d'annonces réalisées pour une campagne en faveur du tabac à cigarettes *American Star*. En couleur. (GER)
51 Annonce figurant dans une campagne de prestige des B.A.T. Cigaretten-Fabriken GmbH: «Fumer, ça crée des liens». (GER)
52 Annonce de magazine (illustration polychrome) pour les vêtements sport et accessoires de la marque *Hang Ten*. Les deux pieds caractérisant la marque se retrouvent dans les palmiers. (USA)

47

48

Steig' aus auf American Star

4,30 3,80

Mild American Blend
Zigaretten-Tabak

**American Star
Jetzt 3,80**

49

Rauchen verbindet.

Die größten Gegensätzlichkeiten finden sich in dieser Gemeinsamkeit: In der Gemeinschaft der Raucher.

Rauchen verbindet Freunde und Feinde, Fremde und Vertraute, Frauen und Männer, alt und jung.

Nicht, als ob das Rauchen die Gegensätze aufhöbe. Und doch.

Findet sich erst eine Gemeinsamkeit, finden sich weitere leichter.

Wie viele Bekanntschaften hat die erste gemeinsame Zigarette anbahnen helfen. Wenn auch meist flüchtige, so flüchtig, wie der Rauch selbst.

Aber auch feste und beständige, so wie das ja mancher gemeinsame Genuß mit sich bringt.

Wie viele fröhliche Verbindungen

hat die erste gemeinsame Zigarette so gestiftet. Einfach weil sie geholfen hat, erste Verlegenheiten zu überwinden, aus denen sich erst so jene Gelegenheiten bilden, bei denen sich Freundschaft oder Liebe sich entzünden kann.

Rauchen verbindet auf vielerlei Weise. Doch wie auch immer, verbindet es immer zur Verbindlichkeit.

B·A·T

Das große Haus des Tabaks.

51

Steig' aus auf American Star

4,30 3,80

Mild American Blend
Zigaretten-Tabak

**American Star
Jetzt 3,80**

50

Hang Ten

HANG TEN

It's one of those dream days. The weather is amazing. Your mind is wandering. And the smile on your face could get you arrested in thirty-seven states.

It's the kind of day Hang Ten sportswear, sports gear and fun stuff were created for. It's enough

to make the toes wiggle on our two little feet.

Now here's something interesting. A guy who really should know better, being entirely too serious.

Ah, perfect. That's the great thing about lipstick. It washes off of cars, and collars, and.

52

43

53

55

54

57

Advertisements
Inserate
Annonces

53, 54 Examples from a series of advertisements for the French mineral water *Perrier*. The rugby players and racing cyclists are painted in strong colours. (FRA)
55, 56 For another mineral water, *Hirschquelle* (Stag's Spring): double spreads of still-life paintings in soft colours. Their theme is today's general longing for what is natural. (GER)
57, 58 Full-colour double spreads from a campaign in magazines to advertise beer brewed by *Veltins*: 57, "The fine manner, always"; 58, "In the best mood of an evening". (GER)
59 Full-colour advertisement for *Gold'n Plump* chicken also used as a brochure, poster and in point-of-sale display. (USA)

53, 54 Beispiele aus einer Serie von Anzeigen für *Perrier*-Mineralwasser. In kräftigen Farben. (FRA)
55, 56 Zwei doppelseitige Zeitschriftenanzeigen in Farbe aus einer Kampagne für *Hirschquelle*-Mineralwasser. Zentrales Thema ist die Sehnsucht nach dem Natürlichen. (GER)
57, 58 Doppelseitige, mehrfarbige Zeitschriften-Inserate aus einer Publikumskampagne für *Veltins*-Bier. (GER)
59 Mehrfarbiges Inserat für *Gold'n-Plump*-Hähnchen aus Minnesota, welche die «Schlacht» gegen die Konkurrenz aus dem Süden durch Frische gewinnen wollen. Das Motiv wurde auch für Broschüren, Innenwerbung und Plakate verwendet. (USA)

53, 54 Exemples d'annonces composant une série publicitaire pour l'eau minérale *Perrier*. Couleurs vives. (FRA)
55, 56 Deux annonces de magazines double page, en couleur, pour une campagne en faveur de l'eau minérale *Hirschquelle* axée sur la nostalgie du retour à la nature. (GER)
57, 58 Annonces de magazines double page, en polychromie, pour une campagne consommateurs des bières *Veltins*. (GER)
59 Annonce polychrome pour les coquelets *Gold'n Plump* du Minnesota, fougueux combattants qui entendent bien gagner la bataille de la fraîcheur contre la concurrence du sud. Le même motif illustre des brochures, affiches et affichettes. (USA)

Die großen Genüsse sind einfacher Natur. │ Die Sehnsucht nach dem Echten und Rechten führt viele zurück zu den Quellen: es duftet wieder nach selbstgebackenem Brot, in den Gärten wächst wieder ungespritztes Obst, und der Wein kann Kennern nicht trocken genug sein. Kein Wunder also, daß auch ein großes stilles Heilwasser aus dem Schwarzwald immer mehr Freunde gewinnt: Hirschquelle. Sie fließt für alle, die zu genießen verstehen. So wie damals, als der Mensch noch kein Wässerchen trüben konnte. *Heilanzeige: Hirschquelle fördert die Funktion von Nieren und Blase und ist harntreibend.* **Hirschquelle. Heilkraft aus dem Schwarzwald.**

56

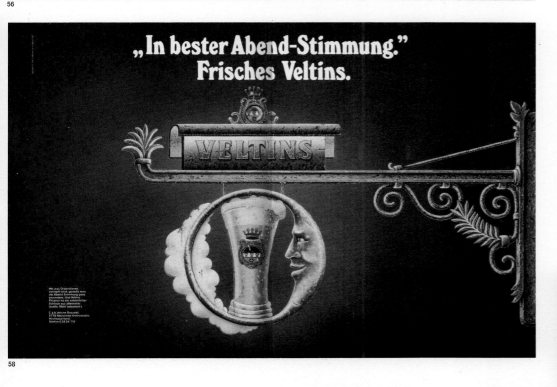

58

59

45

賞与の「賞」は、なぜ貝の字がつくの、お母さん。

60

賞賛の「賛」は、なぜ貝の字がつくの、お母さん。

61

貴重の「貴」は、なぜ貝の字がつくの、おじいちゃん。

62

ARTIST / KÜNSTLER / ARTISTE:

60–62 Todashi Ohashi
63 Henry Brimmer
64, 65 Julie Johnson

DESIGNER / GESTALTER / MAQUETTISTE:

60–62 Hiroshi Wakamatsu
63 Brimmer/Randall
64, 65 Henry Brimmer

ART DIRECTOR / DIRECTEUR ARTISTIQUE:

60–62 Hiroshi Wakamatsu
63–65 Henry Brimmer

AGENCY / AGENTUR / AGENCE – STUDIO:

63–65 Henry Brimmer Design

60–62 Once used as currency in Japan, too, sea-shells are the central motif in this imagebuilding campaign for a bank. Each full-page magazine ad features a detailed illustration of a sea-shell (together with its written character) in brown, beige and yellow shades. (JPN)
63–65 Complete full-page magazine advertisements and illustrative detail, in original size, from a promotional series for the Academy of Art College in San Francisco. (USA)

60–62 Ganzseitige Inserate aus einer Image-Kampagne für eine Bank. Das zentrale Motiv ist jeweils eine Muschel, kombiniert mit dem entsprechenden chinesischen Schriftzeichen. Früher wurde die Muschel in Japan als Zahlungsmittel verwendet. Illustrationen in Braun-, Beige- und Gelbtönen. (JPN)
63–65 Vollständige Anzeigen und Illustration in Originalgrösse aus einer Serie für eine Kunstakademie (Academy of Art College) in San Francisco. (USA)

60–62 Annonces pleine page figurant dans la campagne de prestige d'une banque. Le motif de base est un coquillage combiné avec les caractères chinois adéquats. Les coquillages servaient autrefois de monnaie au Japon. Illustrations en divers bruns, beiges et jaunes. (JPN)
63–65 Annonces complètes et illustration au format original. Série en faveur d'une académie des beaux-arts de San Francisco, l'Academy of Art College. (USA)

63

64

65

47

66

67

68

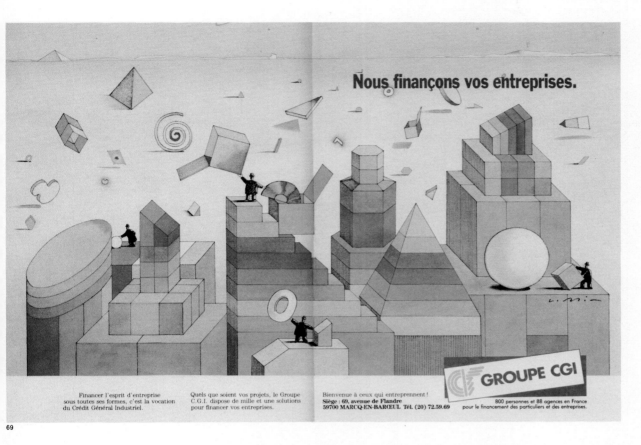

69

ARTIST / KÜNSTLER / ARTISTE:

66, 67 Michael Foreman
68 Milton Glaser
69 Josse Goffin
70 Folon

DESIGNER / GESTALTER / MAQUETTISTE:

66–68, 70 R. David Jenkins

ART DIRECTOR / DIRECTEUR ARTISTIQUE:

66–68, 70 R. David Jenkins
69 Herve Verspirene/Josse Goffin

AGENCY / AGENTUR / AGENCE – STUDIO:

66–68, 70 Ogilvy & Mather
69 Fusion

70

66–68, 70 Complete double spreads and an illustration from a colour campaign advertising the California First Bank. Its trademark, the figure one—is variously interpreted, respectively, by well-known artists from Britain, USA and France. (USA)
69 "We finance your undertaking." Double-spread advertisement for the CGI trade bank. The colourful "buildings" and other figures are on a background of soft tones. (FRA)

66–68, 70 Vollständige doppelseitige Anzeigen und eine der Illustrationen aus einer an Geschäftsleute gerichteten Werbekampagne der California First Bank. Das Signet der Bank, die Eins, wird in den Illustrationen auf verschiedene Art interpretiert. (USA)
69 «Wir finanzieren Ihre Unternehmungen.» Doppelseitiges Inserat der CGI, einer Handelsbank. «Gebäude» und Formen in bunten Farben vor sanft koloriertem Grund. (FRA)

66–68, 70 Annonces double page complètes et l'une des illustrations figurant dans une campagne de la California First Bank destinée aux hommes d'affaires. L'emblème de la banque, le nombre un, est interprété de diverses manières. (USA)
69 Dans cette annonce double page du Crédit Général Industriel, les «bâtiments» et structures apparaissent en couleurs vives sur un fond colorié en tons pastel. (FRA)

71

72

73

74

An die paar wenigen Gelegenheitsleser, denen noch unbekannt ist, welchen Journalismus wir nicht pflegen:

75

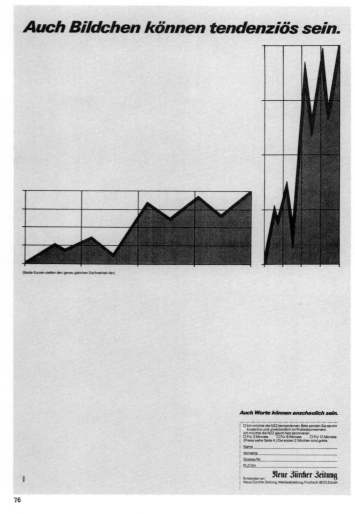

Auch Bildchen können tendenziös sein.

76

Unsere Portefeuille-Analyse
bewahrt Sie
vor Überraschungen.

77

Bei Geldanlagen
kann man auch falsch auf dem
richtigen Pferd sitzen.

78

Advertisements
Inserate
Annonces

Advertisements

Inserate

Annonces

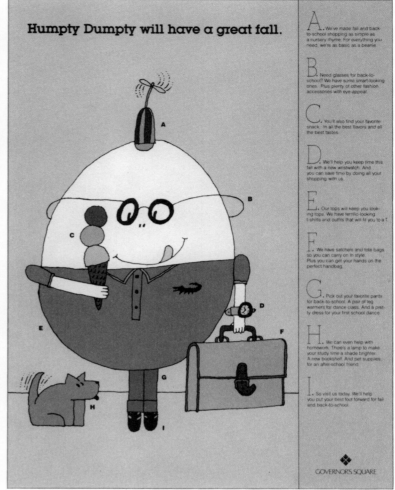

80

81

79 After helping to launch the new national newspaper *USA Today* in other major American markets, its advertising agency marked the New York launch with this ad in its pages. (USA)
80 A savings bank announces the opening of its newest branch, with a black-and-white newspaper ad that illustrates the incentives on offer there during the first week. (USA)
81 Newspaper ad in bright colours for back-to-school clothes and accessories. (USA)
82 Full-page newspaper ad for the so-called "Second Pillar" of support for social security pensions in Switzerland: their additional insurance in the private sector, which is to become obligatory. Full-colour illustration, lettering in red and black on white. (SWI)

79 Ganzseitige Zeitungsanzeige für die Einführung einer Zeitung in New York. (USA)
80 Ankündigung der Eröffnung einer Bankfiliale mit Illustration der speziellen Extras, die während der Eröffnungswoche geboten werden. Zeitungsinserat in Schwarzweiss. (USA)
81 Mehrfarbiges Zeitungsinserat für ein Kaufhaus, das sich speziell auf den Beginn des neuen Schuljahres bezieht. (USA)
82 Ganzseitiges Zeitungsinserat der Rentenanstalt für die sogenannte zweite Säule der Rentenversicherung in der Schweiz, eine obligatorisch werdende Zusatzversicherung durch private Versicherungen. Illustration mehrfarbig, Schrift rot und schwarz. (SWI)

79 Annonce de journal annonçant le lancement d'un nouveau journal à New York. (USA)
80 Annonce de l'ouverture d'une succursale bancaire, illustrant les diverses prestations spéciales fournies pendant la semaine d'inauguration. En noir et blanc. (USA)
81 Annonce de journal polychrome pour un grand magasin. On s'y réfère en particulier à la rentrée scolaire. (USA)
82 Annonce de journal pleine page d'une compagnie d'assurances pour le deuxième pilier de l'assurance-vieillesse en Suisse, soit l'assurance complémentaire devenue obligatoire. Illustration polychrome, texte rouge et noir. (SWI)

82

83

84

85

83, 84 Illustrative detail and complete newspaper ad, in stark black and white, by the Dutch weekly newspaper on socio-economics, *Elseviers Weekblad*. The conclusions from its symposium on "The Industrial Challenge" (available as a supplement or in book form) were summed up by the headlined message: "Wake up, get up and take up the Challenge!" (NLD)
85 Double-page advertisement for *Time* magazine, mainly in shades of blue with white. This referred to its feature on moral and legal aspects to the question of the right to die. (USA)
86–88 Local newspaper advertising for *Bloomingdale's*, the New York department store, for Christmas shopping (Fig. 86) and (Figs. 87, 88) fashion campaigns. (USA)

83, 84 Illustration und vollständiges Zeitungsinserat für eine Wirtschafts-Wochenzeitung, *Elseviers Weekblad*. In Schwarzweiss. (NLD)
85 Doppelseitiges Inserat für die Zeitschrift *Time*. Gegenstand der Illustration (vorwiegend in Blautönen) ist ein Artikel über die Frage nach dem Recht zu sterben. (USA)
86 Inserat für die Ankündigung spezieller Weihnachtsabteilungen und -angebote des New Yorker Kaufhauses *Bloomingdale's*. (USA)
87, 88 Weitere Inserate für *Bloomingdale's*, hier speziell für Mode. (USA)

83, 84 Illustration et annonce de journal complète pour un hebdomadaire économique, *Elseviers Weekblad*. En noir et blanc. (NLD)
85 Annonce double page pour le magazine *Time*. L'illustration, où dominent les tons bleus, se rapporte à un article où l'on discute du droit de l'individu à choisir sa mort. (USA)
86 Annonce servant à présenter divers départements et offres spécifiques de la saison de ventes de Noël du grand magasin newyorkais *Bloomingdale's*. (USA)
87, 88 Deux autres exemples d'annonces pour *Bloomingdale's*, ici pour la mode. (USA)

ARTIST / KÜNSTLER / ARTISTE:

83–85 Brad Holland
86 Jeanne Fisher
87, 88 Antonio Lopez

DESIGNER / GESTALTER / MAQUETTISTE:

87, 88 Darrell Beasley/Larry DaMato

ART DIRECTOR / DIRECTEUR ARTISTIQUE:

85 Rudolph Hoglund/Lily Ho
86 John C. Jay
87, 88 Darrell Beasley

AGENCY / AGENTUR / AGENCE – STUDIO:

83, 84 Noordervliet & Winninghoff/
 Leo Burnett
86–88 Bloomingdale's Adv. Dept.

87

86

88

89 Full page of co-operative advertising that announces the opening of shops and restaurants in the renewed South Street Seaport of New York, where sailing ships used to tie up. (USA)
90, 91 Examples from a series of newspaper ads in full colour by SAS for its non-stop intercity flights: here, for same-day return flights from Stockholm to London and Zurich. (SWE)
92 When the magazine *Executive Travel* conducted a poll among regular business travellers, *Cathay Pacific Airlines* published this black-and-white advertisement to headline their opinion of its service: "Best Airline to the Far East". (CAN)
93 Black-and-white advertisement of a Brazilian newspaper on Freedom-of-the-Press Day. (BRA)
94 Advertisement from a campaign series in a Japanese newspaper for *Suntory* whisky. (JPN)

89 Ganzseitiges Zeitungsinserat als Gemeinschaftswerbung anlässlich der Eröffnung von Restaurants und Läden im alten New Yorker Hafengebiet. (USA)
90, 91 Beispiele aus einer Serie von Zeitungsanzeigen der Fluggesellschaft SAS, hier für Tagesausflüge nach London und Zürich. Mehrfarbige Illustrationen. (SWE)
92 Gegenstand dieses Inserates der *Cathay Pacific Airlines* ist das Ergebnis einer Umfrage des *Executive Travel* Magazins, wonach diese Fluggesellschaft als die beste für den Fernen Osten bezeichnet wird. In Schwarzweiss. (CAN)
93 Anzeige einer brasilianischen Zeitung anlässlich des Tages der Pressefreiheit. (BRA)
94 Aus einer Serie von Zeitungsanzeigen für *Suntory*-Whisky. (JPN)

89 Annonce de journal pleine page. On y trouve une publicité à l'occasion de l'ouverture de divers restaurants et magasins dans l'enceinte du vieux port de New York. (USA)
90, 91 Exemples d'annonces de journaux figurant dans une série publicitaire de la compagnie aérienne SAS: excursions d'une journée à Londres et Zurich. Illustrations polychromes. (SWE)
92 Cette annonce de la compagnie aérienne *Cathay Pacific Airlines* s'inspire des résultats d'une enquête du magazine *Executive Travel* où elle est classée première en ce qui concerne les vols vers l'Extrême-Orient. En noir et blanc. (CAN)
93 Annonce d'un journal brésilien à l'occasion de la Journée de la liberté de la presse. (BRA)
94 Annonce parue dans une série consacrée au whisky *Suntory*. (JPN)

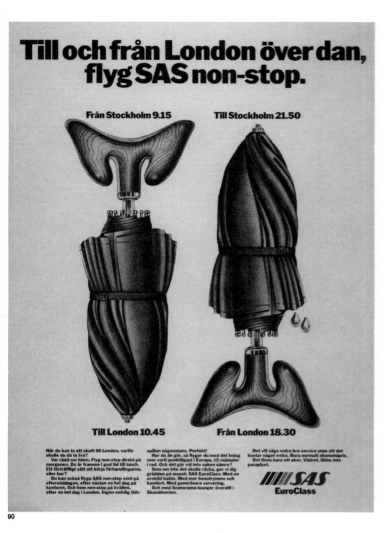

Till och från London över dan, flyg SAS non-stop.

Från Stockholm 9.15 **Till Stockholm 21.50**

Till London 10.45 **Från London 18.30**

När du kan ta ett skutt till London, varför skulle du då ta två?

Var rädd om tiden. Flyg non-stop direkt på morgonen. Du är framme i god tid till lunch. Ett förträffligt sätt att börja förhandlingarna, eller hur?

Du kan också flyga SAS non-stop sent på eftermiddagen, efter nästan en hel dag på kontoret. Och hem non-stop på kvällen, efter en hel dag i London. Ingen onödig tidsspillan någonstans. Perfekt!

Hur du än gör, så flyger du med det bolag som varit punktligast i Europa, 15 månader i rad. Och det gör väl inte saken sämre?

Som om det skulle räcka, ger vi dig grädden på moset: SAS EuroClass. Med en avskild kabin. Med mer benutrymme och komfort. Med generösare servering.

Och med Scanorama-lounger överallt i Skandinavien.

Det vill säga extra bra service utan att det kostar något extra. Bara normalt ekonomipris. Det finns bara ett aber. Vädret. Glöm inte paraplyet.

///// SAS EuroClass

90

Slarva inte bort tiden, flyg SAS non-stop till Zürich.

Från Stockholm 16.00* **Till Stockholm 19.40**

Till Zürich 18.25 **Från Zürich 17.25**

När vi introducerade vår nya non-stop-linje till Zürich i våras, så hade vi vissa förhoppningar. Men resultatet blev faktiskt braksuccé.

Egentligen är det inte så konstigt. Du flyger iväg sent på eftermiddagen efter en hel dag på kontoret. Du flyger hem efter en hel dag i Zürich. Ingen onödig tidsspillan någonstans. Perfekt!

Till råga på allt kommer du hem på kvällen.

Knappast heller det faktum att du flyger med det bolag som varit punktligast i Europa, 15 månader i rad.

Som om det skulle räcka, ger vi dig grädden på moset: SAS EuroClass. Med en avskild kabin. Med mer benutrymme och komfort. Med generösare servering. Och med Business Service Lounger överallt i Skandinavien.

SAS är helt enkelt det bästa sättet att ta vara på tiden. Och pengarna.

För du betalar inget extra. Bara normalt ekonomipris.

*Från 30 oktober ny avgångstid 16.30.

///// SAS EuroClass

91

Quando a censura parou de fazer isto

a Imprensa voltou a ser livre.

7 de Junho. Dia da Liberdade de Imprensa.

A Província do Pará

93

94

57

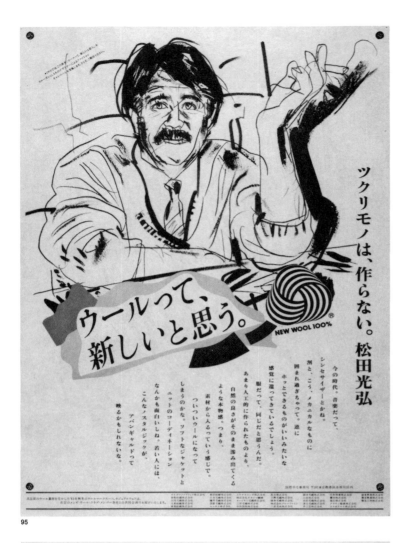

95

96

97

98

ARTIST / KÜNSTLER / ARTISTE:

95, 96 Katsu Yoshida
97, 98 Dominik Burckhardt
99, 100 Mick Brownfield
101 Heinz Edelmann

DESIGNER / GESTALTER / MAQUETTISTE:

95, 96 Mitsuaki Miyamoto
97, 98 Dominik Burckhardt
99, 100 Emile Pater

99

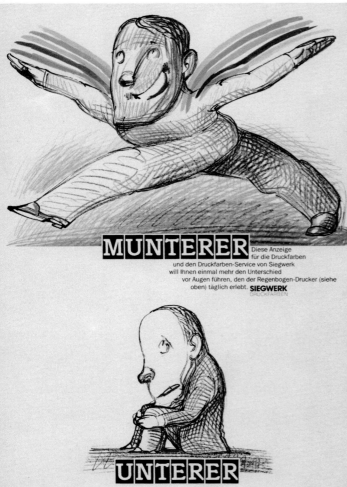

MUNTERER Diese Anzeige
für die Druckfarben
und den Druckfarben-Service von Siegwerk
will Ihnen einmal mehr den Unterschied
vor Augen führen, den der Regenbogen-Drucker (siehe
oben) täglich erlebt. SIEGWERK
DRUCKFARBEN

UNTERER

101

ART DIRECTOR / DIRECTEUR ARTISTIQUE:

95, 96 Yoshifumi Nakashima
97, 98 Dominik Burckhardt
99, 100 Emile Pater
101 Robert Pütz

AGENCY / AGENTUR / AGENCE – STUDIO:

95, 96 J. Walter Thompson
97, 98 Burckhardt, Lüdi
99, 100 Prad B.V.
101 Robert Pütz GmbH

100

95, 96 Examples from an advertising campaign to promote the use of pure wool in Japan. With this black-and-white series in the trade press, the International Wool Secretariat presents full-page portraits of well-known Japanese fashion designers who use pure wool. (JPN)
97, 98 This campaign indicates that *Mediator* television sets are available in a wide range of colours. Advertisements in black and white with, respectively, blue and grey. (SWI)
99, 100 Illustration and ad for *Philips* cassette recorders: "Shudder or enjoy". (NLD)
101 Colour was restricted to the top half of this ad to highlight the difference between a user and a non-user of *Siegwerk* printing colours. (GER)

95, 96 Aus einer Fachzeitungskampagne für das Internationale Wollsekretariat. Zweck der Werbung ist die Förderung der Wolle; in den ganzseitigen Schwarzweiss-Inseraten wird jeweils ein bekannter japanischer Modeschöpfer vorgestellt, der 100% Wolle verwendet. (JPN)
97, 98 Aus einer Inseratenkampagne für *Mediator*-Fernsehapparate, in der auf die grosse Palette der Farbausführungen hingewiesen wird. Schwarzweiss mit Blau (Abb. 97) und Grau (Abb. 98). (SWI)
99, 100 Illustration und Inserat für *Philips*-Tonbandkassetten: «Schaudern oder geniessen.» (NLD)
101 Inserat für *Siegwerk*-Druckfarben, das den Unterschied zwischen einem Verwender dieser Farben (hier in bunten Tönen) und einem Nicht-Verwender (schwarzweiss) zeigt. (GER)

95, 96 Campagne du Secrétariat international de la Laine dans les revues spécialisées. Il s'agit de promouvoir l'usage de la pure laine vierge, par exemple dans la haute couture représentée dans ces annonces noir et blanc par des grands couturiers japonais très connus. (JPN)
97, 98 Exemples d'annonces faisant campagne pour les téléviseurs *Mediator*. On met ici l'accent sur la gamme étendue des coloris: blanc, noir, avec du bleu (fig. 97) et gris (fig. 98) par exemple. (SWI)
99, 100 Illustration et annonce pour les cassettes de magnétophones *Philips*: «Frissonner d'horreur ou connaître l'extase.» (NLD)
101 Annonce pour les encres d'imprimerie *Siegwerk*. La dichotomie fait apparaître en haut l'utilisateur de ces encres (aux couleurs vives), en bas celui qui les ignore (noir-blanc). (GER)

2

Booklets

Folders

Catalogues

Programmes

Broschüren

Faltprospekte

Kataloge

Programme

Brochures

Dépliants

Catalogues

Programmes

A CALL FOR BOOKS, BOOKJACKETS, AND PAPERBACK COVERS

This year, the AIGA will have two simultaneous competitions and exhibitions related to the book arts: the Book Show and the Bookjackets/Paperback Covers Show. There will be one chairman, but separate juries for each competition, and the exhibitions will open simultaneously. The Book Show will consist of books judged as a whole (submitted with or without covers). The Bookjackets/Paperback Covers Show will consist of bookjackets and paperback covers judged as separate entities. All books, bookjackets, and paperback covers for sale that have originated and been designed in the United States or Canada during the period from January 1, 1983 to January 1, 1984 are eligible. Selected entries will be illustrated in *AIGA Graphic Design USA: 5*, our hardbound volume documenting all the work which has comprised the year's competitive exhibitions. All entries should be submitted in the categories listed below. If you are uncertain of the category, it will be placed in the one which will show it to its best advantage for judging.

CATEGORIES

General Trade Books: Books for bookstore distribution (including how-to-do books, cookbooks, craft and hobby books).

Special Trade Books: Books for bookstore distribution which are primarily picture books, photography books, and general distribution books.

Limited Edition and Fine Private Press Books: Collectors' books for fine editions, deluxe art books and all books in which the quality of production, innovation or experimentation is deemed of paramount importance.

Text and Reference Books: All books used for instruction in schools, from elementary and high school texts to college, technical and vocational texts, encyclopedias, atlases, dictionaries and yearbooks.

Juveniles: Books published primarily for children, except texts.

Paperbacks: All books designed for paperback, including mass market.

DEADLINE

All entries must be received by December 16, 1983. Address entries to: The Book Show (or) The Bookjackets/Paperback Covers Show, American Institute of Graphic Arts, 1059 Third Avenue, New York, NY 10021.

102

103

104

102 Large unfolded call for entries for the "AIGA Book Show and Bookjackets/Paperback Covers Show". The illustration is in dark orange-red, green, brown and black. (USA)
103 Concertina folder announcing the new business address of Seitz Yamamoto Moss Inc. Graphic Design Studios. In full colour. (USA)
104 Illustration from a brochure for a college football team known as "The Bear-Cats" of the University of Cincinnati. It was also used for a poster. (USA)

102 Auseinandergefaltete Einladung des American Institute of Graphic Arts (AIGA) zur Teilnahme an zwei Wettbewerben/Ausstellungen, die der Buchkunst gewidmet sind, und zwar der Gesamtgestaltung und den Umschlägen. In Orangerot, Grün, Braun und Schwarz. (USA)
103 Für die Bekanntgabe der neuen Geschäftsadresse des Graphik-Design-Studios Seitz Yamamoto Moss Inc. versandtes Leporello. In Farbe. (USA)
104 Illustration aus einer Broschüre für ein College Football Team, das die «Bär-Katzen» genannt wird. Sie wurde ebenfalls für ein Plakat verwendet. (USA)

102 Invitation dépliée de l'American Institute of Graphic Arts (AIGA) à participer à deux concours-expositions consacrées à l'art du livre (conception d'ensemble et couvertures). Illustration en rouge orangé, vert, brun, noir. (USA)
103 Dépliant en accordéon indiquant la nouvelle adresse du studio Seitz Yamamoto Moss Inc. (USA)
104 Illustration tirée d'une brochure réalisée pour une équipe de football universitaire appelée les Chats-Ours. Illustration utilisée également sous forme d'affiche. (USA)

Booklets / Prospekte / Brochures

105

ARTIST / KÜNSTLER / ARTISTE:

105 Jeff Smith
106 Walter Grieder
107, 108 Olle Eksell
110 Tadanori Yokoo

DESIGNER / GESTALTER / MAQUETTISTE:

106 Walter Grieder
107, 108 Olle Eksell
109 Joyce Ho
110 Tadanori Yokoo
111 Takaaki Matsumoto

ART DIRECTOR / DIRECTEUR ARTISTIQUE:

105 Roger Black
106 Walter Grieder
107, 108 Olle Eksell
109 Janet C. Wright
110 Tadanori Yokoo
111 Takaaki Matsumoto

AGENCY / AGENTUR / AGENCE – STUDIO:

106 Walter Grieder
107 Marianne Pihlgren
109 John Cleveland, Inc.
111 Takaaki Matsumoto

107

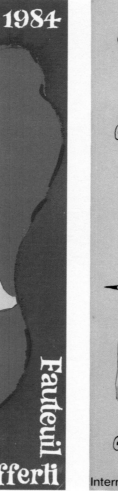

106

International Council of Graphic Design Associations 1963-1983

108

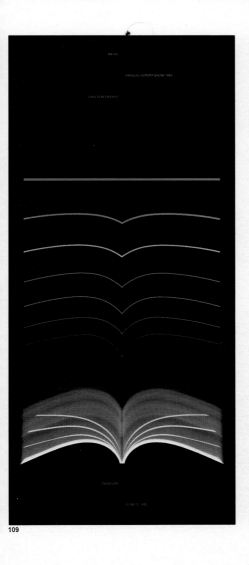

109

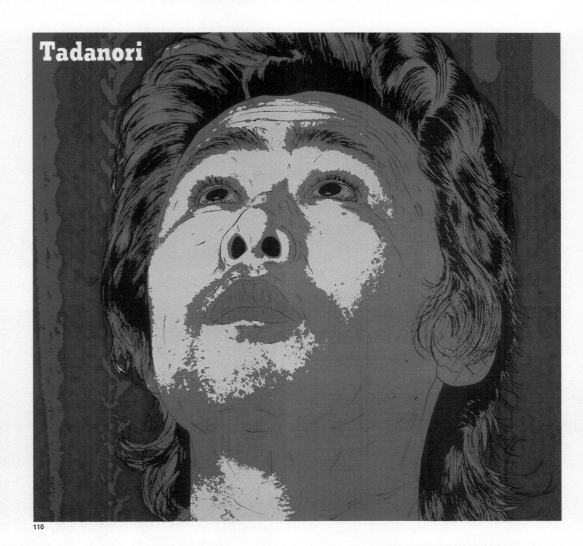

Tadanori

110

105 Call for entries for the AIGA Cover Show. Watercolour illustration with the red hat twice shown. (USA)
106 Cover of a programme for the Basle Fauteuil Theatre. The subject of the entertainment is the Basle Carnival. (SWI)
107 Inside of a folder for company consultants. (SWE)
108 Picture postcard announcing Icograda's congress. Illustrated in full colour. (IRE)
109 Announcement of the deadline for the receipt of entries for the Mead Annual Report Show. (USA)
110 Catalogue cover for an exhibition of the work of the Japanese artist Tadanori Yokoo. (JPN)
111 Invitation with loose imitation rice grains for an exhibition on fake food. Pastel greys, blue and pink. (USA)

105 Einladung zu einem Wettbewerb des AIGA. Thema sind Umschläge verschiedener Kategorien. Aquarell. (USA)
106 Umschlag eines Programms des Fauteuil Theaters. Thema der Vorstellung ist die Basler Fasnacht. (SWI)
107 Innenseite eines Faltprospekts für eine Unternehmens-beratungs-Gruppe. Mehrfarbige Illustrationen. (SWE)
108 Ankündigung einer Tagung der Icograda (International Council of Graphic Design Associations). In Farbe. (IRE)
109 Einladung zur Einreichung von Material für eine Ausstellung über die Gestaltung von Jahresberichten. (USA)
110 Umschlag des Katalogs für eine Ausstellung des japanischen Künstlers Tadanori Yokoo. (JPN)
111 Einladung mit nachgemachten Reiskörnern für eine Ausstellung über imitierte Lebensmittel. (USA)

105 Invitation à un concours AIGA des meilleures couvertures dans diverses catégories. Aquarelle. (USA)
106 Couverture d'un programme du Théâtre Fauteuil de Bâle. La pièce jouée traite du carnaval de Bâle. (SWI)
107 Page intérieure du dépliant d'un groupe de conseils d'entreprises. Illustrations polychromes. (SWE)
108 Annonce d'un meeting d'Icograda (International Council of Graphic Design Associations). Couleur. (IRE)
109 Appel d'envois pour une exposition sur le thème de la conception graphique de rapports annuels. (USA)
110 Couverture du catalogue accompagnant une exposition de l'œuvre de l'artiste japonais Tadanori Yokoo. (JPN)
111 Invitation à une exposition d'aliments factices. Grains de riz reproduits d'après nature. (USA)

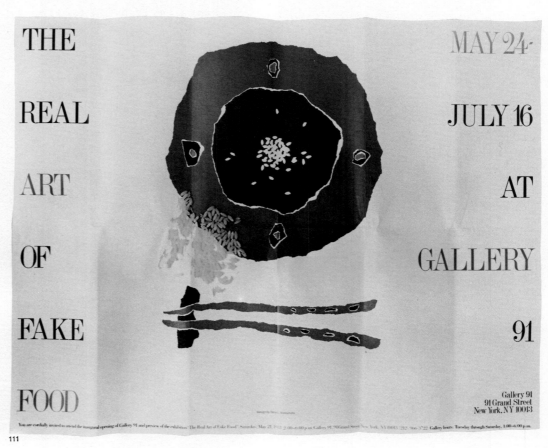

111

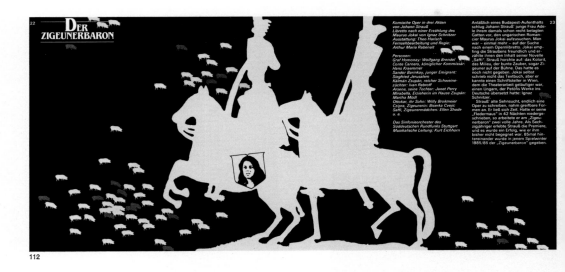

112

114

113

ARTIST / KÜNSTLER / ARTISTE:

112–114 Christof Gassner
115 Lesley Keen
116 Tom Antista
117 Zenji Funabashi

DESIGNER / GESTALTER / MAQUETTISTE:

112–114 Christof Gassner
116 Tom Antista
117 Sakae Kakigi

ART DIRECTOR / DIRECTEUR ARTISTIQUE:

116 Tom Antista
117 Sakae Kakigi

AGENCY / AGENTUR / AGENCE – STUDIO:

112–114 Christof Gassner
117 AZ Inc.

115

116

117

112–114 Double spreads and original-size illustration from a brochure for a German television network entitled "Music on ZDF". Fig. 112: White on black, pale pink and green pigs; Fig. 113: Introductory double spread in black and white; Fig. 114: For a Wagner concert in Neuschwanstein Castle. (GER)
115 "Taking a Line for a Walk. A Homage to the Work of Paul Klee." Card announcing a film on British television. White lines on dark blue background. (GBR)
116 For "Long Beach Blues Festival". Shades of blue. (USA)
117 Inside of an advertising pamphlet to promote vegetable juices for *Kagome*. Strong green, red and yellow tones. (JPN)

112–114 Doppelseiten und Illustration in Originalgrösse aus einer Broschüre des Zweiten Deutschen Fernsehens mit dem Titel «Musik im ZDF». Abb. 112: Weiss auf Schwarz, mit rosafarbenen und grünen Schweinchen; Abb. 113: Einleitende Doppelseite in Schwarzweiss; Abb. 114: Ankündigung eines Wagner-Konzertes im Schloss Neuschwanstein. (GER)
115 «Hommage an das Werk Paul Klees.» Ankündigung eines Films im britischen Fernsehen. Dunkelblau mit Weiss. (GBR)
116 Für ein Blues-Festival am Strand. Zwei Blautöne. (USA)
117 Innenseite einer Werbebroschüre für Gemüsesäfte der Marke *Kagome*. Kräftiges Grün, Rot und Orangegelb. (JPN)

112–114 Doubles pages et illustration au format original d'une brochure de la 2e chaîne TV allemande ZDF intitulée «Musik im ZDF» (Musique sur ZDF). Fig. 112: blanc sur noir, porcelets roses et verts; fig. 113: double page initiale en noir et blanc; fig. 114: annonce d'un concert Wagner au château de Neuschwanstein. (GER)
115 «Hommage à l'œuvre de Paul Klee.» Annonce d'un film consacré au grand artiste suisse/allemand par la Télévision britannique. Bleu foncé, avec du blanc. (GBR)
116 Pour un festival de blues sur une plage. Deux bleus. (USA)
117 Page intérieure d'une brochure publicitaire pour les jus de légumes *Kagome*. Vert vigoureux, rouge, jaune orangé. (JPN)

Booklets / Prospekte / Brochures

118, 119 Double spreads from a furniture catalogue presented in bound book form. Depicted here are "Homo Sedens" and Ingres portrait "Jupiter et Thétis" and also 18th and 19th century divans. Illustrations are in full colour. (ITA)
120–122 From a prospectus for Bösch Engineering Bureau in which the letter B forms the basis for all the illustrations. Shown here are examples for sanitary works and catering kitchen planning, in grey/blue and silver/blue respectively. (SWI)
123, 124 Self-promotion postcards for Jiri Kolar: "Small Tribute to Manet" and "Reading". (FRA)
125, 126 From a small studio magazine showing a pigeon on military assignment and a rat worn as a neckpiece; satirical comments. Linocuts and printed on a handpress. (GER)

118, 119 Doppelseiten aus einem in Buchform gestalteten Katalog für Möbel. Hier «Homo Sedens» und Ingres' «Jupiter und Tethys», sowie Möbel aus dem 18. und 19. Jahrhundert. (ITA)
120–122 Aus einem Prospekt für das Ingenieur-Büro Bösch, in dem der Buchstabe B die Grundlage für alle Illustrationen ist, hier für sanitäre Anlagen und Grossküchenplanung. (SWI)
123, 124 Eigenwerbung für Jiri Kolar: «Kleine Hommage an Manet» und «Lektüre». (FRA)
125, 126 Doppelseiten aus der kleinformatigen Hauszeitschrift des Graphikers Eduard Prüssen. Themen sind die Taube im Militäreinsatz und eine neue Variante des Rattenfells am Kragen. Linolschnitte, auf einer Handpresse gedruckt. (GER)

118, 119 Doubles pages d'un catalogue de meubles présenté en volume. On voit ici l'«Homo Sedens» et «Jupiter et Thétis» d'Ingres, ainsi que des meubles des XVIIIe et XIXe siècles. (ITA)
120–122 Extraits d'un prospectus réalisé pour le bureau d'ingénieurs Bösch. L'initiale de la raison sociale figure comme thème porteur de toutes les illustrations, ici pour des installations sanitaires et des cuisines industrielles. (SWI)
123, 124 Autopromotion de Jiri Kolar: «Petit hommage à Manet», «Lecture». (FRA)
125, 126 Doubles pages du house organ au petit format du graphiste Eduard Prüssen: pigeon militaire; col de fourrure de rat. Linogravures tirées sur une presse à bras. (GER)

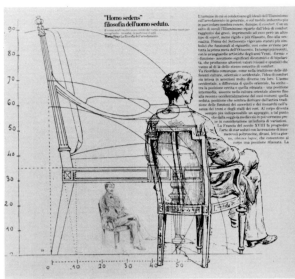

118

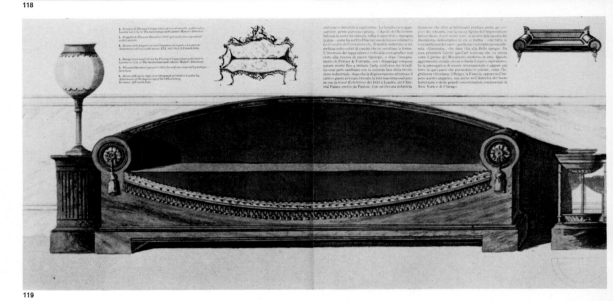

119

120

121

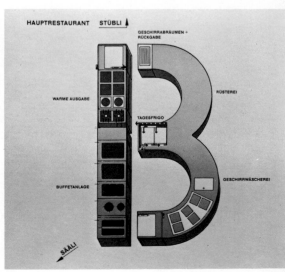

122

ARTIST / KÜNSTLER / ARTISTE:

123, 124 Jiri Kolar
125, 126 Eduard Prüssen

DESIGNER / GESTALTER / MAQUETTISTE:

118, 119 Italo Lupi
120–122 G. Knecht

123

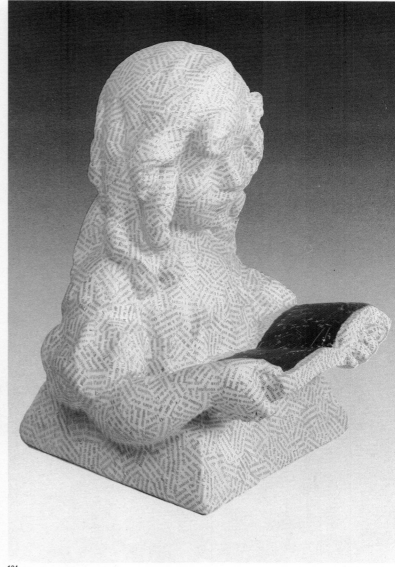

124

ART DIRECTOR / DIRECTEUR ARTISTIQUE:

120–122 Albert Ernst
123, 124 J. Rabascall

AGENCY / AGENTUR / AGENCE – STUDIO:

118, 119 Italo Lupi
120–122 Fabrikatelier am Wasser
123, 124 Atelier Rabascall

125

Löcher, Fransen,
Spitzen. Rüschen,
weiße Handschuhe.
Als jüngste
Zugabe
wird, liebkosend,
Ratte am Kragen
getragen,
lebend,
nicht als Pelz
wie ehedem
bei reichen
Spießern.

126

127

128

129

130

131

132

133

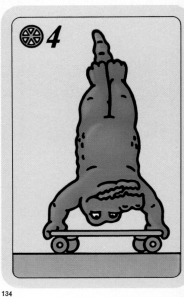

134

Booklets / Prospekte / Brochures

127–134 From a set of playing-cards for the card game entitled "With the Merry Crocodile of *Lacoste*", to promote the *Lacoste* children's collection. The subjects are sports, pastimes and recreation. (GER)
135 The Tucano Club's invitation for its members' welcome-back party after the summer break. The toucan has a blue beak and suit and is portrayed against a black background. (USA)
136 Full colour double spread depicting a polo match from a brochure about a new residential estate in Florida. (USA)
137 Illustration from a brochure describing a new office complex and illustrating the benefits of the surroundings in the south of Connecticut. (USA)

127–134 Kartenillustrationen aus einem Quartettspiel «mit dem lustigen Krokodil von *Lacoste*», zur Verkaufsförderung der *Lacoste*-Kinderkollektion. Thema sind Freizeitbeschäftigungen. (GER)
135 Einladungskarte eines Clubs zur Willkommensparty nach den Sommerferien. In Farbe. (USA)
136 Mehrfarbige Doppelseite mit der Darstellung eines Polo-Spiels aus einer grossformatigen Broschüre über ein neues, exklusives Wohngebiet in Florida. (USA)
137 Aus einer Broschüre für einen neuen Büro-Komplex im Süden Connecticuts. Illustriert sind die Vorzüge der Umgebung. (USA)

127–134 Illustrations figurant sur un jeu de cartes «avec le joyeux crocodile de *Lacoste*» diffusé en promotion des modes enfantines *Lacoste*. Sujets: des activités de loisirs. (GER)
135 Invitation d'un club pour sa première réunion après les vacances d'été. En couleur. (USA)
136 Double page polychrome représentant un match de polo, dans une brochure au grand format réalisée pour la promotion d'une nouvelle zone résidentielle grand luxe en Floride. (USA)
137 Extrait d'une brochure présentant un nouvel ensemble immobilier à usage de bureaux dans le sud du Connecticut. L'accent est mis ici sur les charmes de l'environnement. (USA)

135

136

137

71

138

139

138 Front of a folder for "Interview", a television programme specializing in out-of-the-ordinary advertising. (SWI)
139 Illustration in approximately the original size for a self-promotion card for artist Ponder Goembel. (USA)
140 Poster-sized folder from a visual company profile of *Voko*, a firm producing executive office furniture. (GER)
141 Catalogue illustration for the energy and raw-products combine *Total*. (FRA)

138 Vorderseite eines Faltprospekts für «Interview», ein TV-Magazin für ungewöhnliche Werbung am Fernsehen. (SWI)
139 Illustration, ungefähr Originalgrösse, einer Eigenwerbungskarte der Künstlerin Ponder Goembel. (USA)
140 Aus einem Faltprospekt im Posterformat für Büroprogramme (Möbel, Planung, Ordnungsmittel) von *Voko*. (GER)
141 Katalog-Illustration für den Energie- und Rohstoffkonzern *Total*. (FRA)

138 Recto d'un dépliant promotionnel pour «Interview», un programme de télévision de la publicité hors pair. (SWI)
139 Illustration au format approximativement original, pour la carte autopromotionnelle de l'artiste Ponder Goembel. (USA)
140 Extrait d'un dépliant au format affiche pour les programmes bureaux (meubles, planning, rangement) de *Voko*. (GER)
141 Illustration tirée d'un catalogue du groupe *Total*, spécialisé dans la production d'énergie et les matières premières. (FRA)

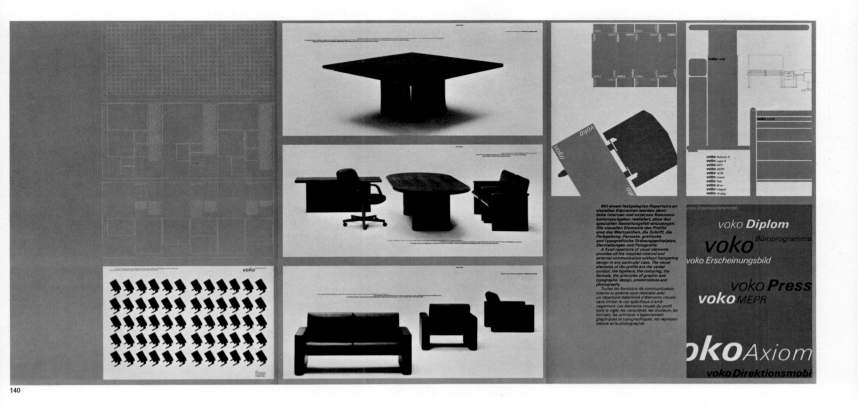

ARTIST / KÜNSTLER / ARTISTE:

142–144 Hans Manusama
145, 147–149 George Tscherny
146 Alain Gauthier

DESIGNER / GESTALTER / MAQUETTISTE:

142–144 Hans Manusama
145, 147–149 George Tscherny

ART DIRECTOR / DIRECTEUR ARTISTIQUE:

145, 147–149 George Tscherny

AGENCY / AGENTUR / AGENCE – STUDIO:

142–144 KLM Studio
145 Chermayeff & Geismar Assoc.
147–149 George Tscherny, Inc.

142

143

Booklets / Prospekte / Brochures

146

142–144 Three-dimensional double cards and complete cover (Fig. 143) of the Royal Dutch Airline KLM's promotional brochure. Fig. 142: Pop-up model of the Airbus A310 in blue, white and silver; Fig. 144: Pop-up of a reclining seat in their Royal Class; gold lettering, blue seat on mustard ground. (NLD)
145 Illustration for a *Xerox* brochure; glasses brown, additions red and black, buff ground. (USA)
146 Card with the illustration "Letter-flowers" as self-promotion for Alain Gauthier. (FRA)
147–149 Covers from a series of city maps and guides featuring major cities on the world routes of *Pan American Airways*. (USA)

142–144 Aufgeklappte, dreidimensionale Doppelkarten und vollständige Kartenvorderseite (Abb. 143) der holländischen Fluggesellschaft KLM. Abb. 142: Falzmodell des Airbus A310, vorwiegend in Blau und Weiss; Abb. 144: Falzmodell eines Sitzes der neuen Royal Class; Schrift in Gold auf senfgelbem Grund. (NLD)
145 Illustration für eine Werbebroschüre der Firma *Xerox*. Brillengestell in Braun, Additionen in Rot und Schwarz. (USA)
146 Karte mit der Illustration «Buchstaben-Blumen» als Eigenwerbung für Alain Gauthier. (FRA)
147–149 Beispiele von Umschlägen aus einer Reihe von Stadtplänen, herausgegeben von *Pan American Airways*. (USA)

142–144 Cartes doubles tridimensionnelles ouvertes et recto complet de carte (fig. 143) pour la compagnie aérienne néerlandaise KLM: Fig. 142: modèle pliant de l'Airbus A310, tons bleu et blanc prédominants; 144: modèle pliant d'un siège de la nouvelle Royal Class; texte or sur fond moutarde. (NLD)
145 Illustration pour une brochure publicitaire de *Xerox*. Monture en brun, additions en rouge et noir. (USA)
146 Carte avec l'illustration «Lettres-fleurs» en guise d'autopromotion, réalisée par Alain Gauthier. (FRA)
147–149 Exemples de couvertures pour une série de plans de villes publiés par *Pan American Airways*. (USA)

royal class

144

145

Rome
City Map and Guide

147

Brussels
City Map and Guide

148

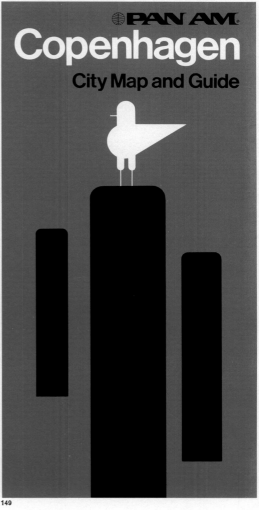

Copenhagen
City Map and Guide

149

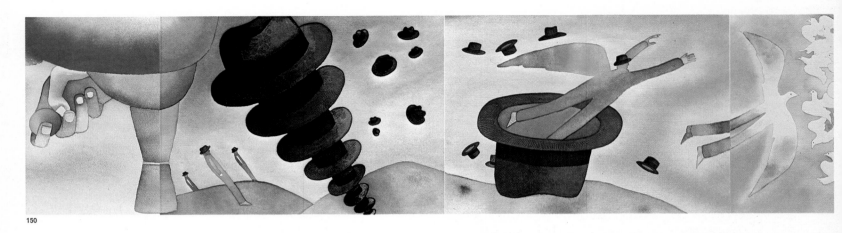

150

151

Booklets / Prospekte / Brochures

Eu carrego...

152

153

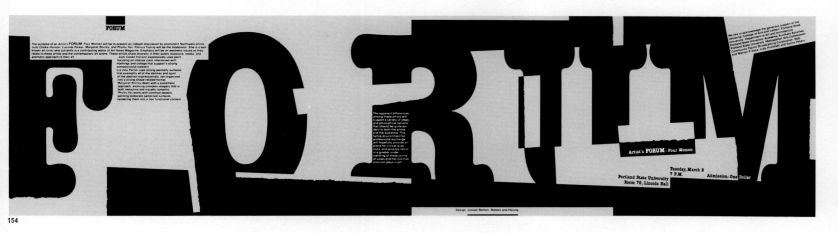

154

150, 151 Examples of double spreads from the concertina-folded book "The Conversation" by Jean Michel Folon and Milton Glaser. (USA)
152 Cover of a folded card; black wheelbarrow on red. Card inside red and black on white. (BRA)
153 The stamped out red and green letters of this greeting card are enclosed loose. (JPN)
154 Invitation card to an artist's forum with title "Four Women". Black and white. (USA)
155 Plastic loose-leaf folder, each leaf representing one square foot of space which can be rented as showrooms for interior furnishings from the International Design Center New York. (USA)

150, 151 Beispiele von Doppelseiten aus dem Leporello-Buch "The Conversation" von Jean Michel Folon und Milton Glaser. (USA)
152 Aufklappbare Karte; aussen schwarz auf Rot, innen rot und schwarz auf Weiss. (BRA)
153 Die ausgestanzten Buchstaben sind dieser Karte lose beigelegt. In Farbe. (JPN)
154 Einladungskarte zu einer Forums-Diskussion mit vier Künstlerinnen. In Schwarzweiss. (USA)
155 Plastikmappe mit losen Blättern aus strukturiertem Papier, herausgegeben vom International Design Center New York für die Vermietung von Showrooms für Inneneinrichtungen. (USA)

150, 151 Exemples de doubles pages contenues dans l'ouvrage à pliage accordéon "The Conversation" de Jean Michel Folon et Milton Glaser. (USA)
152 Carte pliante; extérieur noir sur rouge, intérieur rouge et noir sur blanc. (BRA)
153 Les lettres découpées sont jointes en vrac à cette carte. En couleur. (JPN)
154 Carte d'invitation à une table ronde organisée avec quatre artistes féminins. Noir, blanc. (USA)
155 Dossier plastique à feuillets mobiles de papier structuré, publié par l'International Design Center de New York pour la location de salles d'expositions de déco intérieure. (USA)

155

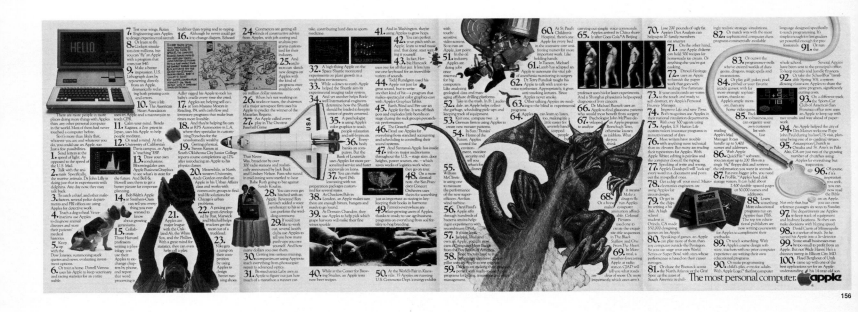

156

157

158

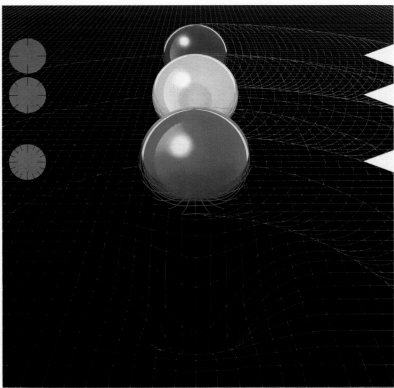

159

160

Booklets / Prospekte / Brochures

156 Prospectus in full colour (as stapled-in supplement for magazines) about the *Apple* Personal Computer and its various applications. (USA)
157, 158 Double spreads from a prospectus about *Linotype*-CRT-Compact Systems. (GER)
159, 160 Illustrations from a brochure about the *Fidelity Guards* computer system. (SAF)
161–162a Covers of brochures about IBM computer systems. Fig. 161 relates to computer graphics, Fig. 162 the IBM Basic programme, Fig. 162 a the IBM series/1 for effective communication within a system. (USA)

156 Mehrfarbiger Prospekt (als eingeheftete Beilage für Magazine) über den *Apple*-Personal-Computer und dessen Verwendungsmöglichkeiten. (USA)
157, 158 Doppelseiten aus einem Prospekt über *Linotype*-CRT-Kompaktsysteme. (GER)
159, 160 Illustrationen einer Broschüre über Computer-Systeme von *Fidelity Guards*. (SAF)
161–162a Vorderseiten von Broschüren über IBM-Computer-Systeme. Abb. 161 betrifft Computer-Graphik, Abb. 162 das IBM-Basic-Programm, Abb. 162a die IBM-Series/1 für effektive Kommunikation innerhalb eines Systems. (USA)

156 Prospectus polychrome (à encarter dans des magazines) présentant l'ordinateur personnel *Apple* et discutant de ses possibilités d'emploi. (USA)
157, 158 Doubles pages d'un prospectus des systèmes compacts *Linotype* CRT. (GER)
159, 160 Illustration d'une brochure consacrée aux systèmes informatiques *Fidelity Guards*. (SAF)
161–162a Rectos de brochures illustrant les systèmes informatiques IBM. La fig. 161 traite des visualisations graphiques sur ordinateur, la fig. 162 du programme Basic IBM, la fig. 162a de la Series IBM/1 assurant une communication efficace à l'intérieur d'un système. (USA)

162

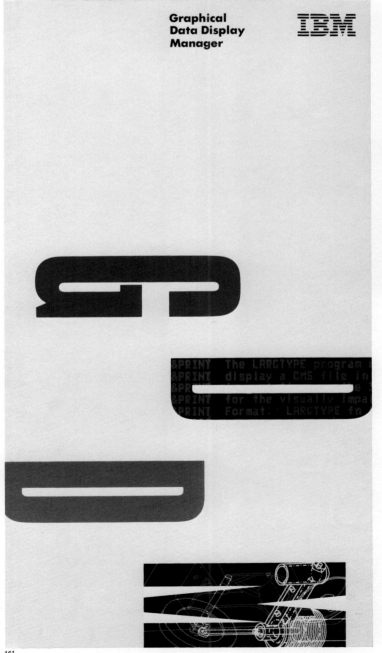

161

162a

ARTIST / KÜNSTLER / ARTISTE:

156 Elwood H. Smith
157, 158 Heinz Edelmann
159, 160 Dirk Voorneveld

DESIGNER / GESTALTER / MAQUETTISTE:

157, 158 Heinz Edelmann
159, 160 Clive Gay
161–162a Jon Craine

ART DIRECTOR / DIRECTEUR ARTISTIQUE:

156 Jim Cox
157, 158 Robert Pütz
159, 160 Clive Gay
161–162a Jon Craine

AGENCY / AGENTUR / AGENCE – STUDIO:

156 Chiat/Day, Inc.
157, 158 Robert Pütz GmbH
159, 160 Pentagraph (Pty) Ltd.
161–162a IBM

Booklets / Prospekte / Brochures

163 This over 13 inch long *Zanders* "Art Pencil" signed by 25 famous artists was distributed to visitors at their stand at the "Art Mate 83" exhibition in Frankfurt/M. (GER)
164 Illustration on the cover of a prospectus for *Cascade* Opaque Offset paper. (USA)
165, 166 From two brochures for the Champion International Corporation in which new paper qualities are introduced. "Marblehead Ivory" is the name of a new colour. (USA)
167 Illustration from an advertising folder for a carbon-paperless copying system. (SWI)
168, 169 Double spread and front cover of a prospectus for the Bezalel Art School. (ISR)
170, 171 Double spread and front cover of a brochure for the printing company *Campec*. (AUS)

163 Dieser 24 cm lange *Zanders* «Art-Stift» mit 25 Signaturen bekannter Künstler wurde an der «Art Mate 83» in Frankfurt/M. an die Messestand-Besucher verteilt. (GER)
164 Illustration auf der Vorderseite eines Prospekts für *Cascade*-Opaque-Offset-Papier. (USA)
165, 166 Aus zwei Broschüren der Champion International Corp., worin neue Papierqualitäten vorgestellt werden. «Marblehead Ivory» ist der Name einer neuen Farbe. (USA)
167 Illustration einer Werbemappe für ein kohlepapierloses Durchschreibesystem. (SWI)
168, 169 Doppelseite und Umschlag-Vorderseite eines Prospekts der Bezalel-Kunstschule. (ISR)
170, 171 Doppelseite und Umschlag-Vorderseite einer Broschüre der Druckerei *Campec*. (AUS)

163 Ce crayon artistique *Zanders*, de 24 cm de long, comportant la signature de 25 artistes de renom, a été distribué aux visiteurs du stand du même nom à l'«Art Mate 83» (Francfort). (GER)
164 Illustration pour le recto d'un prospectus présentant le papier offset opaque *Cascade*. (USA)
165, 166 Extraits de deux brochures de la Champion International Corp. avec de nouvelles qualités de papier. «Marblehead Ivory» est le nom d'un nouveau coloris. (USA)
167 Illustration sur le dossier publicitaire d'un système de calques sans papier carbone. (SWI)
168, 169 Double page et première page de couverture d'un dépliant de l'école d'art Bezalel. (ISR)
170, 171 Double page et première page de couverture d'une brochure de l'imprimerie *Campec*. (AUS)

163

ARTIST / KÜNSTLER / ARTISTE:

164 Warren Eakins
166 Benjamin Perez/
    Gary Stilovich
167 Paul Bergmaier
168, 169 Yarom Vardimon
170, 171 Flett Henderson & Arnold

164

165

166

167

DESIGNER / GESTALTER / MAQUETTISTE:

163 Planungsteam K. Nengelken/
    Werbeabt. Zanders Feinpapiere
164 Warren Eakins
165 Neil Shakery/Lenore Bartz
166 H. L. Chu/Gary Stilovich
167 Christian Lang
168, 169 Yarom Vardimon
170, 171 Flett Henderson & Arnold

ART DIRECTOR / DIRECTEUR ARTISTIQUE:

164 Warren Eakins
165 Neil Shakery
166 H. L. Chu
167 Christian Lang
168, 169 Yarom Vardimon
170, 171 Flett Henderson & Arnold

AGENCY / AGENTUR / AGENCE – STUDIO:

163 Planungsteam K. Nengelken
164 Young & Roehr
165 Jonson Pedersen Hinrichs & Shakery
166 H. L. Chu & Co., Ltd.
167 Ciba-Geigy/Werbung
168, 169 Yarom Vardimon
170, 171 Flett Henderson & Arnold

168

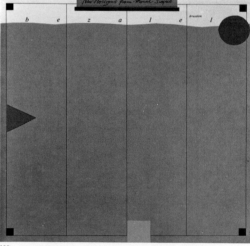

169

170

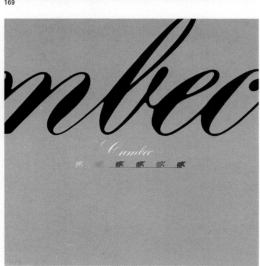

171

DESIGNER / GESTALTER / MAQUETTISTE:

172–177 Gilbert Lesser

ART DIRECTOR / DIRECTEUR ARTISTIQUE:

172–177 Gilbert Lesser

172–177 From the three-dimensional publicity for the magazine *Life*, aimed at attracting potential advertisers. Fig. 172: Cake-mix bowl, spoons and candles for *Life's* fifth birthday; Fig. 173: Feather duster for the advertisers' polished-up image; Fig. 174: Large water ball, "We're going to have a ball.... we'd like you to have one today."; Fig. 175: Small plastic bag unfolding to a larger one; Fig. 176: Dispenser for red-hot sweets (to match red-hot ads); Fig. 177: "Extinguish your media problems with *Life*"-extinguisher. All in red and white. (USA)

172–177 Aus der dreidimensionalen Direktwerbung für die Zeitschrift *Life*, die an potentielle Inserenten gerichtet ist. Abb. 172: Rührschüssel mit Löffeln und Kerzen zum fünften Geburtstag von *Life*; Abb. 173: Staubwedel für ein aufpoliertes Image der Inserenten; Abb. 174: Grosser Wasserball als Symbol für Wohlbefinden; Abb. 175: Kleine Plastiktasche, die sich zu einer grossen auseinanderfalten lässt; Abb. 176: Spender für heisse (scharfe) Bonbons – heiss wie die Werbemöglichkeiten; Abb. 177: Feuerlöscher zum Auslöschen der Werbeprobleme. Alle Objekte rot mit Weiss. (USA)

172–177 Eléments de publicité directe tridimensionnelle pour le magazine *Life*, à l'intention d'annonceurs potentiels. Fig. 172: cuve de mixeur, cuillers et bougies pour le 5e anniversaire de *Life*; 173: plumeau pour épousseter l'image des annonceurs; 174: gros ballon de water-polo symbolisant le bien-être; 175: petit sac plastique qui, déplié, se transforme en grand sac; 176: distributeur de bonbons acidulés donnant du mordant comme les annonces dans *Life*; 177: extincteur à problèmes publicitaires. Tous les objets: rouge, avec du blanc. (USA)

172

173

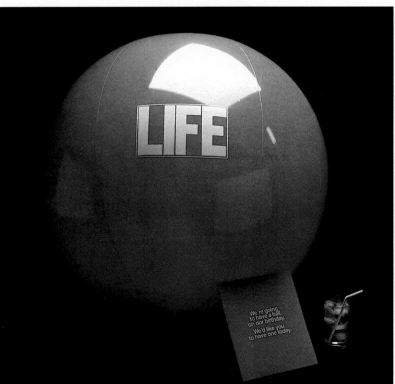

174

175

To get yourself a round redhot
Put a penny in the slot.
To earn yourself a profit clear
Run your ad in LIFE this year.
Here's to red-hot happenings in
1983 (at very low cpms *).

Happy New Year from
your friends at **LIFE**

*LIFE delivers 9,402,000 red-hot readers
for only $.00394 each.

176

LIFE
wishes you the reddest,
hottest, fieriest
of Valentine's Days.

Extinguish your media problems with
LIFE
The magazine that touches America's heart
and sets it on fire.

177

Der Gute Hirt
„Es gibt keine größere Liebe,
als wenn jemand sein
Leben für seine Freunde
hingibt"

178, 179 Double spreads from the exhibition catalogue for the Peruvian painter and sculptor Josué Sanchez Cerron, organized by the International Catholic Mission, *Missio*. (GER)
180 Cartoon by Paul Baringou on "South America 1983". From an exhibition catalogue. (FRA)
181 Cover for the University of Pennsylvania's brochure. Illustrated is rhubarb, which their founder, Benjamin Franklin, introduced into America—among his many other deeds. (USA)
182 Double spread from a brochure for a children's book exhibition in Klingspor Museum. (GER)
183 Front cover of an invitation to a golf tournament on the oldest golfcourse in the world. (USA)

178, 179 Doppelseiten aus dem Katalog für die Ausstellung des peruanischen Malers und Bildhauers Josué Sanchez Cerron, veranstaltet vom internationalen katholischen Missionswerk *Missio*. (GER)
180 Kommentar von Paul Baringou zu «Südamerika 1983». Aus einem Ausstellungskatalog. (FRA)
181 Umschlag einer Broschüre der University of Pennsylvania. Benjamin Franklin, dem Gründer dieser Universität, ist u. a. auch die Einführung des Rhabarbers in die USA zu verdanken. (USA)
182 Doppelseite aus einer Broschüre für eine Bilderbuchausstellung im Klingspor-Museum. (GER)
183 Vorderseite einer Einladung zu einem Golfturnier auf dem ältesten Golfplatz der Welt. (USA)

178, 179 Doubles pages du catalogue d'exposition du peintre et sculpteur péruvien Josué Sanchez Cerron préparé par *Missio*, l'œuvre missionnaire catholique internationale. (GER)
180 Commentaire de Paul Baringou sur «L'Amérique du Sud en 1983». Catalogue d'exposition. (FRA)
181 Couverture d'une brochure de l'Université de Pennsylvanie. Benjamin Franklin, qui a fondé cette université, a aussi introduit la rhubarbe aux Etats-Unis. (USA)
182 Double page d'une brochure pour une exposition de livres d'enfants au Musée Klingspor. (GER)
183 Recto d'une invitation à un tournoi de golf sur les links les plus anciens du monde. (USA)

178

179

180

181

ARTIST / KÜNSTLER / ARTISTE:

178, 179 Josué Sánchez Cerron
180 Paul Baringou
181 Carolyn McIntyre
182 Gert Zeising
183 Chuck Wilkinson

DESIGNER / GESTALTER / MAQUETTISTE:

178, 179 Herbert Wenn
181 Domenica Genovese
182 Walter Wilkes
183 Philip Gips/Dung Nguyen

ART DIRECTOR:

181 Domenica Genovese
183 Philip Gips

AGENCY / AGENTUR / AGENCE:

178, 179 Herbert Wenn
181 North Charles Street
     Design Organization
183 Gips+Balkind+Assoc., Inc.

Der Bandit warf seinen Raub
wie eine müde Rose der
Circusprinzessin Sisiwub zu.
Dabei kopierte er eine Geste des
Filmschauspielers Humphrey Bogart,
eines jener unsterblichen
Celluloid-Idole (!!).

Die Artistin verlor ihren Erwerb (owee)
beim Hofknicks-Aufundab
vor dem im Exil lebenden König
Gageis dem Soundsovielten.
Dieser stürzte sich auf die verlorene
Jugend. Er wollte mit ihr
seine thronlose Zeit totschlagen.

182

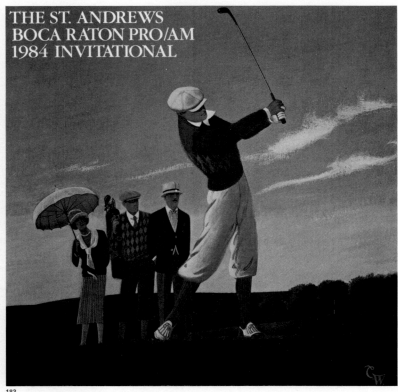

183

ARTIST / KÜNSTLER / ARTISTE:

184, 185 Hans Hillmann
187–191 Michael David Brown/
         Peter Lincoln Dunnigan

DESIGNER / GESTALTER / MAQUETTISTE:

186 Minale, Tattersfield & Partners
187–191 Michael David Brown/
         Chuck Gallis

184

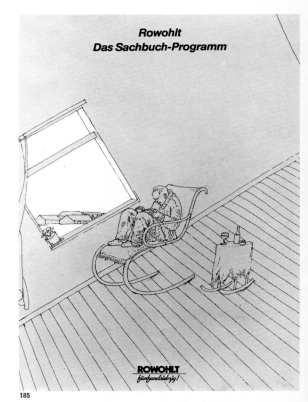

185

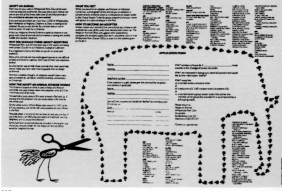

186

Booklets / Prospekte / Brochures

184, 185 Cover illustrations for the *Rowohlt* publishers' catalogue. (GER)
186 Whipsnade Park Zoo invites patrons to "adopt an animal". White and pale blue. (GBR)
187–191 Double spread, illustrations and cover from an information brochure issued by the tax authorities in the United States. Fig. 187: Examples of filled-out tax return forms; Figs. 188–191: Full-page illustrations in full colour and the cover (Fig. 189) portraying American presidents and other famous people, inventions and objects pertaining to American history. (USA)

184, 185 Umschlagillustrationen für Kataloge des *Rowohlt*-Verlags. (GER)
186 Hier wirbt der Londoner Zoo um «Adoptiveltern» für seine Tiere. Weiss und Hellblau. (GBR)
187–191 Doppelseite, Illustrationen und Umschlag einer Informations-Broschüre der Steuerbehörde der Vereinigten Staaten. Abb. 187: Beispiele ausgefüllter Formulare; Abb. 188–191: ganzseitige, mehrfarbige Illustrationen und der Umschlag (Abb. 189) mit Porträts amerikanischer Präsidenten und anderer berühmter Personen, symbolträchtigen Figuren, Dingen und Erfindungen. (USA)

184, 185 Illustrations de couvertures pour des catalogues des Ed. *Rowohlt*. (GER)
186 Ici, le zoo de Londres recherche des «parents adoptifs». Blanc et bleu clair. (GBR)
187–191 Double page, illustrations et couverture d'une brochure d'information des Services fiscaux des Etats-Unis. Fig. 187: exemples de formulaires remplis correctement; fig. 188–191: illustrations polychromes pleine page et couverture (fig. 189), avec les portraits de présidents américains, d'autres célébrités, de personnages, objets et inventions symboliques. (USA)

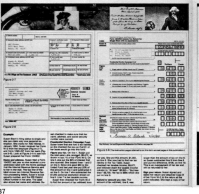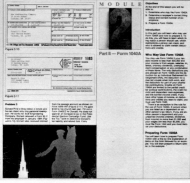

187

ART DIRECTOR / DIRECTEUR ARTISTIQUE:

184, 185 Hans Hillmann
187–191 Chuck Gallis

AGENCY / AGENTUR / AGENCE – STUDIO:

186 Minale, Tattersfield & Partners
187–191 Michael David Brown, Inc.

188

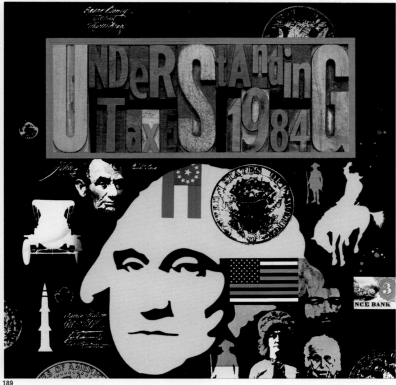

189

190

191

192

ARTIST / KÜNSTLER / ARTISTE:

192, 193 Rafal Olbinski
194 Jorge Sposari
195 Greg MacNair
196, 197 Bob Fortier

DESIGNER / GESTALTER / MAQUETTISTE:

195 David Bartels

ART DIRECTOR / DIRECTEUR ARTISTIQUE:

195 David Bartels

AGENCY / AGENTUR / AGENCE – STUDIO:

195 Bartels & Company, Inc.
196, 197 Reactor

192, 193 Illustrations shown here in original size of self-promotional cards for the Papermania International Studio. (USA)
194 Full-colour illustration for the change-of-address card for a graphic studio. Yellow and white "pencil" skyscrapers; red and white "pencil" bus; blue, yellow and red rainbow—on black. (ARG)
195 Self-promotional piece for an advertising and design agency. The theme promulgated is the company's reliability concerning time, target and budget adherence. Brown on cream paper. (USA)
196, 197 Self-promotional pieces for the Reactor Art & Design Studio and for the illustrator Bob Fortier. Black on white. (CAN)

192, 193 Illustrationen in Originalgrösse für Eigenwerbungskarten des Studios Papermania International. (USA)
194 Mehrfarbige Illustration für die Adressänderungs-Karte eines Graphik-Studios. (ARG)
195 Eigenwerbung eines Werbe- und Design-Studios. Das Thema der Illustration ist Zuverlässigkeit in bezug auf Zeit-, Ziel- und Budget-Einhaltung. Braun auf beigem Papier. (USA)
196, 197 Eigenwerbung für das Reactor Art & Design Studio, beziehungsweise den Illustrator Bob Fortier. Schwarz auf Weiss. (CAN)

192, 193 Illustrations au format original pour les cartes autopromotionnelles du studio Papermania International. (USA)
194 Illustration polychrome pour la carte de changement d'adresse d'un studio d'art publicitaire. (ARG)
195 Autopromotion d'un studio de publicité et de design. L'illustration a pour thème la fiabilité de l'équipe qui tient les délais, respecte les objectifs et le budget. Brun sur papier beige. (USA)
196, 197 Autopromotion pour le Reactor Art & Design Studio respectivement pour l'illustrateur Bob Fortier. Noir sur blanc. (CAN)

194

195

193

197

196

202

ARTIST / KÜNSTLER / ARTISTE:

198, 199 Seymour Chwast
200 Christoph Blumrich
201 James McMullan
202, 203 Lanny Sommese

DESIGNER / GESTALTER / MAQUETTISTE:

198–201 Seymour Chwast

ART DIRECTOR / DIRECTEUR ARTISTIQUE:

198–201 Seymour Chwast
202, 203 Lanny Sommese

AGENCY / AGENTUR / AGENCE – STUDIO:

198–201 Pushpin Lubalin Peckolick, Inc.
202, 203 Lanny Sommese Design

198–201 Cover of a brochure without and with its own transparent overlap on which the clothes only are printed in tones of grey; also two full-page illustrations in full colour. The brochure is for a fitness institute offering comprehensive fitness facilities. (USA)
202, 203 Cover and detail of the illustration from a programme of events for the Central Pennsylvania Festival of the Arts, a visual and performing arts festival. (USA)

198–201 Umschlag ohne und mit dazugehörigem transparenten Papier, auf das die Kleidung in Grautönen aufgedruckt ist, sowie zwei der ganzseitigen Illustrationen aus einer Broschüre für ein Fitness-Institut, das für alle Bedürfnisse ein passendes Programm anbietet. (USA)
202, 203 Umschlag und Detail der Illustration für ein Programmheft des Festivals der darstellenden und visuellen Künste (Central Pennsylvania Festival of the Arts), das alljährlich von der Penn State University und anderen Stellen organisiert wird. (USA)

198–201 Couverture avec et sans le cache transparent où sont imprimés les habits en tons gris, et deux des illustrations pleine page de la brochure d'un institut de culture physique offrant un programme adapté à tous les besoins. (USA)
202, 203 Couverture et détail de l'illustration d'une brochure-programme du festival des arts de spectacle et des arts visuels que la Penn State University organise sous le nom de Central Pennsylvania Festival of The Arts. (USA)

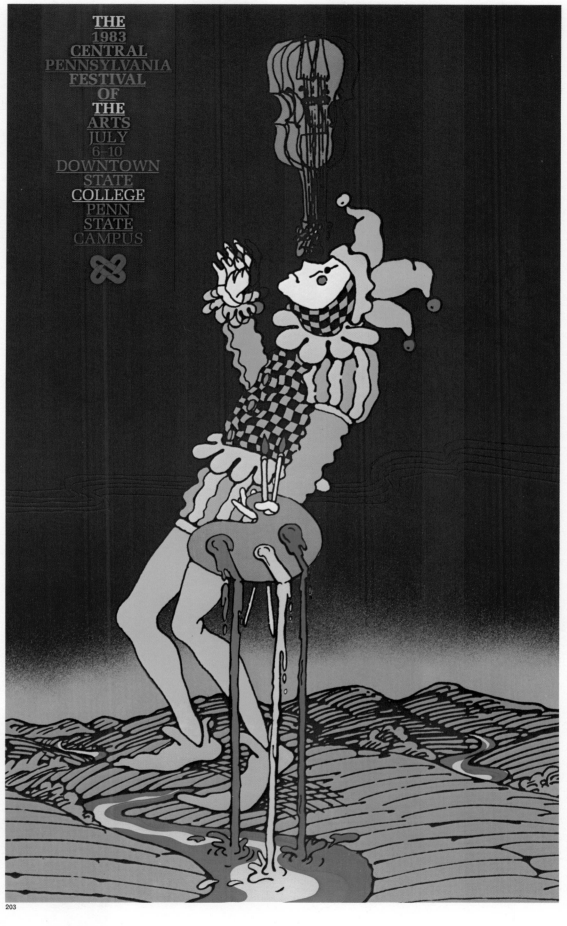

203

Booklets / Prospekte / Brochures

204

ARTIST / KÜNSTLER / ARTISTE:

204 Fred Otnes
205–207 Heinz Edelmann/
　　　　Gerhard Vormwald (Photo)

DESIGNER / GESTALTER / MAQUETTISTE:

205–207 Heinz Edelmann

ART DIRECTOR / DIRECTEUR ARTISTIQUE:

205–207 Robert Pütz

AGENCY / AGENTUR / AGENCE – STUDIO:

205–207 Robert Pütz GmbH

204 Self-promotion card for the American, Fred Otnes. A collage, here in actual size. (USA)
205–207 Cover and double spreads from the first edition of a "magazine" entitled "Creative Network" issued by the advertising agency Robert Pütz as self-promotional literature. This agency is comprised of an international free-lance pool whose policy is the conception of advertising campaigns from the ideas—and not vice versa; hence the reason why no finished work is shown, but only the ideas for creating a campaign. In Figs. 205 and 207 facetious and profound aphorisms, respectively, accompany the illustrations. Fig. 206 is the introductory double spread to the presentation of the idea leading to the corporate image identity for *Nixdorf* computers. (GER)

204 Collage für eine Eigenwerbungskarte des Amerikaners Fred Otnes. (USA)
205–207 Umschlag und Doppelseiten aus einem Heft mit dem Titel «Creative Network», das von der Werbeagentur Robert Pütz herausgegeben wird. Mit diesem Namen bezeichnet die Agentur ihre Zusammenarbeit mit internationalen freien Mitarbeitern, bei der die Konzeption einer Werbekampagne aus der Idee entstehen soll und nicht umgekehrt. Im Heft werden deshalb keine fertigen Werbemittel gezeigt, sondern Ideen, die zu kreativen Kampagnen geführt haben. In Abb. 205 und 207 werden originelle Kommentare zur Werbung präsentiert, Abb. 206 ist die einleitende Doppelseite zu einer Darstellung der Idee, die zum Corporate-Image-Konzept für *Nixdorf*-Computer führte. (GER)

204 Collage pour une carte autopromotionnelle de l'Américain Fred Otnes. (USA)
205–207 Couverture et doubles pages d'une brochure publiée par l'agence de publicité Robert Pütz sous le titre de «Creative Network». Ce terme désigne un réseau international de designers indépendants associés à l'agence, chez qui l'idée précède la conception d'une campagne publicitaire, contrairement à ce qui se fait souvent ailleurs. D'où la présentation, dans cette brochure, non pas de produits finis, mais des idées qui les ont inspirés. Fig. 205 et 207: commentaires percutants de l'action publicitaire. Fig. 206: double page initiale introduisant l'idée qui a servi de détonateur à la conception de l'image globale de marque des ordinateurs *Nixdorf*. (GER)

205

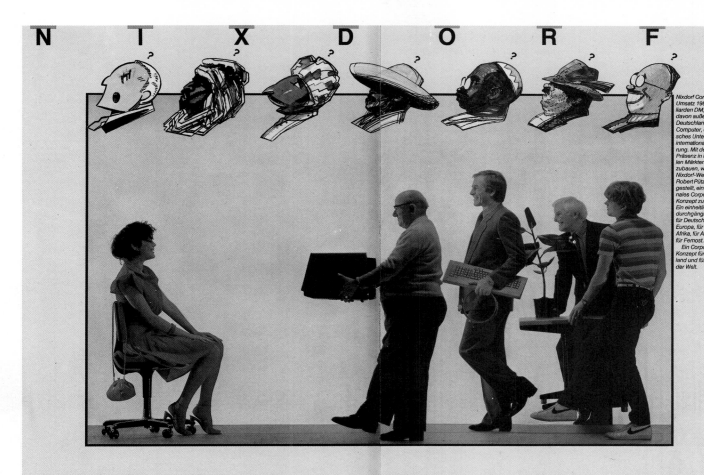

**In Germany and
33 countries worldwide**

Nixdorf Computer. Umsatz 1982: 2,3 Milliarden DM, 54 Prozent davon außerhalb Deutschlands. Nixdorf Computer, ein deutsches Unternehmen mit internationaler Orientierung. Mit dem Ziel, die Präsenz in internationalen Märkten weiter auszubauen, wurde der Nixdorf-Werbeagentur Robert Pütz die Aufgabe gestellt, ein internationales Corporate Image-Konzept zu entwickeln. Ein einheitliches und durchgängiges Konzept für Deutschland, für Europa, für Amerika, für Afrika, für Australien und für Fernost.
Ein Corporate Image-Konzept für Deutschland und für 33 Länder der Welt.

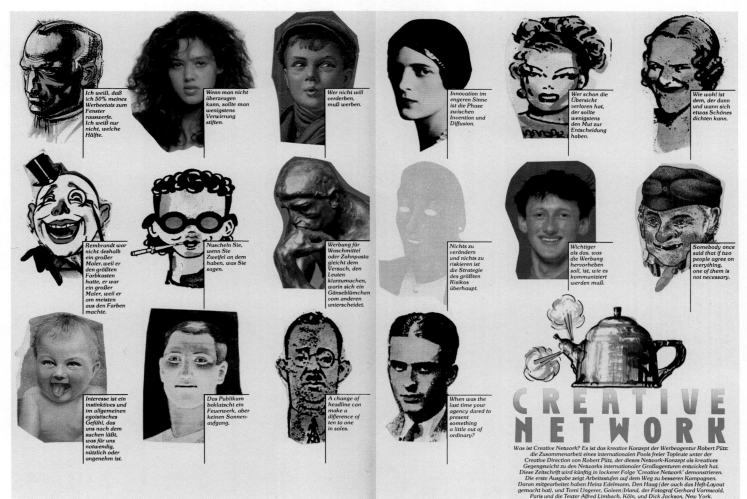

Ich weiß, daß ich 50% meines Werbeetats zum Fenster rauswerfe. Ich weiß nur nicht, welche Hälfte.

Wenn man nicht überzeugen kann, sollte man wenigstens Verwirrung stiften.

Wer nicht will verderben, muß werben.

Innovation im engeren Sinne ist die Phase zwischen Invention und Diffusion.

Wer schon die Übersicht verloren hat, der sollte wenigstens den Mut zur Entscheidung haben.

Wie wohl ist dem, der dann und wann sich etwas Schönes dichten kann.

Rembrandt war nicht deshalb ein großer Maler, weil er den größten Farbkasten hatte, er war ein großer Maler, weil er am meisten aus den Farben machte.

Nuscheln Sie, wenn Sie Zweifel an dem haben, was Sie sagen.

Werbung für Waschmittel oder Zahnpasta gleicht dem Versuch, den Leuten klarzumachen, worin sich ein Gänseblümchen vom anderen unterscheidet.

Nichts zu verändern und nichts zu riskieren ist die Strategie des größten Risikos überhaupt.

Wichtiger als das, was die Werbung hervorheben soll, ist, wie es kommuniziert werden muß.

Somebody once said that if two people agree on everything, one of them is not necessary.

Interesse ist ein instinktives und im allgemeinen egoistisches Gefühl, das uns nach dem suchen läßt, was für uns notwendig, nützlich oder angenehm ist.

Das Publikum beklatscht ein Feuerwerk, aber keinen Sonnenaufgang.

A change of headline can make a difference of ten to one in sales.

When was the last time your agency dared to present something a little out of ordinary?

CREATIVE NETWORK

Was ist Creative Network? Es ist das kreative Konzept der Werbeagentur Robert Pütz: die Zusammenarbeit eines internationalen Pools freier Topleute unter der Creative Direction von Robert Pütz, der dieses Network-Konzept als kreatives Gegengewicht zu den Networks internationaler Großagenturen entwickelt hat. Diese Zeitschrift wird künftig in lockerer Folge 'Creative Network' demonstrieren. Die erste Ausgabe zeigt Arbeitsstufen auf dem Weg zu besseren Kampagnen. Daran mitgearbeitet haben Heinz Edelmann, Den Haag (der auch das Heft-Layout gemacht hat), und Tomi Ungerer, Goleen/Irland, der Fotograf Gerhard Vormwald, Paris und die Texter Alfred Limbach, Köln, und Dick Jackson, New York.

ARTIST / KÜNSTLER / ARTISTE:

211, 212 Michael Everitt
213 Al Hirschfeld
214 Reven T. C. Wurman (Photo)

DESIGNER / GESTALTER / MAQUETTISTE:

208–214 Richard Saul Wurman

ART DIRECTOR / DIRECTEUR ARTISTIQUE:

208–210, 213, 214 Richard Saul Wurman/
Allison Ann Goodman
211, 212 Richard Saul Wurman/
Michael Everitt

■ In this double spread samples are shown from a series of handbooks presenting American cities and sports, published by Access Press, Inc., of which Richard Saul Wurman is President and Creative Director. The city guidebooks offer numerous plans and a wealth of information on culture, history, landmarks, attractions, shops, hotels etc.; the sports guides, conceived as television viewers' guides, contain everything the viewer sports-devotee wants to know about his favourite sports. The guidebooks are of handy slim tall-pocket format.

■ Auf dieser Doppelseite werden Beispiele aus einer Handbuchreihe über amerikanische Städte und Sport vorgestellt, die von Access Press, Inc., herausgegeben wird. (R.S. Wurman ist Präsident und Creative Director.) Die Stadtführer bieten neben zahlreichen Plänen ausführliche Informationen über Kultur, Geschichte, Sehenswürdigkeiten und Veranstaltungen; die Sportführer enthalten neben den Veranstaltungskalendern alles, was der Zuschauer über die verschiedenen Disziplinen wissen sollte. Die Bände haben ein praktisches, schlankes Taschenformat.

■ Cette double page présente des exemples tirés d'une série de manuels sur le thème des villes et des sports d'Amérique, publiés par Access Press, Inc., dont Richard Saul Wurman est président et directeur créatif. Les guides relatifs aux villes contiennent de nombreuses cartes, des informations sur la culture, l'histoire, les curiosités et les manifestations; les guides relatifs aux sports fournissent le programme des manifestations de la discipline choisie en même temps qu'une foule de renseignements. Format de poche mince, pratique.

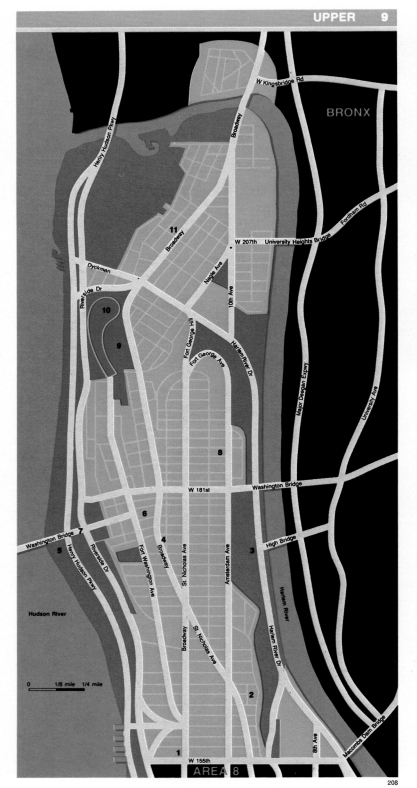

208

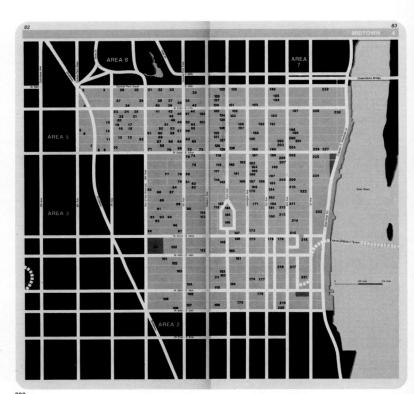

209

211

208–210, 213, 214 From the *Access* Guidebook to New York City. Figs. 208, 209: Plans of parts of the Manhattan area; Fig. 210: Sample of a double spread with information about buildings (here about the World Trade Center); Fig. 213: Black-and-white illustration for a page on culture information; Fig. 214: Cover illustration in full colour. (USA)
211, 212 Double spreads from the *Access* Television Viewers' Guide to the Olympic Games in Los Angeles, offering information on archery and gymnastics. (USA)

208–210, 213, 214 Aus dem *Access*-Stadtführer für New York City. Abb. 208, 209: Pläne für Teilbereiche von Manhattan; Abb. 210: Beispiel einer Doppelseite mit Informationen über Gebäude (hier über das World Trade Center); Abb. 213: Illustration für eine Seite mit Kulturinformationen; Abb. 214: Umschlag mit mehrfarbiger Illustration. (USA)
211, 212 Doppelseiten aus dem *Access*-Handbuch über die Olympischen Spiele in Los Angeles für Fernsehzuschauer, hier mit Informationen über Bogenschiessen und Gymnastik. (USA)

208–210, 213, 214 Guide *Access* de la ville de New York. Fig. 208, 209: cartes de diverses secteurs de Manhattan; fig. 210: exemple de double page renseignant sur les bâtiments (ici, le World Trade Center); fig. 213: illustration d'une page de renseignements culturels; fig. 214: couverture ornée d'une illustration en polychromie. (USA)
211, 212 Doubles pages du guide *Access* consacré aux Jeux Olympiques de Los Angeles, à l'intention des téléspectateurs; renseignements sur le tir à l'arc et la gymnastique. (USA)

213

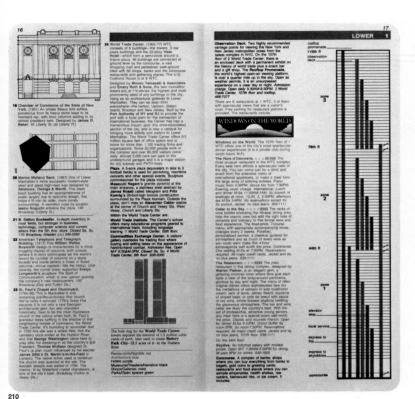

210

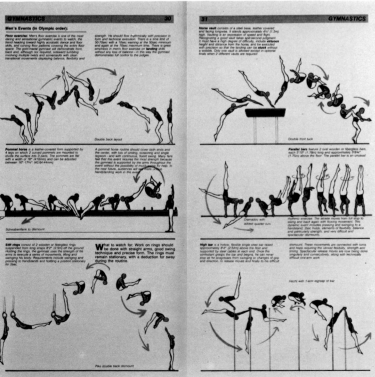

212

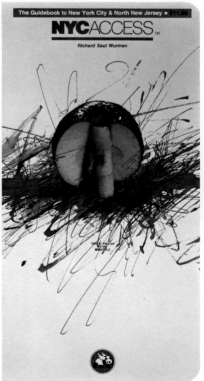

214

GOOD EVENING, LADIES AND GENTLEMEN. I'M SO HAPPY TO BE HERE TONIGHT. BECAUSE WITH THE MONEY I MAKE FROM THIS PERFORMANCE I'M GOING TO BUY MYSELF A SLEEK NEW JAGUAR WITH LEATHER INTERIOR AND SILVER INSTEAD OF CHROME. DO YOU LIKE MY NEW WHITE FOX? IT WAS DESIGNED FOR ME IN FRANCE. I PLAYED CHOPIN FOR THAT.

„1980". Ein Stück von Pina Bausch

Ein Mann besitzt ein Pferd und das Pferd rennt davon. Ein Freund sagt zu ihm: „Das tut mir leid für Dich." Der Mann antwortet: „Ich weiß nicht, ob es gut oder schlecht ist." Das Pferd kommt zurück mit einem zweiten Pferd. Der Freund sagt: „Ah, Du hast aber Glück!" Der Mann antwortet wieder: „Ich weiß nicht, ob es gut oder schlecht ist." Der Mann gibt das zweite Pferd seinem Sohn und der ist darüber sehr glücklich. Der Sohn besteigt das Pferd und

DREI MARK

Theater der Welt '81 Köln 12.–28.Juni

215

Squat Theatre: „Mr. Dead & Mrs. Free"

The men passionately hunted shells looking for pearls and one of them, a Brooklyn police man, had the luck to collect quite a lot. "Dear wife", he wrote, "I am coming home soon, want to open a jewelry store in midtown, I already got the name for it: Mr. DEAD & Mrs. FREE. How do you like it, honey?"

In diesem Augenblick bricht Krieg aus. Alle jungen Männer werden eingezogen, nur der Sohn nicht, weil er ein gebrochenes Bein hat. Der Freund sagt: „Oh, was für ein Glück für ihn." Der Mann sagt: „Ich weiß nicht, ob es gut oder schlecht ist."

Yoshi Oida: „Interrogations"

fällt herunter. Er bricht sich das Bein. Der Freund sagt: „Oh, so ein Pech!" Der Mann sagt: „Ich weiß nicht, ob es gut oder schlecht ist."

DER MOPS BELLTE KRITISCH, DER LAKAI GLOTZTE, SEIN HERR PUTZTE SICH DIE NASE UND MYLADY SAGTE:„A FINE EXHIBITION, VERY FINE INDEED!"

Heinrich Heine

216

215–218 For a programme in newspaper format for the World Theatre Festival in Cologne. Fig. 215: Cover with table of contents and quotations, black and white with yellow; Fig. 216: First page with quotations, black and white with red mask; Fig. 217: Double spread with quotations and information on the production of the opening performance, black and white with yellow; Fig. 218: Programme supplement in smaller format, black and white with red. (GER)
219 Cover of a press folder for publicity material about a television production of *King Lear*, starring Sir Laurence Olivier. Yellow crown, royal blue cloak. (USA)
220 Cover in full colour for a dance festival covering all styles of dancing. (ITA)
221 Vertical concertina-fold as invitation to a film premiere about American architecture. (USA)

215–218 Für ein im Zeitungsformat erschienenes Programmheft des internationalen Theater-Festivals in Köln. Abb. 215: Umschlag mit Zitaten und Inhaltsübersicht, schwarzweiss mit Gelb; Abb. 216: Erste Seite mit Zitaten, schwarzweiss mit roter Maske; Abb. 217: Doppelseite mit Informationen und Zitaten zur Eröffnungsvorstellung, schwarzweiss mit Gelb; Abb. 218: Beigefügte Spielplanübersicht in kleinerem Format, schwarzweiss mit Rot. (GER)
219 Vorderseite einer Pressemappe für Unterlagen über eine Fernsehaufführung von *König Lear*, mit Sir Laurence Olivier in der Hauptrolle. In Farbe. (USA)
220 Umschlag des Programms für Tanzveranstaltungen während Festwochen in Comacchio. (ITA)
221 Leporello als Einladung für eine Filmvorführung über moderne amerikanische Architektur. (USA)

217

218

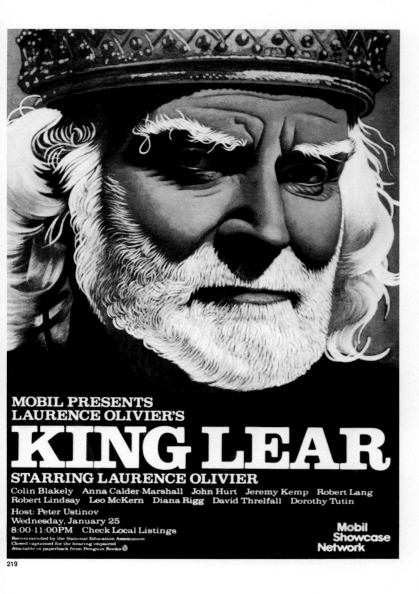

219

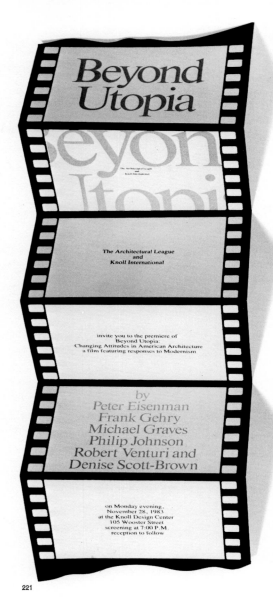

221

215–218 Pour un programme du Festival international du théâtre de Cologne publié sous forme de journal. Fig. 215: couverture ornée de citations, avec le sommaire, noir, blanc et jaune; fig. 216: première page de citations, noir et blanc, masque rouge; fig. 217: double page d'informations et de citations pour la soirée d'inauguration du festival, noir, blanc et jaune; fig. 218: programme annexé, petit format, noir, blanc et rouge. (GER)
219 Recto d'une documentation presse contenant des informations sur une dramatique avec Sir Laurence Olivier (*Le Roi Lear*). En couleur. (USA)
220 Couverture du programme de danse du Festival de Comacchio. (ITA)
221 Invitation pliée en accordéon: projection d'un film sur l'architecture américaine. (USA)

220

Booklets / Prospekte / Brochures

ARTIST / KÜNSTLER / ARTISTE:

215–218 Heinz Edelmann/Klaus Mohr
219 Paul Davis
220 Ilde Ianigro

DESIGNER / GESTALTER / MAQUETTISTE:

215–218 Heinz Edelmann/Klaus Mohr
219 Paul Davis
220 Marisa Rizzato
221 Takaaki Matsumoto

ART DIRECTOR / DIRECTEUR ARTISTIQUE:

215–218 Klaus Mohr
219 Paul Davis
220 Ilde Ianigro
221 Harold Matossian/
     Takaaki Matsumoto

AGENCY / AGENTUR / AGENCE-STUDIO:

219 Doyle Dane Bernbach, Inc.
220 Coopstudio
221 Knoll Graphics

222

223

Booklets / Prospekte / Brochures

222, 223 Two pages from a catalogue for Andrzej Dudzinski's exhibition entitled "The Spectators" at the National Theatre, London. Dudzinski's famous "Dudi Bird" cartoon figure has become, in this series of paintings, the "watchbird" in life's theatre. Accompanying the illustrations are comments about theatre audiences dating back to the 16th century. (GBR)
224 Collage with stamps as self-promotion for the illustrator Marie-Louise Cusack. (CAN)
225 From one of the beauty books issued by the cosmetic firm *Shiseido*; the double spread shown here is used in a self-promotion catalogue entitled "Cut Out" for the artist. (JPN)
226 "Casa Batlló, Barcelona." Drawing used as self-promotion for Robin Ward. (GBR)

222, 223 Zwei Seiten aus einem Katalog für eine Ausstellung von Andrzej Dudzinski, die unter dem Titel «Die Zuschauer» im Londoner National Theatre stattfand. Zu den Bildern gehören Kommentare aus verschiedenen Jahrhunderten über das Theaterpublikum. (GBR)
224 Collage mit Briefmarken als Eigenwerbung der Illustratorin Marie-Louise Cusack. (CAN)
225 Aus einem vom japanischen Kosmetikkonzern *Shiseido* herausgegebenen Schönheitsbuch; hier als Doppelseite in einem Eigenwerbungskatalog des Künstlers verwendet. (JPN)
226 «Casa Batlló, Barcelona.» Illustration als Eigenwerbung für Robin Ward. (GBR)

222, 223 Pages d'un catalogue d'exposition («Les Spectateurs») d'Andrzej Dudzinski pour le National Theatre de Londres. Les tableaux sont accompagnés de commentaires sur le public de théâtre au cours des siècles. (GBR)
224 Collage de timbres-poste, autopromotion de l'illustratrice Marie-Louise Cusack. (CAN)
225 Extrait d'un manuel de beauté publié par le groupe des cosmétiques *Shiseido*, utilisé sur une double page du catalogue autopromotionnel de l'artiste. (JPN)
226 «Casa Batlló, Barcelona.» Illustration utilisée pour les besoins promotionnels de l'artiste Robin Ward. (GBR)

224

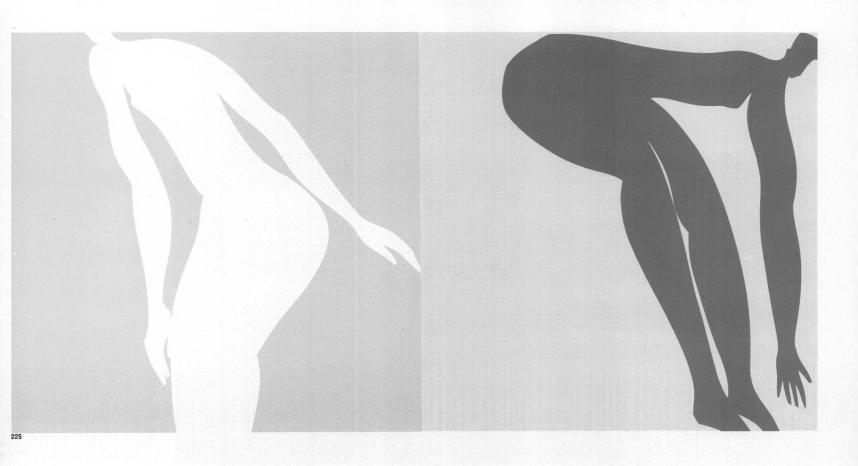

227

ARTIST / KÜNSTLER / ARTISTE:

227 Fred Otnes
228, 229 Anthony Rutka

DESIGNER / GESTALTER / MAQUETTISTE:

228, 229 Anthony Rutka
230, 231 Rosmarie Tissi

ART DIRECTOR / DIRECTEUR ARTISTIQUE:

228, 229 Anthony Rutka

AGENCY / AGENTUR / AGENCE – STUDIO:

228, 229 Rutka & Weadock
230, 231 Odermatt & Tissi

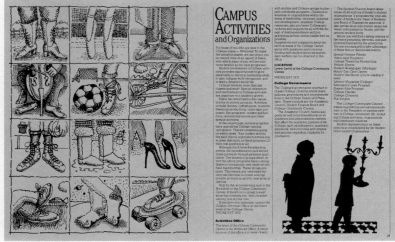

228

229

227 Collage for a self-promotional card for the American Fred Otnes. (USA)
228, 229 Double spreads from a college student handbook—a guide relating to the college's policies, regulations and services. Themes of the illustrations in Fig. 228 are protection services and keeping a motor vehicle on the campus. In Fig. 229 the illustrations depict the numerous activities the college has to offer and its governance structure. Black on yellow paper. (USA)
230, 231 Covers of offer-folders for the printers Anton Schöb. Fig. 231 relates to the firm's 35 years in business and also to the 35 members of its staff. (SWI)

227 Collage für eine Eigenwerbungskarte des Amerikaners Fred Otnes. (USA)
228, 229 Doppelseiten aus einem Handbuch für die Studenten eines College, mit Informationen über Schulregeln, Dienstleistungen und Veranstaltungen. Die Themen der Illustrationen in Abb. 228 sind ein Erste-Hilfe- und Schutzdienst sowie die Fahrzeughaltung, in Abb. 229 geht es um Veranstaltungen und die Verwaltung des College. Schwarz auf gelbem Papier. (USA)
230, 231 Vorderseiten von Offerten-Mappen der Buch- und Offsetdruckerei Anton Schöb. Abb. 231 bezieht sich unter anderem auf das 35jährige Bestehen. (SWI)

227 Collage pour la carte autopromotionnelle de l'Américain Fred Otnes. (USA)
228, 229 Doubles pages du guide de l'étudiant d'un collège universitaire contenant des informations sur les règlements, prestations et manifestations. Les sujets des illustrations de la fig. 228: premiers soins, sécurité, admission des véhicules. La fig. 229 se réfère aux manifestations et l'administration du collège. Noir sur papier jaune. (USA)
230, 231 Recto de documentations d'offres de l'imprimerie typo/offset Anton Schöb. Dans la fig. 231, on fait référence, entre autres, aux 35 années d'activité de la firme. (SWI)

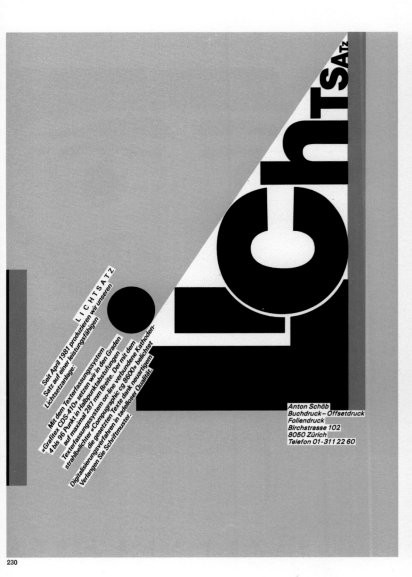

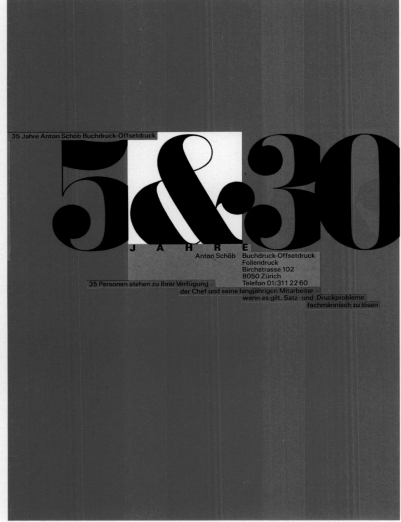

230

231

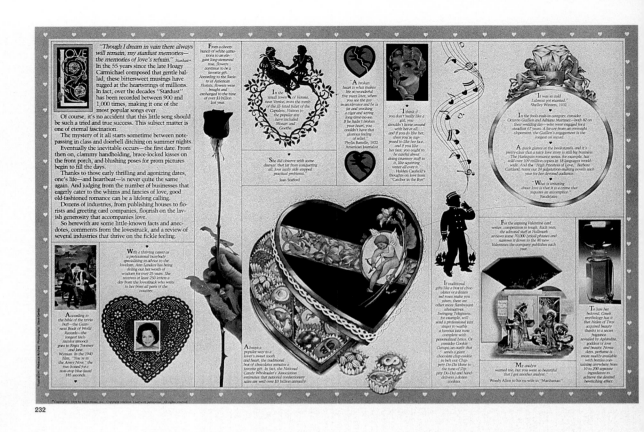

232

ARTIST / KÜNSTLER / ARTISTE:

232 Gary Viskupic/Bud Thon/
    Rebecca Archey
234 William Wondriska/
    Larry Plourde (Photo)
235 Jeff Jackson
236 Mario Carrieri
237 Margaret Hathaway

DESIGNER / GESTALTER:

232 Kit Hinrichs/Barbara Vick
233 Denise Rogo
234 William Wondriska
235 Paul Fiala
236 Takaaki Matsumoto
237 Margaret Hathaway

ART DIRECTOR:

232 Kit Hinrichs
233 Joseph Martino
234 Gordon Bowman
235 Paul Fiala
236 Harold Matossian/
    Takaaki Matsumoto

AGENCY / AGENTUR / AGENCE:

232 Jonson Pedersen Hinrichs
    & Shakery
234 Wondriska Associates
235 Paul Fiala & Assoc.
236 Knoll Graphics
237 Reactor

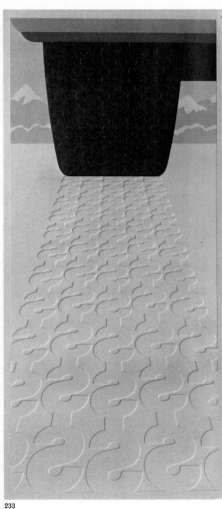

233

234

→ Ideal angina prophylaxis for these periods would therefore combine rapid onset, predictable potency and long duration of action.

→ Up to now, that kind of protection did not exist in a single preparation.

235

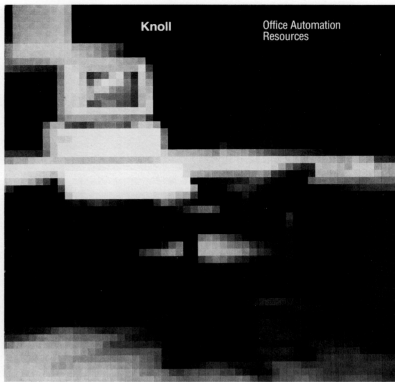

Knoll Office Automation Resources

236

237

232 Double spread in full colour on the theme of love, from which the various branches of industry flourish (e. g. makers of cards, florists, chocolate and perfumery manufacturers). (USA)
233 Concertina-fold; recto with tyre imprint symbolising dollar notes blind embossed. "More mileage in the luxury drive" heads tabulation proving that a certain magazine reaches more wealthy people than other magazines, thus a better prospect for auto advertising. (USA)
234 Announcement of a performance of *The Nutcracker*, danced by the Hartford Ballet. (USA)
235 Double spread from an information brochure about a medicament with prophylactic properties to guard against Angina Pectoris in periods of high attack probability. (USA)
236 Full-colour cover from a brochure about office computer support products. (USA)
237 Large format self-promotional card for Margaret Hathaway. Black-and-white drawing. (CAN)

232 Mehrfarbige Doppelseite zum Thema Liebe, von dem verschiedene Industriezweige (z. B. Karten-produzenten, Floristen, Schokoladen- und Parfumhersteller) profitieren. (USA)
233 Leporello-Vorderseite, deren Reifen-Profile in Dollarform blindgeprägt sind. Statistiken sollen beweisen, dass mit Anzeigen für neue Autos in einer bestimmten Zeitschrift mehr vermögende Kunden erreicht werden als in anderen. (USA)
234 *Der Nussknacker*, getanzt vom Hartford-Ballett, wird hiermit angekündigt. (USA)
235 Doppelseite aus einer Informations-Broschüre über ein Medikament mit prophylaktischen Eigen-schaften als Schutz vor Angina-Pectoris-Anfällen in Stress-Situationen. (USA)
236 Mehrfarbige Vorderseite einer Broschüre über Büro-Mobiliar rund um den Computer. (USA)
237 Grossformatige Eigenwerbungskarte für Margaret Hathaway. Zeichnung in Schwarzweiss. (CAN)

232 Double page polychrome sur le thème de l'amour qui profite à différentes branches de l'industrie (fabricants de cartonnages, fleuristes, chocolatiers, parfumeurs). (USA)
233 Recto d'un dépliant en accordéon. Les profils de pneus sont gaufrés à sec en forme de dollars. Les statistiques sont censées démontrer que la publicité pour les voitures neuves atteint plus de clients fortunés dans un magazine donné que dans d'autres. (USA)
234 Annonce d'une interprétation du *Casse-Noisette* par le ballet Hartford. (USA)
235 Double page d'une brochure d'information sur un médicament utilisé dans la prophylaxie de l'angine de poitrine. (USA)
236 Recto polychrome d'une brochure sur les meubles de bureau associés à l'ordinateur. (USA)
237 Carte au grand format servant à la promotion de l'artiste Margaret Hathaway. (CAN)

103

238

239

240

ARTIST / KÜNSTLER / ARTISTE:

238–241 Greg MacNair
242, 243 Design Center

DESIGNER / GESTALTER / MAQUETTISTE:

238–241 David Bartels/Bill Kumke
242, 243 Bruce Naftel
244–248 D. C. Stipp/Brent Croxton

ART DIRECTOR / DIRECTEUR ARTISTIQUE:

238–241 David Bartels
242, 243 Bruce Naftel
244–248 D. C. Stipp/Brent Croxton

AGENCY / AGENTUR / AGENCE – STUDIO:

238–241 Bartels & Company, Inc.
242, 243 Design Center/Western Michigan University
244–248 Richards, Sullivan, Brock & Associates

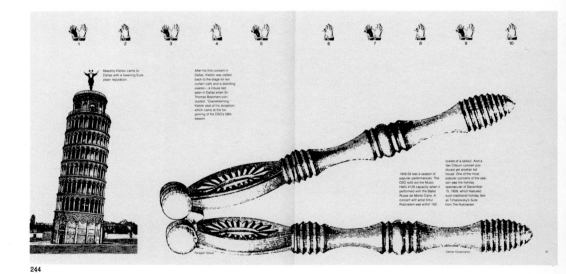

244

247

238–241 Illustrations and complete double spread from a booklet in which a consulting service for churches is offered. The positioning of the fingers symbolizes in Fig. 238 the church, in Fig. 239 the steeple, in Fig. 240 the open doors and in Fig. 241 the people. (USA)
242, 243 From an events calendar of the College of Fine Arts, Western Michigan University. (USA)
244–248 Double spreads and recto of cover from a brochure in book form for the Dallas Symphony Orchestra. The historical development, music directors and conductors are presented. In black and white and ochre/beige. (USA)

238–241 Illustrationen und vollständige Doppelseite aus einem Prospekt, worin eine Organisation den Kirchen Beratungsdienste anbietet. Die Fingerstellungen symbolisieren die Kirche, den Kirchturm, das Öffnen der Türen und das Volk. (USA)
242, 243 Aus einem Veranstaltungskalender der Fakultät für bildende Künste, Western Michigan University. (USA)
244–248 Doppelseiten und Umschlag-Vorderseite einer Broschüre in Buchform für das Dallas Symphony Orchester. Die geschichtliche Entwicklung, Musikdirektoren und Dirigenten werden darin vorgestellt. In Schwarzweiss und Ockerbeige. (USA)

238–241 Illustrations et double page complète d'un prospectus où une organisation propose ses conseils aux Eglises. Les positions de mains symbolisent l'église (fig. 238), le clocher de l'eglise (fig. 239), l'ouverture des portes (fig. 240), le peuple (fig. 241). (USA)
242, 243 Extraits d'un calendrier de manifestations publié par la Faculté des beaux-arts de la Western Michigan University. (USA)
244–248 Doubles pages et 1re page de couverture d'une brochure de l'Orchestre Symphonique de Dallas publiée sous forme de livre. On y présente l'historique, les directeurs et les chefs d'orchestre de cette institution. Noir, blanc et beige ocré. (USA)

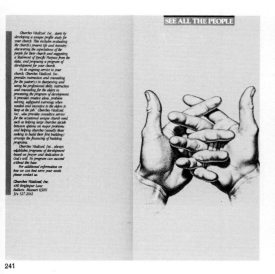

241

242

243

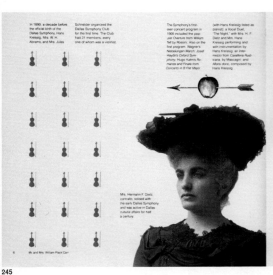

245

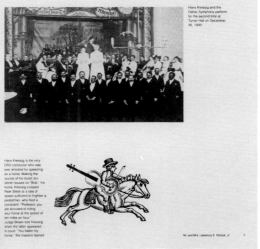

246

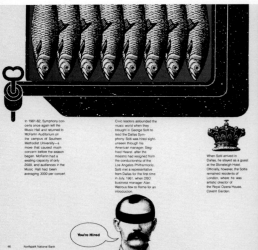

248

Booklets / Prospekte / Brochures

249

250

251

249–251 A single illustration split into three sections and used for covers, box wrap and poster for a government field day programme to promote community fitness and health. (CAN)
252 Cover of an advertising composite containing ads of various firms which appeared in the *Wall Street Journal*. (USA)
253 Catalogue cover with stamped out profiles promoting the *Mona Lisa* line in optical frames. All pages are laminated. (ISR)
254, 255 Illustration and complete front cover for a trade fair on shop interiors in Japan. (JPN)

249–251 Dreiteilige Illustration, deren einzelne Sektoren u. a. als Umschläge und Plakate für ein Regierungsprogramm über Fitness und Nahrung verwendet wurden. (CAN)
252 Umschlag einer Werbemappe mit verschiedenen Firmeninseraten, die im *Wall Street Journal* erschienen sind. (USA)
253 Katalog-Umschlag mit ausgestanzten Profilen für *Mona-Lisa*-Brillenmodelle. Alle Katalog-Seiten sind laminiert. (ISR)
254, 255 Illustration und vollständige Umschlag-Vorderseite für eine Ausstellungsmesse in Japan. (JPN)

249–251 Illustration tripartite, dont les différentes sections ont été utilisées comme couvertures et affiches pour un programme gouvernemental de santé physique et alimentaire. (CAN)
252 Couverture d'un dossier publicitaire du *Wall Street Journal* contenant des exemples d'annonces publiées. (USA)
253 Couverture de catalogue aux profils découpés, pour les modèles de lunettes *Mona Lisa*. Toutes les pages laminées. (ISR)
254, 255 Illustration et première page de couverture où elle figure. Pour une foire-exposition au Japon. (JPN)

252

253

254

255

ARTIST / KÜNSTLER / ARTISTE:

249–251 James Tughan
252 Lonni Sue Johnson
254, 255 Kazumasa Nagai

DESIGNER / GESTALTER / MAQUETTISTE:

240–251 James Tughan / Paul Hodgson
252 Doris Halle
253 Maurice Arbel
254, 255 Kazumasa Nagai

ART DIRECTOR / DIRECTEUR ARTISTIQUE:

249–251 Paul Hodgson
252 Doris Halle
253 Maurice Arbel
254, 255 Kazumasa Nagai

AGENCY / AGENTUR / AGENCE – STUDIO:

249–251 Spencer Francey
253 Maurice Arbel (Piha)
254, 255 Nippon Design Center

Booklets / Prospekte / Brochures

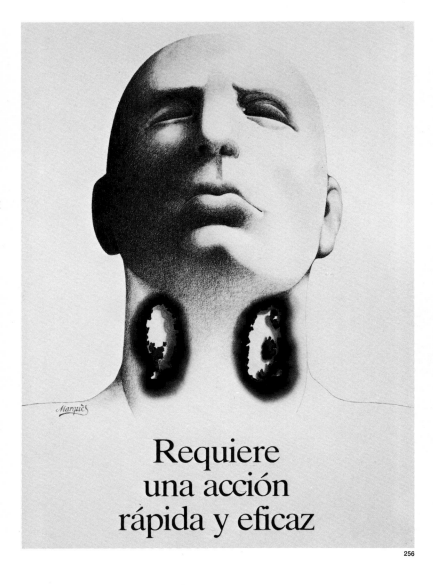

Requiere
una acción
rápida y eficaz

256

Cuando
estalla
la tossssss...

257

Booklets / Prospekte / Brochures

258

259

ARTIST / KÜNSTLER / ARTISTE:

256, 257 Joan Marquès Bach
258–261 Christian Lang

DESIGNER / GESTALTER / MAQUETTISTE:

256, 257 Joan Marquès Bach
258–261 Christian Lang

ART DIRECTOR / DIRECTEUR ARTISTIQUE:

256, 257 Joan Marquès Bach
258–261 Christian Lang

AGENCY / AGENTUR / AGENCE – STUDIO:

256, 257 Joan Marquès Bach
258–261 Ciba-Geigy/Werbung

256, 257 Front covers of brochures about medical products. Fig. 256: Tonsillitis "requires fast and effective treatment"; Fig. 257: "When the cough explodes…" (SPA)
258–261 Illustrations in black and white for brochures about a medicament for the treatment of geriatric depression. Fig. 260 shows the complete front cover of one of the folded brochures. (SWI)

256, 257 Beispiele von Umschlag-Vorderseiten für Broschüren über Arzneimittel. Abb. 256: Mandelentzündung «verlangt ein schnelles und wirksames Handeln»; Abb. 257: «Wenn der Husten explodiert…» (SPA)
258–261 Broschüren-Illustrationen in Schwarzweiss für ein Medikament gegen Altersdepression. Abb. 260 zeigt die vollständige Vorderseite einer dieser Broschüren. (SWI)

256, 257 Exemples de premières pages de couvertures de brochures pharmaceutiques. Fig. 256: l'amygdalite «exige une intervention rapide et efficace»; fig. 257: «Quand la toux explooooose…» (SPA)
258–261 Illustrations de brochures, noir et blanc, pour un remède de la dépression du grand âge. Fig. 260 recto complet du dépliant. (SWI)

260

261

3

Newspaper Illustrations
Magazine Covers
Magazine Illustrations
Weekend Supplements
Trade Magazines
House Organs
Annual Reports
Book Covers

Zeitungs-Illustrationen
Zeitschriften-Umschläge
Zeitschriften-Illustrationen
Wochenendbeilagen
Fachzeitschriften
Hauszeitschriften
Jahresberichte
Buchumschläge

Illustrations de journaux
Couvertures de périodiques
Illustrations de périodiques
Suppléments dominicaux
Revues professionnelles
Journaux d'entreprise
Rapports annuels
Couvertures de livres

262

263

265

266

264

ART DIRECTOR / DIRECTEUR ARTISTIQUE:

264 Nancy Kent
265 Robert Neubecker
266 Lynn Staley
267 Broc Sears

PUBLISHER / VERLEGER / EDITEUR:

262 The Miami News
263 Herald Tribune
264 The New York Times
265 Inx Inc.
266 The Boston Globe
267 The Dallas Morning News

262 Illustration for the "Lifestyle" section of *The Miami News* offering advice on the "premenstrual syndrome". (USA)
263 From *The International Herald Tribune* for an article on Yugoslavia's need for reform without army intervention. (USA)
264 How to cook possum. From *The New York Times*. (USA)
265 For a newspaper comment on a "not guilty" verdict. (USA)
266 From *The Boston Globe*, also used for a programme. (USA)
267 "Inside Nicaragua". An illustration from *The Dallas Morning News* for an article about the Sandinista regime. (USA)

262 Illustration für einen Beitrag mit Ratschlägen für Frauen mit premenstruellen Beschwerden, aus der Zeitung *Miami News*. (USA)
263 Aus einem Artikel in der *International Herald Tribune* über die Notwendigkeit demokratischer Reformen in Jugoslawien. (USA)
264 «Wie man ein Oppossum kocht.» *The New York Times*. (USA)
265 Zeitungskommentar zu einem Gerichtsurteil, das «nicht schuldig wegen Unzurechnungsfähigkeit» lautete. (USA)
266 Illustration für eine Buchmesse des *Boston Globe*. (USA)
267 Das sandinistische Regime Nicaraguas ist Gegenstand dieser Illustration zu einem Artikel in *Dallas Morning News*. (USA)

262 Illustration pour la section «Lifestyle» des *Miami News*: conseils pour bien se préparer aux douleurs des règles. (USA)
263 Pour un article de l'*International Herald Tribune*: comment réformer la Yougoslavie sans que l'armée intervienne. (USA)
264 Comment cuire un opossum. *The New York Times*. (USA)
265 Pour un commentaire d'acquittement judiciaire. (USA)
266 Illustration du *Boston Globe*, pour une foire. (USA)
267 «Au Nicaragua». Illustration pour un article du *Dallas Morning News* sur le régime sandiniste. (USA)

ARTIST / KÜNSTLER / ARTISTE:

262 Dale Brubaker
263 Francisco Graells (Pancho)
264 Randall Enos
265 Vivienne Flesher
266 Tom Lulevitch
267 Novle Rogers

DESIGNER / GESTALTER / MAQUETTISTE:

262 Dale Brubaker
266 Lynn Staley
267 Clif Bosler

267

113

268–270 Three illustrations in full colour for the covers of the food section "Taste" in *The Minneapolis Star*. Fig. 268 is entitled "Nothing Taxing"; the play on the word "taxing" is shown by the incomplete tax-returns on the man's desk while he searches for a not-too-taxing meal. Fig. 269 concerns green vegetables and is entitled "Offbeat Greens" and Fig. 270 "For Women Only" is after Picasso's "Les Demoiselles d'Avignon". (USA)
271 An illustration for an article in *The New York Times* suggesting that King Hussein should be more receptive to Arab/Israeli peace moves. (USA)
272 A black-and-white illustration for a book review in *The Boston Globe*. The tale is about the adventures of a burglar in New York. (USA)

268–270 Ganzseitige Illustrationen in Farbe für die Vorderseite des Kochrezept-Sektors im *Minneapolis Star*. Abb. 269 basiert auf einem Wortspiel mit dem englischen Ausdruck für Steuern (taxes) und leichte (non-taxing) Kost; Abb. 269 betrifft Gemüse und Abb. 270, Pablo Picassos «Les Demoiselles d'Avignon» nachempfunden, trägt den Titel «Nur für Frauen». (USA)
271 Illustration für einen Artikel in der *New York Times*, in dem es um eine aktivere Rolle König Husseins bei den Friedensbemühungen im Nahen Osten geht. (USA)
272 Illustration für eine Buchbesprechung im *Boston Globe*. Gegenstand des Buches sind die Abenteuer eines Einbrechers in New York. (USA)

268–270 Trois illustrations en polychromie pour les couvertures de la section Alimentation («Taste») du *Minneapolis Star*. Fig. 268: jeu de mots sur «taxing», qui désigne à la fois la déclaration d'impôts et un menu éprouvant pour l'organisme. La fig. 269 concerne les légumes verts. La fig. 270, «Réservé aux femmes», s'inspire des «Demoiselles d'Avignon» de Pablo Picasso. (USA)
271 Illustration pour un article paru dans le *New York Times*, qui critique le roi Hussein pour son manque d'enthousiasme pour les propositions de paix arabo-israéliennes. (USA)
272 Illustration noir-blanc pour un compte rendu de livre dans le *Boston Globe*: les aventures d'un cambrioleur à New York. (USA)

ARTIST / KÜNSTLER / ARTISTE:

268, 269 Todd Grande
270 Barbara Redmond
271 Cathy Hull
272 Anthony Russo

DESIGNER / GESTALTER / MAQUETTISTE:

270 Barbara Redmond
272 James Pavlovich

ART DIRECTOR:

268, 269 Michael Carroll
270 Barbara Redmond
271 Jerelle Kraus
272 James Pavlovich

AGENCY / AGENTUR / AGENCE:

270 Barbara & Patrick Redmond
Design Inc.

PUBLISHER / VERLEGER / EDITEUR:

268–270 Minneapolis Star
and Tribune
271 The New York Times
272 The Boston Globe

Taste / Nothing taxing — Minneapolis Star and Tribune
Wednesday April 13 / 1983 1T

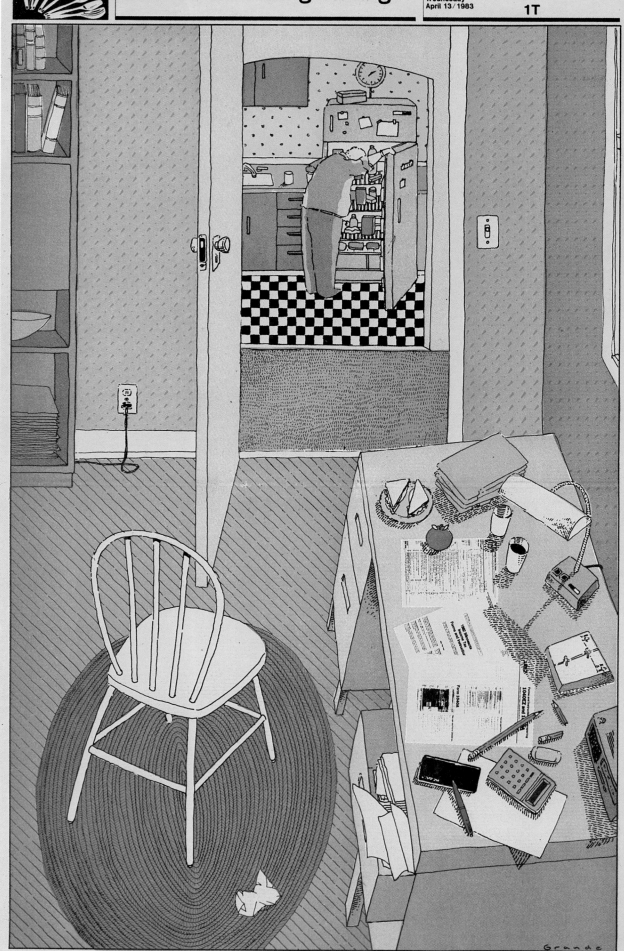

268

269

271

270

272

273

275

274

276

Newspaper Illustrations

273 For the cover of the "Living" column in the *Boston Sunday Globe*, illustrating an article entitled "Waiting with style". (USA)
274 To illustrate the cover of the "Viewpoint" column in *The Miami Herald* offering a doctor's views on the ethics of treating the aged and chronically sick. (USA)
275, 276 Illustration and complete page of *The New York Times*. The subject was the alleged bipartisan consensus on the two political issues—Central America and arms control. (USA)
277 From *The Progressive* magazine illustrating an article on rising libel lawsuit costs. (USA)

273 «Mit Stil warten.» Illustration für einen Beitrag in der Sonntagsausgabe des *Boston Globe*. (USA)
274 Für den Beitrag eines Arztes in der «Standpunkt»-Kolumne des *Miami Herald*, in dem es um die Ethik in der Betreuung von alten und chronisch kranken Menschen geht. (USA)
275, 276 Illustration und vollständige Seite aus der *New York Times*. Thema ist die angebliche Übereinstimmung der beiden Parteien der USA in zwei Fragen: Mittelamerika und Rüstungskontrolle. (USA)
277 Für einen Artikel in dem Magazin *The Progressive*, in dem es um die Selbstzensur der Medien aus Angst vor den hohen Bussgeldstrafen bei Verleumdungsprozessen geht. (USA)

273 Pour la couverture de la section «Living» du *Boston Sunday Globe*. Illustration d'un article sur «l'art d'attendre avec panache». (USA)
274 Illustration de la couverture de la section «Viewpoint» du *Miami Herald*: un médecin donne son avis sur le comportement moral vis-à-vis des vieillards et des malades chroniques. (USA)
275, 276 Illustration et page complète du *New York Times*. Il s'agit de la prétendue unité de vues au Parlement sur deux problèmes politiques – Amérique centrale, désarmement. (USA)
277 Pour le magazine *The Progressive*: renchérissement des procès pour diffamation. (USA)

277

Newspaper Illustrations
Zeitungs-Illustrationen
Illustrations de journaux

278

279

ARTIST / KÜNSTLER / ARTISTE:

278, 279 Brad Holland
280 Andrezej Dudzinski
281, 282 Pétur Halldórsson

278, 279 Complete page and black-and-white illustration from *The New York Times* for an article on the official East/West prevarications in the arms-control negotiations. (USA)
280 From the "Science Section" in *The Boston Globe* illustrating an article on the race between industry and government to offer financial support to university scientists and the impact on their research. (USA)
281, 282 Two black-and-white illustrations for the Icelandic newspaper *Morgunblaðið Reykjavík*. (ICE)

278, 279 Vollständige Seite und Schwarzweiss-Illustration für einen Beitrag mit Vorschlägen für die Abrüstungsverhandlungen zwischen Ost und West; aus der *New York Times*. (USA)
280 Für einen Artikel im *Boston Globe* über den Wettlauf zwischen Industrie und Regierung in der finanziellen Unterstützung von Universitäts-Wissenschaftlern und über die Auswirkungen auf die Forschungsarbeit. (USA)
281, 282 Zwei Illustrationen in Schwarzweiss für die isländische Zeitung *Morgunblaðið Reykjavík* (ICE)

278, 279 Page complète et illustration noir et blanc du *New York Times*: article stigmatisant la valse-hésitation des deux grands engagés dans la négociation pour le désarmement. (USA)
280 Illustration pour la section «Science» du *Boston Globe*: il est question de la surenchère à laquelle se livrent gouvernement et industrie pour financer la recherche universitaire. (USA)
281, 282 Deux illustrations noir et blanc pour le quotidien islandais *Morgunblaðið Reykjavík*. (ICE)

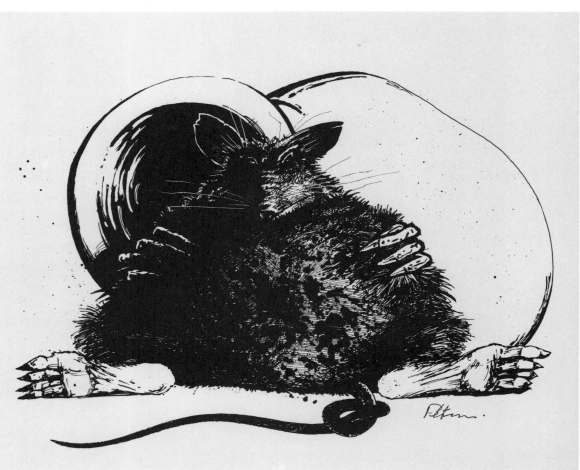

281

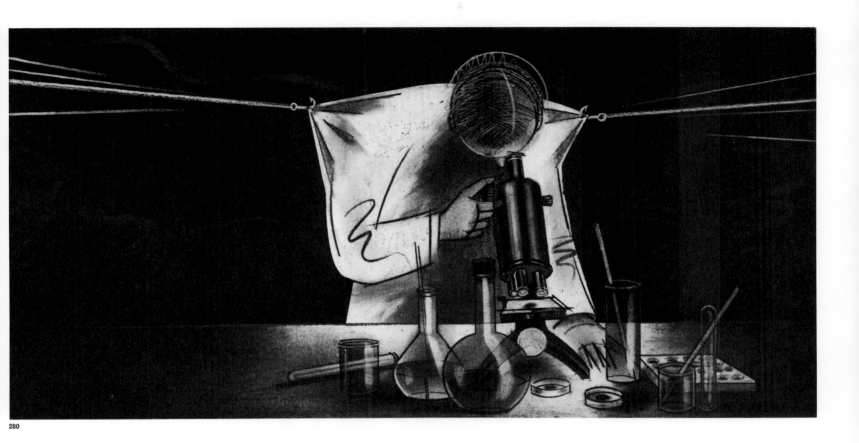

280

DESIGNER / GESTALTER / MAQUETTISTE:

280 Holly Nixholm
281, 282 Pétur Halldórsson

ART DIRECTOR / DIRECTEUR ARTISTIQUE:

278, 279 Jerelle Kraus
280 Holly Nixholm

AGENCY / AGENTUR / AGENCE – STUDIO:

281, 282 Pétur Graphic Design

PUBLISHER / VERLEGER / EDITEUR:

278, 279 The New York Times
280 The Boston Globe
281, 282 Morgunbladid Reykjavík

282

283

284

ARTIST / KÜNSTLER / ARTISTE:

283–286 Bruno Liberati
287, 288 Frances Jetter

ART DIRECTOR / DIRECTEUR ARTISTIQUE:

287, 288 John McCleod

PUBLISHER / VERLEGER / EDITEUR:

283–286 Jornal do Brasil
287, 288 Inx Inc.

286

285

283–286 Illustrations for the *Jornal do Brasil*, "Especial" section. Figs. 283 and 284 show the complete page and illustration for an article about the growth in political power of the rural workers in the northeast region; Fig. 285 illustrates a feature on the economic-social depression in the northeast and Fig. 286 "This Year Brazil will Eat Less"—alluding to changes in cereal production and the effects of the recession on the consumer's eating habits. (BRA)
287 Illustration in black and white for several newspapers, entitled "Nuclear Screams", after Edvard Munch's "The Shriek". (USA)
288 Illustration published in several newspapers for an article on the subject "Social Security cut to the bone". (USA)

283–286 Illustrationen für das *Jornal do Brasil*. Abb. 283, 284: vollständige Seite und Illustration für einen Artikel über das wachsende politische Gewicht der Landarbeiter in der nordöstlichen Region; Abb. 285: für einen Artikel über die schlechte sozial-wirtschaftliche Lage im Nordosten; Abb. 286: «Dieses Jahr wird Brasilien weniger essen» – Anspielung auf die schlechte Getreideproduktion und deren Auswirkung auf die Essgewohnheiten der Konsumenten. (BRA)
287 In verschiedenen Zeitungen veröffentlichte Illustration mit dem Titel «Atom-Schreie», nach Edvard Munchs «Der Schrei». (USA)
288 Kommentar zur Reduktion der Rentenversicherungen. In verschiedenen Zeitungen veröffentlichte Schwarzweiss-Illustration. (USA)

283–286 Illustrations pour la section «Especial» du *Jornal do Brasil*. Les fig. 283 et 284 représentent la page complète et l'illustration d'un article sur l'accès au pouvoir politique des ouvriers agricoles de la région du nord-est; la fig. 285 illustre un article sur la dépression socio-économique dans le nord-est; la fig. 286 («Cette année, le Brésil mangera moins») se rapporte aux transformations affectant la production céréalière et à la consommation en période de récession. (BRA)
287 Illustration noir et blanc publiée dans plusieurs journaux. Elle s'intitule «Cris d'angoisse nucléaire» et s'inspire du «Cri» d'Edvard Munch. (USA)
288 Illustration reproduite dans divers journaux, en marge d'un article sur «la sécurité sociale décharnée jusqu'à l'os» par des coupes sombres. (USA)

287

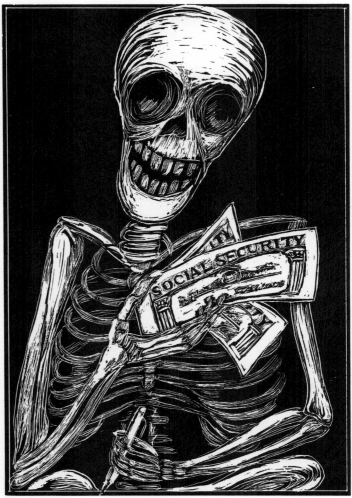

288

289

289–291 Woodcuts as illustrations taken from the "Overnight" section of the Brazilian weekly satirical newspaper *Pasquim*. This column comments in brief on current political and financial topics. (BRA)
292, 293 Woodcuts from the *Jornal do Brasil*, illustrating articles (Fig. 292) on people's submersion in the flow of economic crises and recession and (Fig. 293) on political franchise, entitled "Ways and Alternatives". (BRA)

289–291 Holzschnitt-Illustrationen in Schwarzweiss aus der satirischen Wochen-Zeitung *Pasquim*, für eine Seite mit kurzen Kommentaren zu politischen und finanzwirtschaftlichen Fragen. (BRA)
292, 293 Holzschnitte aus der Zeitung *Jornal do Brasil*. Abb. 292 illustriert einen Artikel über die Auswirkungen der Wirtschaftskrise für die Bevölkerung; Abb. 293 zeigt den Kreis gegenseitiger Beeinflussung in der Politik, zentrales Thema eines Artikels über politische Rechte, Ziele und Erwartungen. (BRA)

289–291 Illustrations tirées de la section «Overnight» du journal brésilien *Pasquim*, où l'on trouve de brefs commentaires des actualités politiques et financières du pays. (BRA)
292 Gravure sur bois illustrant un article du *Jornal do Brasil*. On y représente l'immersion des Brésiliens dans le flot des crises économiques. (BRA)
293 Gravure sur bois pour le *Jornal do Brasil*. L'article, intitulé «Chemins et alternatives», traite des privilèges en politique. (BRA)

292

290

291

ARTIST:

289–293 Rubem Campos Grilo

PUBLISHER / VERLEGER / EDITEUR:

289–291 Pasquim
292, 293 Jornal do Brasil

293

294

295

ARTIST / KÜNSTLER / ARTISTE:

294, 297 Rubem Campos Grilo
295 Cathy Hull
296, 298 Randall Enos

DESIGNER / GESTALTER / MAQUETTISTE:

296 Donna Albano

ART DIRECTOR / DIRECTEUR ARTISTIQUE:

296 Donna Albano
298 Steve Heller

PUBLISHER / VERLEGER / EDITEUR:

294, 297 Jornal do Brasil
295, 298 The New York Times
296 The Boston Globe

294 Woodcut as illustration for an article about the economy. From the newspaper *Jornal do Brasil*. (BRA)
295 "The stranger's stare—baleful or beckoning?" For a feature in *The New York Times*. (USA)
296 Illustration in about the original size from the food section in the *Boston Globe* and relating to the excitement (for Americans) of shopping in Europe's traditional markets. Here Florence's "Mercato Centrale". (USA)
297 Woodcut illustration entitled "Graphics" from the newspaper *Jornal do Brasil*. (BRA)
298 For a book review in *The New York Times*. The book is about horseracing. (USA)

294 Holzschnitt als Illustration eines Wirtschaftsartikels in der Zeitung *Jornal do Brasil*. (BRA)
295 «Der Blick des Fremden – wütend oder einladend?» Für einen Beitrag in der *New York Times*. (USA)
296 Illustration, ungefähr Originalgrösse, aus dem Kochrezept-Sektor des *Boston Globe*. Hier geht es um den für Amerikaner aufregenden Einkauf auf den europäischen Warenmärkten. (USA)
297 Holzschnitt-Illustration mit dem Titel «Graphik» aus der Zeitung *Jornal do Brasil*. (BRA)
298 Für die Besprechung eines Buches, in dem es um ein Rennpferd geht. Aus der *New York Times*. (USA)

294 Gravure sur bois illustrant un article du *Jornal do Brasil* sur l'économie du pays. (BRA)
295 «Le regard de l'étranger – sinistre ou invitant?» Pour un article du *New York Times*. (USA)
296 Illustration approximativement grandeur nature pour la section Alimentation du *Boston Globe*: le plaisir qu'il y a pour les Américains à faire les marchés traditionnels d'Europe, ici Florence. (USA)
297 Illustration (gravure sur bois) pour le *Jornal do Brasil*. Titre: «Graphisme». (BRA)
298 Pour un compte rendu de livre dans le *New York Times*. Ouvrage sur les courses de chevaux. (USA)

296

297

298

125

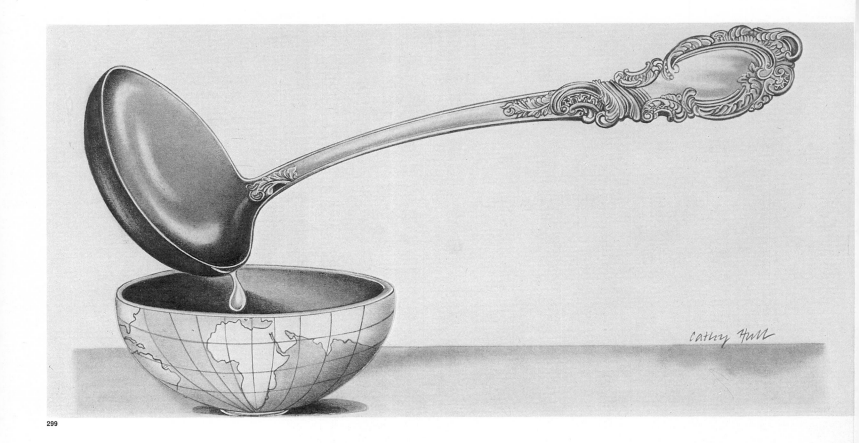

299

301   302

300

Newspaper Illustrations
Zeitungs-Illustrationen
Illustrations de journaux

ARTIST / KÜNSTLER / ARTISTE:

299 Cathy Hull
300 Henrick Drescher
301 Marguerita
302 Rafal Olbinski
303 Eugene Yelchin

DESIGNER / GESTALTER / MAQUETTISTE:

303 Lynn Staley

ART DIRECTOR / DIRECTEUR ARTISTIQUE:

299, 302 Jerelle Kraus
300 John McCleod
301 George Delmerico
303 Lynn Staley

PUBLISHER / VERLEGER / EDITEUR:

299, 302 The New York Times
300 Inx Inc.
301 The Village Voice
303 The Boston Globe

303

299 "No Thanks to Give" is the title of an article in the Thanksgiving Day edition of *The New York Times*. A black-and-white illustration referring to the malnutrition in the third world and urging wealthier nations to pledge aid. (USA)
300 An illustration published in several newspapers for articles concerning America's persuasion of Europe to accept the Pershing missiles. (USA)
301 From *Voice*; illustrating a film review. (USA)
302 Illustration for an article in *The New York Times* lending an ear to the plea, "Rescue Public Radio". (USA)
303 For *The Boston Globe's* "Dining Out" column, illustrating an article on where to eat the Japanese dish "Sushi". (USA)

299 «Kein Anlass zum Dank.» Schwarzweiss-Illustration für einen Artikel in der Erntedanktags-Ausgabe der *New York Times*. Thema ist die Hungersnot in der Dritten Welt und die dringend benötigte Hilfe der reicheren Nationen. (USA)
300 Kommentar zu den Bemühungen der Vereinigten Staaten, die europäische Jugend für die Pershing-Raketen zu gewinnen. Die Illustration wurde in diversen Zeitungen gezeigt. (USA)
301 Für die Besprechung eines Films in der *Voice*. (USA)
302 Illustration für einen Artikel in der *New York Times* über die finanziellen Schwierigkeiten von Radiosendern. (USA)
303 Für die kulinarische Kolumne des *Boston Globe*, hier mit Informationen über «Sushi», ein spezielles japanisches Gericht, und Restaurantempfehlungen. (USA)

299 «Pas de grâces à rendre»: titre d'un article de l'édition du *New York Times* publiée à l'occasion du Thanksgiving (littéralement: action de grâces) américain. Illustration noir-blanc sur la faim dans le monde et l'aide nécessaire des nantis. (USA)
300 Illustration reproduite dans divers journaux pour des articles discutant de l'insistance des Américains pour que les Européens acceptent leurs missiles Pershing. (USA)
301 Compte rendu d'un film, dans *Voice*. (USA)
302 Illustration pour un article du *New York Times* en faveur de l'action «Venez au secours de la radio publique». (USA)
303 Pour la section «Restaurants» du *Boston Globe*: où trouver le plat japonais «sushi» traditionnel. (USA)

304

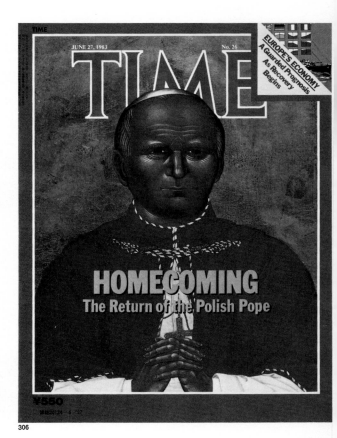

306

305

309

304, 305 Covers of *The New Yorker* magazine; Fig. 304 in shades of green, lilac lettering; Fig. 305: blue sculpture on a brown base. (USA)

306, 307 Covers of *Time* magazine. Fig. 306 is the International edition; papal vestments in red and white, yellow ground; Fig. 307: Great Kremlin Palace in red, grey, blue and yellow on pale blue ground. (USA)

308 Complete page of *Time* magazine. The illustration is for the cover story and is about the perils of cocaine addiction. (USA)

309 Cover of the book magazine *Lire*. The illustration alludes to a feature on the follies and truths about China. (FRA)

310 A yellow diagonal shaft of sunlight and a terra-cotta flowerpot on a sky-blue background for the spring cover of the Canadian magazine *Avenue*. (CAN)

311 Cover illustration of the pre-Christmas edition of *Astrapi* magazine. (FRA)

307

308

310

311

ARTIST / KÜNSTLER / ARTISTE:

304, 305 Eugene Mihaesco
306 Kinuko Craft
307 James Marsh
308 Ed Soyka
310 Wendy Wortsman
311 Josse Goffin

DESIGNER / GESTALTER:

307, 308 Nigel Holmes
309 Jean-Pierre Cliquet
310 Jonathan Rogers

ART DIRECTOR:

304, 305 Lee Lorenz
306–308 Rudolph Hoglund
309 Jean-Pierre Cliquet
310 Jonathan Rogers
311 Claude Delafosse

PUBLISHER / VERLEGER:

304, 305 The New Yorker
306–308 Time, Inc.
309 Groupe Express
310 Avenue
311 Bayard Presse

304, 305 Umschläge der Zeitschrift *The New Yorker*. Abb. 304: In Grün-, Blau- und Lilatönen, lila Schrift; Abb. 305: Blaue Skulptur auf braunem Grund. (USA)
306, 307 Mehrfarbige Umschläge des *Time*-Magazins. Abb. 306: Für eine internationale Ausgabe zum Besuch des Papstes in seiner Heimat Polen; Abb. 307: «Das KGB heute. Andropows Augen beobachten die Welt.» (USA)
308 Illustration für eine Titelgeschichte über Kokain im *Time*-Magazin. (USA)
309 Umschlag-Vorderseite des Büchermagazins *Lire*. Illustriert wird ein Artikel mit dem Titel «Dummheiten und Wahrheiten über China». (FRA)
310 Ein gelber Streifen Sonnenlicht auf graublauem Grund mit Terracotta-Topf als Umschlag-Illustration der Zeitschrift *Avenue*. (CAN)
311 Umschlag der Vorweihnachtsnummer des Kindermagazins *Astrapi*, die Geschenkvorschläge enthält. Warme Farbtöne, Schrift gelb und rot. (FRA)

304, 305 Couvertures complètes du magazine *The New Yorker*; fig. 304: divers verts, texte lilas; fig. 305: sculpture bleue sur socle brun. (USA)
306, 307 Couvertures complètes du magazine *Time*. Fig. 306: édition internationale; vêtements rouge et blanc du Pape, fond jaune; fig. 307: Grand Palais du Kremlin; rouge, gris, bleu, jaune sur fond bleu pâle. (USA)
308 Page complète du magazine *Time*. L'illustration se rapporte au titre en couverture: les dangers de la cocaïnomanie. (USA)
309 Couverture complète du magazine des livres *Lire*. L'illustration se rapporte à un article sur l'interprétation correcte des mœurs chinoises. (FRA)
310 Un trait diagonal de soleil jaune et un pot de fleurs de terre cuite sur un fond bleu ciel pour la couverture de printemps du magazine *Avenue*. (CAN)
311 Couverture complète de l'édition du magazine *Astrapi* précédant Noël. (FRA)

Magazine Covers
Zeitschriftenumschläge
Couvertures de périodiques

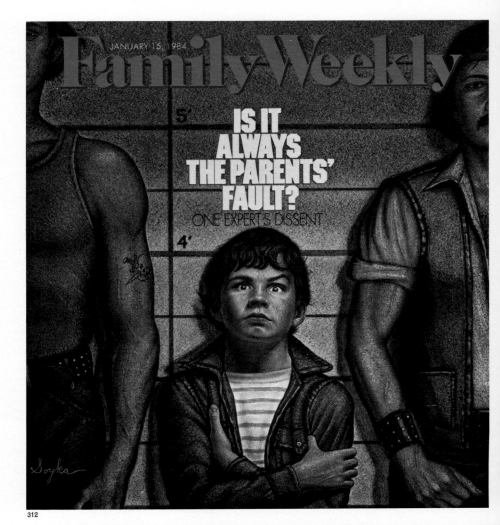

312

312 Cover of the *Family Weekly* magazine, in dark subdued tones. This issue includes a feature on "The Killer Kids". (USA)
313 This illustration on the cover of *The Boston Globe Magazine* shows the "palette" of leisure activities in the U.S. Pen-and-ink and crayon. (USA)
314 Cover of *La Gola*, an Italian co-operative magazine devoted to food. (ITA)
315 The illustration on this cover of the *Family Weekly* magazine is after Grant Wood's "American Gothic". (USA)
316 Complete page from the Christmas issue of the *Chicago Tribune* magazine. (USA)
317 Pencilled figures and background with coloured headware for the cover of the German *TransAtlantik* magazine. (GER)

312 Umschlag des Magazins *Family Weekly* in dumpfen, rötlichen Farbtönen. Die Illustration bezieht sich auf einen Artikel über «mordende Kinder». (USA)
313 Umschlag-Illustration für *The Boston Globe Magazine*, mit einer Palette der Freizeitmöglichkeiten in den USA. Tusche und Farbstift. (USA)
314 Umschlag des italienischen Magazins *La Gola*, zum Thema Nahrung. (ITA)
315 Illustration nach Grant Woods «American Gothic» für einen Artikel in *Family Weekly* über die Gründe, weshalb Ehen scheitern können. (USA)
316 Umschlag für die Weihnachtsausgabe des Magazins *Chicago Tribune*. (USA)
317 Figuren und Hintergrund dieser Umschlag-Illustration für *TransAtlantik* sind mit Bleistift, die Kopfbedeckungen mit Farbstift gezeichnet. (GER)

312 Couverture complète du magazine *Family Weekly*, où figure un article sur les «tueurs enfants». (USA)
313 Couverture complète du *Boston Globe Magazine*. Palette des activités de loisirs aux Etats-Unis. Dessin à la plume et crayon couleur. (USA)
314 Couverture complète de *La Gola*, un magazine de coopérateurs italiens consacré à l'alimentation et aux besoins vitaux. (ITA)
315 Illustration de couverture (ici complète) pour le magazine *Family Weekly*, dans le style de Grant Wood. (USA)
316 Pour l'édition de Noël du magazine *Chicago Tribune*. (USA)
317 Personnages et arrière-plan crayonnés, couvre-chefs couleur. Couverture du magazine *TransAtlantik*. (GER)

315

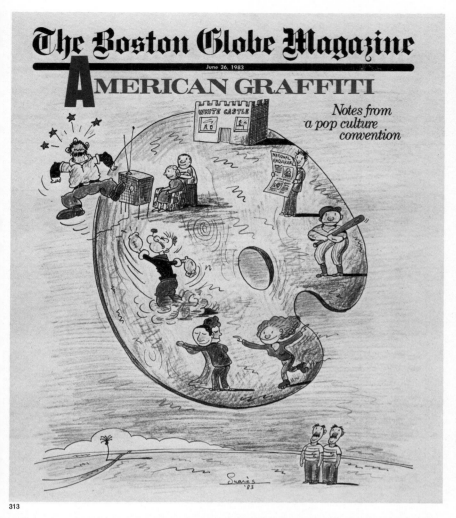

The Boston Globe Magazine
June 26, 1983

AMERICAN GRAFFITI

*Notes from
a pop culture
convention*

313

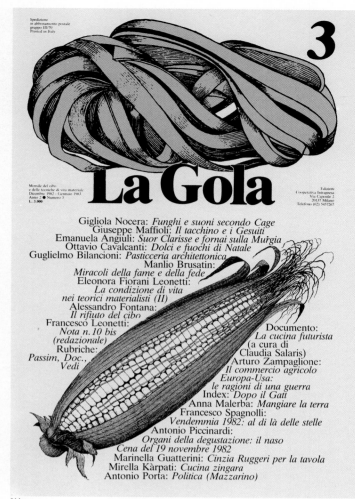

3

La Gola

Spedizione
in abbonamento postale
gruppo III/70
Printed in Italy

Mensile del cibo
e delle tecniche di vita materiale
Dicembre 1982 - Gennaio 1983
Anno 2 ● Numero 3
L. 3.000

Edizioni
Cooperativa Intrapresa
Via Caposile 2
20137 Milano
Telefoni (02) 5457267

Gigliola Nocera: *Funghi e suoni secondo Cage*
Giuseppe Maffioli: *Il tacchino e i Gesuiti*
Emanuela Angiuli: *Suor Clarisse e fornai sulla Murgia*
Ottavio Cavalcanti: *Dolci e fuochi di Natale*
Guglielmo Bilancioni: *Pasticceria architettonica*
Manlio Brusatin:
Miracoli della fame e della fede
Eleonora Fiorani Leonetti:
*La condizione di vita
nei teorici materialisti (II)*
Alessandro Fontana:
Il rifiuto del cibo
Francesco Leonetti:
*Nota n.10 bis
(redazionale)*
Rubriche:
*Passim, Doc.,
Vedi*

Documento:
La cucina futurista
(a cura di
Claudia Salaris)
Arturo Zampaglione:
*Il commercio agricolo
Europa-Usa:
le ragioni di una guerra*
Index: *Dopo il Gatt*
Anna Malerba: *Mangiare la terra*
Francesco Spagnolli:
Vendemmia 1982: al di là delle stelle
Antonio Piccinardi:
Organi della degustazione: il naso
Cena del 19 novembre 1982
Marinella Guatterini: *Cinzia Ruggeri per la tavola*
Mirella Kàrpati: *Cucina zingara*
Antonio Porta: *Politica (Mazzarino)*

314

Chicago Tribune
Magazine Dec. 25, 1983 Section 10

GOOD CHEER
A tasty holiday feast
of Christmas lore

316

TRANS ATLANTIK

Januar 1/1984   Acht Mark   B 5183 E

Bodo
Kirchhoff:
Bundeswehr
made
in USA

Micky
Remann:
Legenden aus
dem Meer

Patricia
Highsmith:
Mörder
a la carte

317

318

319

321

322

318–324 Covers in full colour for the humoristic, satirical magazine *Nebelspalter*. Fig. 318: "Half-heard plus half-seen adds up to one total opinion"; blue jacket, yellow hair, green background; Fig. 319: this issue includes a thirty-page literature supplement; Fig. 320 offers mental "food for thought"; in Fig. 321 the black dog is watching realistic flames on television in the fireplace; Fig. 322 shows the problems of choosing between eight television channels; Fig. 323 satirically illustrates the current craze for walkman headphones and introduces a new type "now with vision"; Fig. 324 is a humorous allusion to the bathing season and appeared in a summer issue. (SWI)

318–324 Mehrfarbige Umschläge, von Wolf Barth illustriert, für die humoristisch-satirische Wochenzeitschrift *Nebelspalter*. Abb. 318: Jacke in Blau, gelbes Haar, grüner Hintergrund, weisse Schrift; Abb. 319: Kleidung und *Nebelspalter*-Schrift blau, mehrfarbige Buchrücken; Abb. 320: «Geistige Nahrung» wird hier angeboten. Grüner Hintergrund; Abb. 321: Illustration einer «gemütlichen Silvesterfeier» vor dem Bildschirm; Abb. 322: Von der Schwierigkeit, zwischen verschiedenen Fernseh-Kanälen auszuwählen; Abb. 323: Neueste «Erfindung»: der Walkman zum Hören und Sehen. Schwarz, Blau und Weiss überwiegen; Abb. 324: Illustration für die Juli-Nummer des *Nebelspalter*. (SWI)

320

Magazine Covers

ARTIST / KÜNSTLER / ARTISTE:
318–324 Barth

ART DIRECTOR / DIRECTEUR ARTISTIQUE:
318–324 Franz Mächler

PUBLISHER / VERLEGER / EDITEUR:
318–324 Nebelspalter-Verlag

323

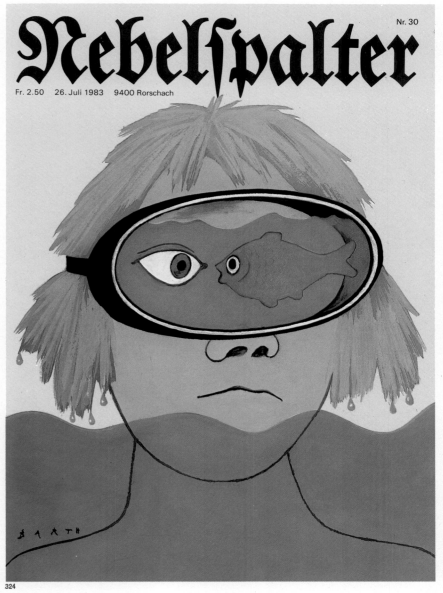

324

318–324 Couvertures complètes en polychromie pour le magazine satirique *Nebelspalter*. Fig. 318: «Entendu à moitié et vu à moitié permet de se faire une opinion complète»; veston bleu, cheveux jaunes, fond vert. Fig. 319: ce numéro contient un supplément littéraire de trente pages. La fig. 320 offre de la «nourriture spirituelle». Dans la fig. 321, le chien noir observe les flammes réalistes de la télévision dans la cheminée. La fig. 322 montre le choix difficile entre huit chaînes de télé. La fig. 323 tourne en dérision la mode du walkman en y ajoutant une nouveauté, la «vision comprise». La fig. 324 est une référence humoristique à la saison balnéaire. (SWI)

327

325

326

328

ARTIST / KÜNSTLER / ARTISTE:

325, 326 Franciso Graells (Pancho)
327, 328 Hermenegildo Sábat

DESIGNER / GESTALTER / MAQUETTISTE:

325, 326 Jean-Pierre Cliquet
327, 328 Hermenegildo Sábat

ART DIRECTOR:

325, 326 Sylvie Marcovitch
327, 328 Hermenegildo Sábat

PUBLISHER / VERLEGER / EDITEUR:

325 Le Monde de la Musique
326 Groupe Express
327, 328 Idea Magazine

325 Portrait of the composer Serge Rachmaninov in a French music magazine. (FRA)
326 Illustration for the book magazine *Lire*, portraying the political writer Raymond Aron in connection with a feature on his newly published memoirs. (FRA)
327 Portrait of Walter Rathenau in original size, illustrating one of a series of features on industrialists. (Rathenau was a Berliner and industrial moralist, and, as Germany's Minister for Foreign Affairs, signed the peace treaty with Russia in 1922 and was assassinated that same year.) Presenting this series was the magazine *Idea*. (ARG)
328 Full-colour portrait of Henry Laurence Gantt (1861–1919). An illustration from the same series (see Fig. 327) which appeared in the business magazine *Idea*. (ARG)

325 Aus *Le Monde de la Musique*. Ganzseitiges Porträt von Serge Rachmaninov. (FRA)
326 Ganzseitiges Porträt des politischen Schriftstellers Raymond Aron in dem Literaturmagazin *Lire*, im Zusammenhang mit einer Besprechung seiner Memoiren. (FRA)
327, 328 Porträts des ehemaligen deutschen Reichsaussenministers und Industriellen Walter Rathenau und des amerikanischen Ingenieurs Henry Laurence Gantt (1861–1919) innerhalb einer Reihe über industrielle Theoretiker in der Wirtschaftsfachzeitschrift *Idea*. Hier geht es um Rathenaus sozialpolitisches Engagement und seine Schriften über die Gefahren der «Mechanisierung des Lebens» und um Gantts Bemühungen und Publikationen hinsichtlich sozialer Verbesserungen und Organisierung der Industriearbeiter. (ARG)

325 Portrait du compositeur Serge Rachmaninov, paru dans *Le Monde de la Musique*. (FRA)
326 Illustration pleine page pour un article à l'occasion de la publication des Mémoires de l'écrivain et historien Raymond Aron, paru dans le magazine littéraire *Lire*. (FRA)
327, 328 Portraits de l'ancien ministre des Affaires étrangères du Reich allemand, l'industriel Walter Rathenau, et de l'ingénieur américain Henry Laurence Gantt (1861–1919), dans une série du magazine économique *Idea* consacrée aux théoriciens de l'industrie. Il s'agit ici de l'engagement sociopolitique de Rathenau, qui mit en garde contre «la mécanisation de la vie», et de l'œuvre de Gantt en faveur des ouvriers industriels. (ARG)

329

ARTIST / KÜNSTLER / ARTISTE:

329, 330 Edward Sorel
331 Seymour Chwast
332 James Marsh
333 Brad Holland

DESIGNER / GESTALTER:

329, 331, 332 Judy Garlan
330, 333 Terry Brown

ART DIRECTOR:

329, 331, 332 Judy Garlan
330, 333 Terry Brown

PUBLISHER / VERLEGER / EDITEUR:

329–333 The Atlantic Monthly

330

Magazine Illustrations
Zeitschriften-Illustrationen
Illustrations de périodiques

329–333 Illustrations taken from *The Atlantic Monthly*. Fig. 329: pen-and-ink drawing for a regular feature entitled "First Encounters"; this is a first encounter between Captain John Smith and Pocahontas. Fig. 330: Full-colour illustration for the "First Encounter" series; this time it is James Joyce and T. S. Eliot who are portrayed; predominantly brown shades. Fig. 331: Illustration in full colour for a non-fiction article entitled "The Next American Frontier". Fig. 332 illustrates a short story entitled "Real Seasons", an illustration in full colour. Fig. 333 is a black-and-white illustration for an article on the President, entitled "Ronald Reagan and the Techniques of Deception". (USA)

329–333 Illustrationen aus dem Magazin *The Atlantic Monthly*. Abb. 329: Tuschzeichnung für regelmässig erscheinende Artikel unter dem Titel «Erste Begegnung». Sie zeigt eine erste Begegnung zwischen Kapitän John Smith und Pocahontas; Abb. 330: Illustration in Brauntönen für die «Erste Begegnung» zwischen James Joyce und T. S. Eliot; Abb. 331: «Die neuen amerikanischen Pioniere.» Mehrfarbige Illustration auf dunkelgrünem Hintergrund; Abb. 332 illustriert eine Kurzgeschichte mit dem Titel «Richtige Jahreszeiten». Violett-blaue Abendstimmung; Abb. 333: «Ronald Reagan und die Technik der Täuschung.» In Schwarzweiss. (USA)

329–333 Illustrations tirées du magazine *The Atlantic Monthly*. Fig. 329: Dessin à l'encre de Chine pour une série d'articles intitulée «Première rencontre». On y voit celle entre le capitaine John Smith et Pocahontas; fig. 330: illustration, divers bruns, de la «première rencontre» entre James Joyce et T. S. Eliot; fig. 331: «Les nouveaux pionniers américains», polychromie sur fond vert foncé; la fig. 332 illustre une nouvelle parue sous le titre de «Saisons véritables» – ambiance sérale bleu violet; fig. 333: «Ronald Reagan et la technique de l'illusionnisme», en noir et blanc. (USA)

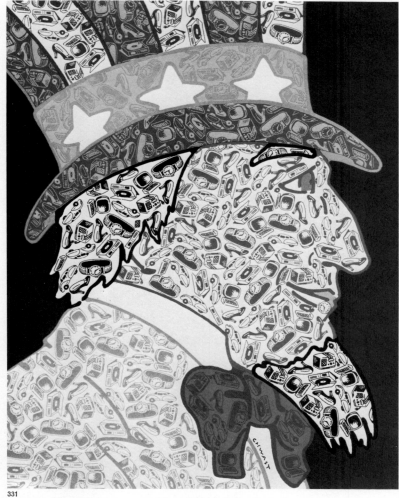

331

332

333

Magazine Illustrations

ARTIST / KÜNSTLER / ARTISTE:

334–336 Brad Holland

DESIGNER / GESTALTER / MAQUETTISTE:

336 Judy Garlan

ART DIRECTOR:

334, 334a Andrew Epstein/Bett McLean
335, 335a Ken Smith/Su Pogany
336 Judy Garlan

PUBLISHER / VERLEGER / EDITEUR:

334–335a 13–30 Corporation
336 The Atlantic Monthly

334

338

339

340

341

ARTIST / KÜNSTLER / ARTISTE:
338–342 Guy Billout

DESIGNER / GESTALTER / MAQUETTISTE:
338–340, 342 Judy Garlan

ART DIRECTOR / DIRECTEUR ARTISTIQUE:
338–340, 342 Judy Garlan
341 Derek Ungless

PUBLISHER / VERLEGER / EDITEUR:
338–340, 342 The Atlantic Monthly
341 Rolling Stone

342

338–340, 342 Full-page illustrations, all in full colour, from *The Atlantic Monthly* magazine. Fig. 338 is entitled "Latitude 90°N, Longitude 0°"; Fig. 339: "The Edge", red-brown, beige and blue tones; Fig. 340 is entitled "Time Line", rose-beige, blue and black; Fig. 342: "Phobia". (USA)
341 "New York City, 1987" is the title of this illustration from the *Rolling Stone* magazine, showing the famous "iron". The accompanying story is about an impending glacial age hitting New York in 1987. The buildings are mainly in rust-red tones, on a cold blue background. (USA)

338–340, 342 Ganzseitige Illustrationen aus der Zeitschrift *The Atlantic Monthly.* Abb. 338: «Breitengrad 90°N, Längengrad 0°»; Abb. 339: «Der Rand», Braunrot, Beige und Blautöne; Abb. 340: «Gleis der Zeit», Beigerosa-Töne, Blau und Schwarz; Abb. 342: «Phobie». (USA)
341 «New York City 1987.» Ganzseitige Illustration aus der Zeitschrift *Rolling Stone*, mit dem berühmten «Bügeleisen». In der dazugehörigen Geschichte geht es um eine neue Eiszeit, die New York 1987 überrollt. Vorwiegend in kalten Blau- und Rostrottönen. (USA)

338–340, 342 Illustrations pleine page pour le magazine *The Atlantic Monthly.* Fig. 338: «Latitude 90°N, longitude 0°»; fig. 339: «Le bord», rouge brun, beige, divers bleus; fig. 340: «Rail du temps», divers rose beige délicats, bleu et noir; fig. 342: «Phobie». (USA)
341 «New York en 1987.» Illustration pleine page dans le magazine *Rolling Stone*, avec le fameux «fer à repasser». Le récit qui l'accompagne met en scène une nouvelle période glaciaire qui sonne le glas de New York en 1987. Divers bleus et rouille de tonalité froide. (USA)

Magazine Illustrations

343

344

345

346

347

ARTIST / KÜNSTLER / ARTISTE:

343 Mark English
344–347 Eugene Mihaesco

DESIGNER / GESTALTER / MAQUETTISTE:

343, 347 Terry Brown
344–346 Irene Ramp

ART DIRECTOR / DIRECTEUR ARTISTIQUE:

343, 347 Terry Brown
344–346 Rudolph Hoglund

PUBLISHER / VERLEGER / EDITEUR:

343, 347 The Atlantic Monthly
344–346 Time, Inc.

343 Full-page illustration for an article entitled "Freud and the Seduction Theory" in *The Atlantic Monthly* magazine. (USA)
344–346 Illustrations in full colour for a cover story in *Time* magazine. The subject is coping with stress. (USA)
347 Illustration in black and white and pale yellow for an article entitled "The Cartel that Never Was" concerning the OPEC countries; for *The Atlantic Monthly* magazine. (USA)

343 Ganzseitige Illustration für einen Artikel über «Freud und die Verführungstheorie» in *Atlantic Monthly*. (USA)
344–346 Mehrfarbige Illustrationen für einen Leitartikel in der Rubrik «Medizin» der Zeitschrift *Time*. Thema ist die Bewältigung von Stress. (USA)
347 Für einen Artikel über die OPEC in *Atlantic Monthly:* «Das Kartell, das es nie gab.» Schwarzweiss und Hellgelb. (USA)

343 Illustration pleine page pour un article sur «Freud et la théorie de la séduction», dans *Atlantic Monthly*. (USA)
344–346 Illustrations polychromes pour un article sur la résistance au stress dans la section «Médecine» du magazine *Time*. (USA)
347 Pour un article de l'*Atlantic Monthly* sur l'OPEC, «le cartel qui n'a jamais existé». Noir, blanc, jaune clair. (USA)

348

349

350

Magazine Illustrations

ARTIST / KÜNSTLER / ARTISTE:
348–350 Randall Enos
351 Bascove

DESIGNER / GESTALTER / MAQUETTISTE:
348–351 Patrick JB. Flynn

ART DIRECTOR / DIRECTEUR ARTISTIQUE:
348–351 Patrick JB. Flynn

PUBLISHER / VERLEGER / EDITEUR:
348–351 The Progressive

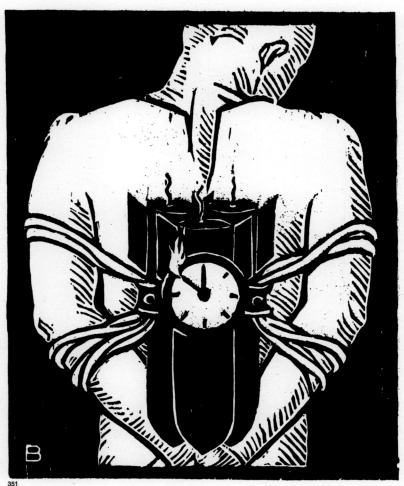

351

348–351 Illustrations in black and white for *The Progressive* magazine. Fig. 348: "Atom and Eve"; in original size, illustrating a feature on the nuclear industry's promotion directed towards women; Figs. 349, 350: Illustrating an article about six Salvadorans who took flight during the war; Fig. 351 illustrates an article about the artists' stand against militarism. (USA)

348–351 Schwarzweiss-Illustrationen aus dem Magazin *The Progressive*. Abb. 348: «Atom und Eva», ganzseitig, für einen Artikel über die Versuche der Kernkraftindustrie, die Frauen zu überzeugen; Abb. 349, 350: für Kriegserlebnisberichte von Flüchtlingen aus El Salvador; Abb. 351: ganzseitige Illustration für einen Artikel über die Opposition von Künstlern gegenüber dem Militarismus. (USA)

348–351 Illustrations noir et blanc dans le magazine *The Progressive*. Fig. 348: «Atome et Eve», pleine page, pour un article sur la campagne de l'industrie atomique auprès des femmes; fig. 349, 350: pour des récits de guerre de réfugiés salvadoriens; fig. 351: illustration pleine page pour un article sur les artistes opposés au militarisme. (USA)

Magazine Illustrations

352

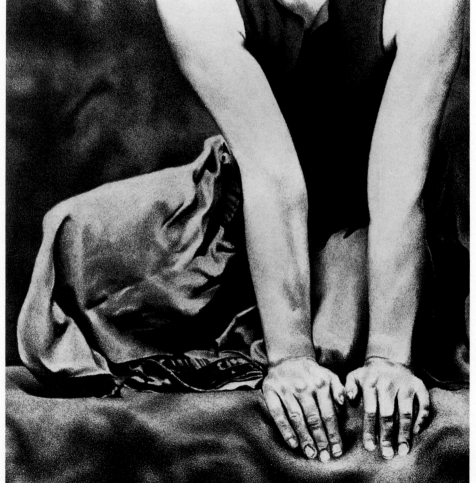

353

352 For a story in *Playboy*. The plot is the kidnapping and interrogation of a Palestinian terrorist by the Israelis. Yellow and mid-blue. (USA)
353 For a story about a girl potter in *the Saturday Night* magazine. She is wearing a violet skirt and a rust-coloured blouse. (USA)
354 Full-page illustration for the "Interpretation of Dreams" column in the *Eltern* magazine. This article concerns dreams about pregnancy and birth. Green labyrinth, blue foetus and sky, face beige with blue, on black ground. (GER)
355 Illustration for a ribald poem by La Fontaine about a nun. From *Playboy*. (USA)
356 Full-page illustration for "Mr. Mike's America", a story in *Playboy*. (USA)
357 Cover of the *Town & Country's* Annual Racing Guide. Globe in green and yellow, jockey's cap pink, background yellow, pink and blue. (USA)

352 Für eine Geschichte im *Playboy*, in der es um Gefangennahme und Verhör eines palästinensischen Terroristen durch die Israelis geht. Gelb und Mittelblau. (USA)
353 Illustration für eine Geschichte über eine Töpferin, in *Saturday Night*. Violetter Rock, rostrote Bluse. (USA)
354 Ganzseitige Illustration für die Rubrik «Traumdeutung» der Zeitschrift *Eltern*. Der Beitrag befasst sich mit Träumen von Schwangerschaft und Geburt. Grünes Labyrinth, blauer Fötus und Himmel, Gesicht beige mit Blau auf Schwarz. (GER)
355 Für einen spöttischen Vers von La Fontaine. Aus *Playboy*. (USA)
356 Ganzseitige Illustration für «Mr. Mike's America», aus *Playboy*. (USA)
357 Umschlag eines Veranstaltungskalenders für Pferderennen, herausgegeben von *Town & Country*. Globus grün und gelb, Hintergrund gelb, rosa und blau. (USA)

352 Pour un récit de *Playboy*, où il est question de l'arrestation et de l'interrogatoire d'un terroriste palestinien par les Israéliens. Jaune, bleu moyen. (USA)
353 Illustration d'un récit dont l'héroïne est une potière, dans *Saturday Night*. Jupe violette, blouse rouille. (USA)
354 Illustration pleine page pour la section «Interprétation des rêves» du magazine *Eltern*. L'article discute de la signification des rêves de grossesse et de naissance. Labyrinthe vert, fœtus bleu, ciel bleu, visage beige, avec du bleu, sur noir. (GER)
355 Pour une poésie satirique de La Fontaine sur une religieuse. Dans *Playboy*. (USA)
356 Illustration pleine page pour «Mr. Mike's America», un récit de *Playboy*. (USA)
357 Couverture d'un calendrier de manifestations hippiques publié par *Town & Country*. Globe terrestre vert et jaune, fond jaune, rose, bleu. (USA)

354

355

356

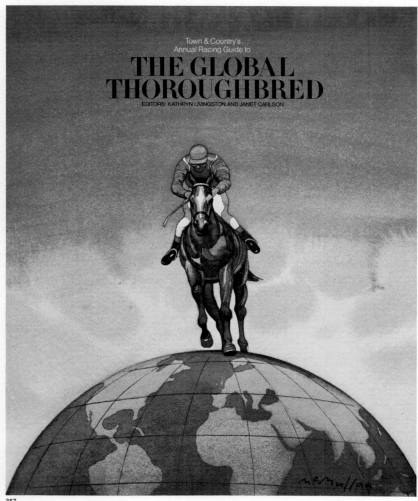

357

358

ARTIST / KÜNSTLER / ARTISTE:

358 Marvin Mattelson
359 Nacho Soriano
360 Marshall Arisman

DESIGNER / GESTALTER / MAQUETTISTE:

358 Judy Garlan
360 Art Spiegelman

ART DIRECTOR / DIRECTEUR ARTISTIQUE:

358 Judy Garlan
359 Nacho Soriano

PUBLISHER / VERLEGER / EDITEUR:

358 The Atlantic Monthly
359 PSOE – El Socialista
360 Raw Magazine

Magazine Illustrations
Zeitschriften-Illustrationen
Illustrations de périodiques

358 For an article in *The Atlantic Monthly* referring to the need for more funds for basic plant science. Dollar notes can be seen on the cabbage heart. (USA)
359 For an article in the Spanish magazine *El Socialista* which appeared during the time of Calvo Sotelo's government. (SPA)
360 Illustration for a story in *Raw* magazine. (USA)

358 Illustration für einen Artikel, in dem es um die für die Landwirtschaft notwendige Forschung geht. Dollarnoten werden auf den inneren Kohlblättern sichtbar. Aus *The Atlantic Monthly*. (USA)
359 Illustration für einen Artikel in der spanischen Zeitschrift *El Socialista*, der während der Regierungszeit von Calvo Sotelo erschien. (SPA)
360 Ganzseitige Illustration für eine Geschichte in der Zeitschrift *Raw*. (USA)

358 Illustration d'un article où il est question de la recherche agricole. Des billets en dollars apparaissent sur les feuilles intérieures du chou. Paru dans *The Atlantic Monthly*. (USA)
359 Illustration pour un article du magazine espagnol *El Socialista* paru sous le gouvernement de Calvo Sotelo. (SPA)
360 Illustration pleine page pour un récit paru dans le magazine *Raw*. (USA)

359

361

362

A

B

C

D

E

F

363

364

365

Magazine Illustrations

361 "Cactus Jack"; an illustration on a page entitled "Western Art" in the *Texas Monthly* magazine. Green face with white thorns, brown hat. (USA)
362 Full-page illustration in green tones for an article in *Saturday Night* for a feature about SS Master Sergeant Helmut Rauca who was arrested in Canada in 1982. (CAN)
363 From an article in the *New York Times Magazine* about American industry. (USA)
364 "Snow White and Several Dwarfs"; an illustration to a story in *Chicago* magazine. (USA)
365 "The Birth of Bebop"; for an article in *Esquire* about a Harlem jazz club where, in the nineteen-forties, musicians such as Dizzy Gillespie, Thelonius Monk, Roy Eldridge and Charlie Parker played. (USA)

361 «Kaktus-Jack», Illustration einer Seite mit dem Titel «Western-Kunst» in der Zeitschrift *Texas Monthly*. Grünes Gesicht mit weissen Stacheln, brauner Hut. (USA)
362 Ganzseitige Illustration in Grüntönen für einen Artikel in *Saturday Night* über den 1982 in Kanada verhafteten ehemaligen SS-Stabsfeldwebel Helmut Rauca. (CAN)
363 Aus einem Beitrag im *New York Times Magazine* über die amerikanische Industrie. (USA)
364 «Schneewittchen und mehrere Zwerge», Illustration zu einer Geschichte in *Chicago*. (USA)
365 Für einen Beitrag in *Esquire* über ein Jazz-Lokal in Harlem, in dem in den vierziger Jahren u. a. Dizzy Gillespie, Thelonius Monk, Roy Eldridge und Charlie Parker spielten. (USA)

361 «Cactus-Jack», illustration d'une page intitulée «L'art du far-ouest», dans le magazine *Texas Monthly*. Visage vert, piquants blancs, sombrero marron. (USA)
362 Illustration pleine page, tons verts, pour un article de *Saturday Night* sur l'ancien sergent-chef SS Helmut Rauca arrêté au Canada en 1982. (CAN)
363 Pour un article du *New York Times Magazine* sur l'état de l'industrie américaine. (USA)
364 «Blanche-Neige et divers nains», illustration d'un récit paru dans *Chicago*. (USA)
365 Pour un article rétrospectif d'*Esquire* sur une salle de jazz de Harlem, qui vit se produire dans les années 40 Dizzy Gillespie, Thelonius Monk, Roy Eldridge, Charlie Parker, etc. (USA)

were relatively small. If another team offered a player who made $100,000 a year $15,000 more, he would often stay put. If it offered him $300,000, he was gone.

I thought that Simon and Garfunkel, in that lovely song, asked the wrong question. It should not have been "Where have you gone, Joe DiMaggio?" but, rather, in an age when players can make their own decisions, "Where are you going . . . ?"

I think, now, I know.

Since DiMaggio was a white superstar with exceptional right-handed power, and since the Yankees and the Red Sox have one of the last surviving true rivalries in sports, I believe Joltin' Joe, if he were still playing, would be going to the Red Sox for a cool $3,000,000 a year, plus a fat Fenway Franks endorsement deal. After all, it is clear that he and George Steinbrenner would have long since been estranged. DiMaggio's innate grace, his consummate talent and his unwillingness

366

ARTIST / KÜNSTLER / ARTISTE:

366 Teresa Fasolino
367 Alain Gauthier
368 Marvin Mattelson
369 Robert Giusti

DESIGNER / GESTALTER / MAQUETTISTE:

368 Bruce Hansen
369 Liz Siroka

ART DIRECTOR / DIRECTEUR ARTISTIQUE:

366 Tom Staebler/Len Willis
367 Annick Geille
368 Tom Staebler
369 Elizabeth Woodson

PUBLISHER / VERLEGER / EDITEUR:

366, 368 Playboy Enterprises, Inc.
367 Playboy France
369 Omni Publications International Ltd.

367

368

369

366 Illustration from a *Playboy* feature about an ageing baseball star. (USA)
367 Illustrating an excerpt from a Philippe Sollers' novel in *Playboy* magazine. (FRA)
368 From *Playboy*, to illustrate an article saying that the American media suggest there is a return to the old Puritan morality. Statue of Liberty poison-green, blue sky. (USA)
369 For an article in *Omni* entitled "Animal Feminism" in which, according to animal behaviourists, female animals of certain species dominate the males. (USA)

366 Illustration aus einem *Playboy*-Artikel über einen alternden Baseball-Star. (USA)
367 Für einen im *Playboy* erschienenen Auszug eines Romans von Philippe Sollers. (FRA)
368 Eine neue puritanische Sex-Moral innerhalb der amerikanischen Medien ist Gegenstand des *Playboy*-Artikels, zu dem diese Illustration gehört. Freiheitsstatue giftgrün, Himmel hellblau. (USA)
369 Für einen Artikel in *Omni*. Thema sind Ergebnisse der Tierverhaltensforschung, gemäss welchen die weiblichen Tiere bei einigen Spezies die Männchen eindeutig dominieren. (USA)

366 Illustration d'un article de *Playboy* sur une vedette vieillissante du base-ball. (USA)
367 Pour les bonnes feuilles d'un roman de Philippe Soller publiées dans *Playboy*. (FRA)
368 L'article de *Playboy* d'où est tirée cette illustration fait état d'une nouvelle morale puritaine des médias américains en matière de sexualité. Statue verte, ciel bleu clair. (USA)
369 Pour un article d'*Omni*. On y passe en revue les résultats acquis en éthologie au sujet des espèces chez qui la femelle domine indiscutablement le mâle. (USA)

Magazine Illustrations

370

371

Magazine Illustrations
Zeitschriften-Illustrationen
Illustrations de périodiques

374

370 "The Attila Tapes". Illustration for a humorous article in *The Atlantic Monthly*. (USA)
371 Illustration for a magazine story. The dog is dressed in a red coat with a yellow bone pattern. (GER)
372, 373 Double spreads in full colour from the magazine *Grazia*. Fig. 372 illustrates a story entitled "Tea with the Diva"; Fig. 373 refers to the changing attitudes to procreation in the light of scientific advances, e. g. the pill and artificial insemination. (ITA)
374 Full-page illustration for a *Penthouse* article about the circumstances leading to the brutal murder of four churchwomen in El Salvador. (USA)
375 "Roboclone". Can a robot duplicate itself? It can, according to an article in *Omni* for which this is the illustration. (USA)

370 Illustration für einen humoristischen Beitrag in *The Atlantic Monthly*: «Die Atilla-Bänder.» (USA)
371 Illustration für eine Magazin-Geschichte. Hund in rotem Mäntelchen mit gelben Knochen. (GER)
372, 373 Doppelseiten mit mehrfarbigen Illustrationen aus dem Magazin *Grazia*. Abb. 372 bezieht sich auf eine Geschichte mit dem Titel «Tee mit der Diva»; Sexualität und umwälzende Veränderungen wie Geburtenkontrolle und künstliche Befruchtung sind das Thema in Abb. 373. (ITA)
374 Ganzseitige Illustration für einen *Penthouse*-Artikel über die Umstände der Ermordung von vier Amerikanerinnen (drei Nonnen und eine Sozialarbeiterin) in El Salvador. (USA)
375 Für einen *Omni*-Beitrag über Roboter-Utopien. (USA)

370 Illustration d'un article humoristique dans l'*Atlantic Monthly*. (USA)
371 Illustration d'un récit publié en magazine. Chien au manteau rouge, os jaune. (GER)
372, 373 Doubles pages du magazine *Grazia*, en polychromie. La fig. 372 se rapporte à une histoire intitulée «Thé avec la diva»; la 373 traite de la sexualité et des bouleversements qui l'affectent – le contrôle des naissances, l'insémination artificielle. (ITA)
374 Illustration pleine page pour un article de *Penthouse* sur les circonstances de l'assassinat de quatre Américaines (trois religieuses, une assistante sociale) au Salvador. (USA)
375 Pour un article d'*Omni* sur les robots. (USA)

UN TÉ
CON
LA DIVA

*Racconto di
Dorothy Parker*

Nel mondo che cambia, la continuazione stessa della
specie umana sta assumendo connotazioni nuove

UNA DONNA
UN UOMO
FORSE
UN BAMBINO

In pochi anni conquiste
scientifiche senza precedenti
(la contraccezione e la
fecondazione artificiale) hanno
portato alla scissione fra
la sessualità e la procreazione,
trasformando i rapporti
uomo-donna e padre-madre-
figlio: una rivoluzione
culturale, entusiasmante ma
inquietante, che richiede
una seria riflessione per evitare
il rischio che l'essere
umano perda la sua identità.

*di Paolo Francioli
disegni di Jaume Cluet*

ARTIST / KÜNSTLER / ARTISTE:

370 Mel Furukawa
371 Bengt Fosshag
372, 373 Jaume Cluet
374, 375 Marshall Arisman

DESIGNER / GESTALTER / MAQUETTISTE:

370 Judy Garlan
371 Bengt Fosshag
375 Liz Siroka

ART DIRECTOR / DIRECTEUR ARTISTIQUE:

370 Judy Garlan
371 Bengt Fosshag
372, 373 Romano Vitale
374 Richard Bleiweiss
375 Elizabeth Woodson

PUBLISHER / VERLEGER / EDITEUR:

370 The Atlantic Monthly
372, 373 Arnoldo Mondadori
374 Penthouse International
375 Omni Publications International Ltd.

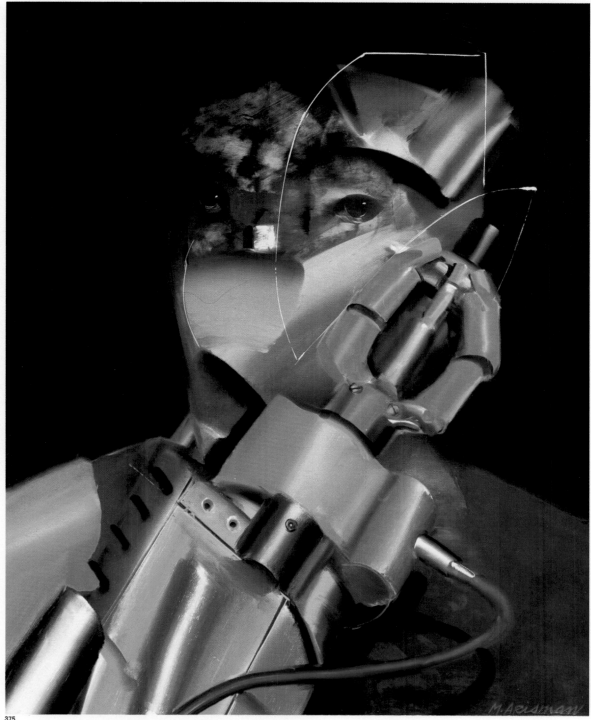

381

381 For a story in *Esquire* about the dreams and fears of a Jew. (USA)
382 One of five illustrations for a feature on the murder of a Toronto policeman in *Saturday Night* magazine. Mainly mournful grey tones splashed with red blood. (CAN)
383 Illustration for a story in the *Boston Magazine* about a murder that happened in a small neighbourhood store. In grey and brown with red. (USA)

381 Für eine Geschichte in *Esquire* über Träume und Ängste eines Juden. (USA)
382 Eine von fünf Illustrationen für einen Artikel in *Saturday Night* über die Ermordung eines Polizisten in Toronto. Vorwiegend düstere Graugrüntöne, rotes Blut. (CAN)
383 Illustration für eine Geschichte im *Boston Magazine* über einen Mord, der sich in einem kleinen Quartierladen abspielte. In Grau und Braun mit Rot. (USA)

381 Pour un récit, dans *Esquire*, qui relate les rêves et les angoisses d'un Juif. (USA)
382 L'une des cinq illustrations d'un article de *Saturday Night* où il est question du meurtre d'un policier à Toronto. Tons vert gris lugubres, sang rouge. (CAN)
383 Illustration pour un récit du *Boston Magazine* qui met en scène un meurtre commis dans une petite boutique de quartier. Gris et brun, avec du rouge. (USA)

382

383

ARTIST / KÜNSTLER / ARTISTE:

381 Miro Malish
382 Sue Coe
383 Terry Widener

DESIGNER / GESTALTER / MAQUETTISTE:

382 Louis Fishauf

ART DIRECTOR / DIRECTEUR ARTISTIQUE:

381 Robert Priest
382 Louis Fishauf
383 Stan McCray

AGENCY / AGENTUR / AGENCE – STUDIO:

381 Reactor Art & Design Ltd

PUBLISHER / VERLEGER / EDITEUR:

381 Esquire, Inc.
382 Saturday Night Magazine
383 Boston Magazine

Magazine Illustrations
Zeitschriften-Illustrationen
Illustrations de périodiques

YEAR OF THE
H O R S E

The art of winning it racing/By Barry Callaghan

It all began in the South China Sea, in Macáo, where I'd gone to play the casinos, crowding into the gaming rooms with Chinese who stood sleepless for hours waiting for someone to surrender a chair at the tables, and then holding onto that chair with a squint-eyed right for two hours, a day, two... stamina and a little luck, stamina and the clatter of the steel ball in the wheel as the hours slipped away, lost, all sense of time lost, playing fantan and roulette until I went out, suddenly bored by the ache in my shoulders, satisfied that I had the price of pearls in my pocket, and then, only a few feet from the door, the ocean slapped against the breakwall, and so I went for a walk along the ocean road, calmed by that curious watery milk-light before dawn...

everything so fresh, cleansed: but there were no birds crying along the shore, and the air seemed empty, empty and still.

Macáo did not seem right for me, so I went to a temple and had tea with an old monk under a huge tree that was three trees twisted together and had bits onto the fortune sticks, and then went back to Hong Kong on one of the jetfoil boats, passing between islands that are stone bumps in the sea, arriving at last at the Peninsula Hotel, a place of grace that caters to dreams, surrounded by the rich and reputable, producers and perhaps a gunrunner, exquisite women and the odd seraphead. I strode between Silver Clouds, the white stone lions at the door, and little feet in white suits wearing white pillbox hats, and found my friend George Yemac—lean and

sleek and greying at the temples—and he said, "Hello, can you get up at 4 in the morning? You should come with me and see the horses."

In the morning hours, in the cold dark hours overcast with no stars in the sky, I found myself hunched against the cold beside a racetrack, and there were great amber floodlights high in the morning mist, suspended flowers, but I couldn't see anything, not around the turns in the rail, but I heard the muffled sound of hoofs and suddenly a huge horse broke into the half-light, lunging past. "Aie, she's a might slow this morning," said the small Cork trainer, clocking the horse and staring into the gloom, waiting. Other horses, appearing out of the dark, disappeared. *Continued on page 71*

Continued on page 71

The Day the
Money Stopped

The day the world upended. You remember the date: July 17, or March 4, or perhaps September 27, when it all happened and everything suddenly became different. Nothing—barring accidents of course—happens in one day, but when the money stops, that's the way it seems.
By Eve Rockett

384 Full-colour double spread for an article in *Toronto Life Magazine* about horse-racing. (CAN)
385 "The Day the Money Stopped"; an introductory double spread for a story in *Homemaker's Magazine*. Autumn colouring with dollar bills falling as leaves. (CAN)
386 For an article in *City Woman* Magazine about the role mentors play in leading women through the maze of corporate management. (CAN)
387 From the *Texas Monthly* magazine. One of four illustrations for an article about an axe murder and the subsequent trial. This is the fourth and illustrates the trial. (USA)

384 Einleitende Doppelseite für einen Beitrag über Pferderennen in *Toronto Life Magazine*. (CAN)
385 «Der Tag, an dem kein Geld mehr kam.» Einleitende Doppelseite für eine Geschichte in *Homemakers Magazine*. In Orange, Rot, Gelb, Braun und Grün. (CAN)
386 Illustration für einen Beitrag in *City Woman Magazine*. Zentrales Thema ist die Frage, wie Frauen mit Betriebs-Managementproblemen fertig werden und die Rolle, die Ratgeber dabei spielen. (CAN)
387 Für einen Artikel in *Texas Monthly* über einen mit einer Axt verübten Mord. Diese Illustration bezieht sich auf den anschliessenden Prozess. (USA)

384 Double page initiale d'un article du *Toronto Life Magazine*: courses de chevaux. (CAN)
385 «Le jour où l'argent cessa d'arriver.» Double page initiale d'un récit publié dans le *Homemakers Magazine*. Orange, rouge, jaune, brun, vert. (CAN)
386 Illustration pour un article du *City Woman Magazine* où l'on discute des problèmes de gestion d'entreprise qui se posent aux femmes et du rôle que jouent les conseillers en management. (CAN)
387 Pour un article du *Texas Monthly* consacré à un meurtre odieux où l'arme du crime était une hache. L'illustration se rapporte au procès qui s'ensuivit. (USA)

Magazine Illustrations

ARTIST / KÜNSTLER / ARTISTE:

384 Julius Ciss
385 Miro Malish
386 James Tughan
387 Jeff Smith

DESIGNER / GESTALTER / MAQUETTISTE:

386 James Tughan
387 Fred Woodward

ART DIRECTOR / DIRECTEUR ARTISTIQUE:

384 James Ireland/Lindsay Beadry
385 Ursula Kaiser
386 Barb Solowan
387 Fred Woodward

AGENCY / AGENTUR / AGENCE – STUDIO:

385 Reactor Art & Design Ltd

PUBLISHER / VERLEGER / EDITEUR:

384 Toronto Life Magazine
385, 386 Comac Communications Ltd
387 Texas Monthly, Inc.

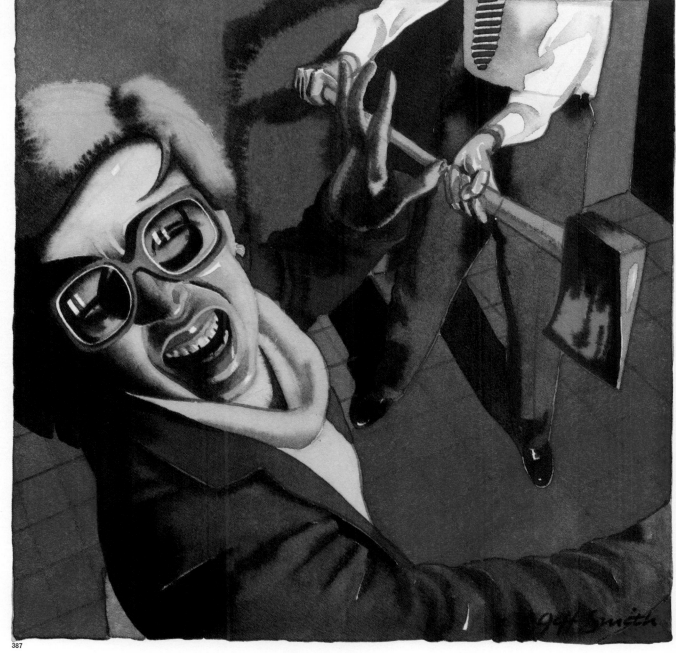

387

Magazine Illustrations

388 Full-page illustration for a story in *Ms* magazine about a son's remembrance of his mother. (USA)
389 Illustration for the "Western Art" page from the *Texas Monthly*. This title is "Urbanization". (USA)
390, 391 For Truman Capote's reminiscences of his friend Tennessee Williams; in *Playboy*. These full-page portraits of the famous playwright are by Andy Warhol. (USA)
392 Illustration in brown and green tones on a pale background for a play by R. E. Sherwood. (USA)
393 A full-page illustration for a short story by Truman Capote entitled *Miriam* in *Carina*. The flowers, girl's dress and hair are in off-white on a dark, sombre ground. (GER)
394 Full-page portrait for an article in the magazine *Rolling Stone*. (USA)

388 Ganzseitige Illustration für eine Geschichte im *Ms*-Magazin, mit dem Titel «Der Bastard». (USA)
389 Illustration mit dem Titel «Verstädterung» für die «Western-Kunst»-Seite von *Texas Monthly*. (USA)
390, 391 Für Truman Capotes Erinnerungen an seinen Freund Tennessee Williams, im *Playboy*. Ganzseitige Porträts des berühmten Schriftstellers von Andy Warhol. (USA)
392 Illustration in Braun- und Grüntönen mit hellem Hintergrund für ein Theaterstück von R. E. Sherwood. (USA)
393 «Der unheimliche Gast.» Ganzseitige Illustration für eine Kurzgeschichte von Truman Capote in *Carina*. Blumen, Kleid und Haare des Mädchens in gräulichem Weiss, sonst verhaltene, dunkle Farben. (GER)
394 Ganzseitiges Porträt für einen Beitrag in der Zeitschrift *Rolling Stone*. (USA)

388 Illustration pleine page pour une nouvelle publiée dans le magazine *Ms*, «Le Bâtard». (USA)
389 Illustration intitulée «Urbanisation» pour la page d'«Art du far-ouest» du *Texas Monthly*. (USA)
390, 391 Pour un texte de Truman Capote évoquant le souvenir de son ami Tennessee Williams, dans *Playboy*. Portraits pleine page du célèbre écrivain par Andy Warhol. (USA)
392 Illustration aux tons bruns et verts, sur fond clair, pour une pièce de R. E. Sherwood. (USA)
393 «L'Hôte inquiétant.» Illustration pleine page pour une nouvelle de Truman Capote publiée dans *Carina*. Fleurs, robe, chevelure blanc grisâtre, le reste en tons sombres, retenus. (GER)
394 Portrait pleine page pour un article publié dans le magazine *Rolling Stone*. (USA)

389

388

392

ARTIST / KÜNSTLER / ARTISTE:

388 Paola Piglia
389 Scott Reynolds
390, 391 Andy Warhol
392 Dagmar Frinta
393 Katrin Lindley
394 Philip Hays

DESIGNER / GESTALTER:

389 Fred Woodward/David Kampa
390, 391 Kerig Pope
392 Michael Mendelsohn

160

390

391

393

394

ART DIRECTOR / DIRECTEUR ARTISTIQUE:

388 Kati Korpijaakko
389 Fred Woodward
390, 391 Tom Staebler
392 Michael Mendelsohn

PUBLISHER / VERLEGER / EDITEUR:

388 Ms Magazine
389 Texas Monthly, Inc.
390, 391 Playboy Enterprises, Inc.
392 The Franklin Library
393 Burda Verlag

161

Magazine Illustrations

396

395

399

395 Illustration for a feature about sex in the Forum section of the *Penthouse* magazine. (USA)
396 For a memoir by Irwin Shaw in *Playboy*, recalling what he has learned about manhood through experience. A mainly black-and-white portrait, with brown and grey tones on the skin. (USA)
397 An illustration in brown shades from *Saturday Night*. It relates to an article on the murder of a Toronto policeman and the history of the firearm which killed him. (CAN)
398 Black-and-white illustration from the *Radio Guide* for an article about the late night radio series "A Little Night Music". The article is entitled "The Sandman Cometh". (CAN)
399 From *Quest* magazine for a feature about men losing the battle of the sexes and their fight to win back their lost rights. Symbol in pale grey, green T-shirt, on orange-red ground. (CAN)
400 "Eye to Eye with Mr. T." A sombre-toned illustration for a story in *Playboy* magazine. (USA)
401 For an illustration in *The Boston Globe Magazine*. In black-and-white with beige tones. (USA)

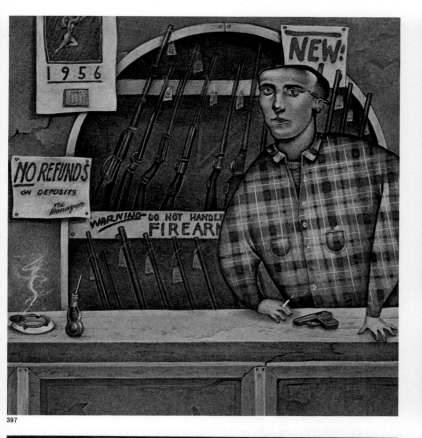

397

398

400

401

395 Illustration für einen Beitrag über Sex im Forum-Sektor des Magazins *Penthouse*. (USA)
396 Für einen Beitrag in *Playboy* über die Erfahrungen eines Mannes und was es heisst, ein Mann zu sein. Illustration vorwiegend in Schwarz und Weiss, mit Braun- und Grautönen auf der Haut. (USA)
397 Illustration in Brauntönen aus *Saturday Night*. Sie bezieht sich auf den Waffenkauf in einem Sportgeschäft, den Anfang einer Geschichte, die mit einem Mord endet. (CAN)
398 Schwarzweiss-Illustration aus *Radio Guide* für einen Artikel über eine regelmässige Nacht-Sendung mit dem Titel «Eine kleine Nachtmusik». (CAN)
399 Für einen Artikel in *Quest* über Männer, die versuchen, ihre durch die Frauenemanzipation verlorenen Rechte zurückzugewinnen. Hellgraues Symbol, grüne Kleidung, Hintergrund orangerot. (CAN)
400 «Auge in Auge mit Mr. T.» Illustration in dunklen Tönen für eine Geschichte in *Playboy*. (USA)
401 Für einen Beitrag in *The Boston Globe Magazine*. In Schwarzweiss mit Beige-Tönen. (USA)

395 Illustration pour un article de sexualité du magazine *Penthouse*, section Forum. (USA)
396 Pour un article de *Playboy* où un homme parle de ses expériences et où l'on définit ce que c'est qu'un homme. Illustration noir et blanc, avec divers bruns et gris sur la peau. (USA)
397 Illustration aux tons bruns parue dans *Saturday Night*. Elle se rapporte à l'achat d'une arme dans un magasin de sport, début d'une histoire qui se termine par un meurtre. (CAN)
398 Illustration noir et blanc dans *Radio Guide* pour un article sur une émission nocturne permanente intitulée «Une Petite Sérénade». (CAN)
399 Pour un article de *Quest* sur les hommes qui tentent de reconquérir leurs droits lésés par l'émancipation des femmes. Emblème gris clair, vêtements verts, fond rouge orangé. (CAN)
400 «Face à face avec M. T.» Illustration aux tons sombres pour un article de *Playboy*. (USA)
401 Pour un article du *Boston Globe Magazine*. Noir et blanc, tons beiges. (USA)

402

403

402, 403 Illustration and introductory double spread from *Saturday Night* for an article entitled "Journey into Fear", about a TV reporter who was hit by a shell in Lebanon. Blue clothes, bed and pillowcase, red blood-splashes, green and blue interior. (CAN)
404 Full-page illustration from *The New York Time Magazine* about the combination of changes in modern society (including TV and less supervision) which has led to precocious children. (USA)

402, 403 Illustration und einleitende Doppelseite für einen Beitrag in *Saturday Night*. Es geht um einen Reporter, der im Libanon von einer Granate getroffen wird. Blau und Grün mit Rot. (CAN)
404 Ganzseitige Illustration aus dem Magazin der *New York Times* für einen Artikel über die veränderten Umstände, unter denen Kinder heute aufwachsen und die Konsequenzen. Die Illustration bezieht sich auf eine der Ursachen für die Veränderung, das Fernsehen. (USA)

402, 403 Illustration et double page initiale d'un article de *Saturday Night*. Il y est question d'un reporter blessé par un obus sur le théâtre de guerre libanais. Bleu, vert, rouge. (CAN)
404 Illustration pleine page, dans le *New York Times Magazine*, pour un article sur les transformations qui affectent le cadre de vie des enfants d'aujourd'hui et le dénaturent sensiblement. Ici, c'est la télévision qui est sur la sellette. (USA)

404

ARTIST / KÜNSTLER / ARTISTE:

402, 403 Julian Allen
404 R.O. Blechman

DESIGNER / GESTALTER / MAQUETTISTE:

402, 403 Joel Cuyler

ART DIRECTOR / DIRECTEUR ARTISTIQUE:

402, 403 Louis Fishauf
404 Roger Black

PUBLISHER / VERLEGER / EDITEUR:

402, 403 Saturday Night Publishing Services
404 The New York Times

Magazine Illustrations

Magazine Illustrations
Zeitschriften-Illustrationen
Illustrations de périodiques

ARTIST / KÜNSTLER / ARTISTE:

405 Philip Hays
406 John Lykes
407 Alain Gauthier
400 Michael B. Morgan

ART DIRECTOR:

406, 408 Roger Carpenter
407 François Ruy Vidal

PUBLISHER / VERLEGER / EDITEUR:

406, 408 Galliard Press
407 Alain Pierson

405 Illustration for a magazine story. White robe, pale blue sky, dark wall, brown basket with green peas. (USA)
406, 408 Two examples of the full-page illustrations accompanying song lyrics in *Radio Eyes*. Fig. 406 illustrates Randy Newman's "Short People" and Fig. 408 relates to the lyrics of Lou Reed's "Walk on the Wild Side". (USA)
407 Full-page illustration for a song by Tino Rossi, from *Song-book*. (FRA)

405 Illustration für eine Kurzgeschichte. Weisses Gewand vor hellblauem Himmel, dunkle Mauer, brauner Korb mit grünen Erbsen. (USA)
406, 408 Zwei Beispiele von ganzseitigen Illustrationen zu den Texten von Songs, in *Radio Eyes*. Abb. 406 bezieht sich auf Randy Newmans «Short People», Abb. 408 auf Lou Reeds «Walk on the wild side». (USA)
407 Ganzseitige Illustration für ein Lied von Tino Rossi, aus *Song-book*. (FRA)

405 Illustration d'un récit publié en magazine. Vêtement blanc sur ciel bleu clair, mur sombre, corbeille marron, petits pois verts. (USA)
406, 408 Deux exemples d'illustrations pleine page accompagnant le texte de chansons dans *Radio Eyes*. La fig. 406 se rapporte aux «Short People» (Petites Gens) de Randy Newman, la 408 au «Walk on the wild side» de Lou Reed. (USA)
407 Illustration pleine page pour une chanson de Tino Rossi, dans *Song-book*. (FRA)

405

406

407

Magazine Illustrations
Zeitschriften-Illustrationen
Illustrations de périodiques

ARTIST / KÜNSTLER / ARTISTE:

409　Giora Carmi
410, 411　Lou Beach
412　Barbara Nessim

ART DIRECTOR / DIRECTEUR ARTISTIQUE:

409　Giora Carmi
410, 411　Roger Carpenter
412　Kati Korpijakko

PUBLISHER / VERLEGER / EDITEUR:

410, 411　Galliard Press
412　Ms Magazine

412

411

409 Illustration in brown with orange-yellow on beige, with the title "Death Sentence". (ISR)
410, 411 Illustration and complete double spread accompanying the song lyrics of Debra Ayall's "Never Say Never", taken from *Radio Eyes*. See also Figs. 406, 408. (USA)
412 Produced on a computer for an article on computer-aided design in the *Ms* magazine. (USA)

409 Illustration in Braun mit Orangegelb auf Beige, mit dem Titel «Todesurteil». (ISR)
410, 411 Illustration und vollständige Doppelseite für den Song «Never say never» von Debora Ayall, aus *Radio Eyes*. Siehe auch Abb. 406, 408. (USA)
412 Für einen Artikel über Techniken der Computer-Graphik im *Ms*-Magazin. (USA)

409 Illustration en brun, avec du jaune orangé sur beige: «Sentence capitale». (ISR)
410, 411 Illustration et double page complète pour la chanson «Never say never» de Debora Ayall, dans *Radio Eyes*. Cf. les fig. 406, 408. (USA)
412 Pour un article sur les créations graphiques assistées par ordinateur. Magazine *Ms*. (USA)

Magazine Illustrations

413 Full-page illustration from a series in *Playboy* on the state of the sexual union. Here the article tries to assess sex in married life. (USA)
414 Introductory double spread for a feature in *Omni* about extrasensory perception and psychic remote viewing. Pale blue paper, white lettering on black ground. (USA)
415 "The Race"; black-and-white illustration for a serial in *Stern* concerning a Scottish long-distance runner in Los Angeles. (GER)

413 Ganzseitige Illustration für eine Serie im *Playboy* über sexuelle Verhaltensnormen verschiedener Gruppen, hier mit Anspielung auf Sex in der Ehe. (USA)
414 Einleitende Doppelseite für einen Beitrag in *Omni*, bei dem es um die Fähigkeiten geht, dank psychischer Kraft Ereignisse über Entfernungen hin zu sehen. (USA)
415 «Das Rennen.» Illustration in Schwarzweiss für einen Fortsetzungsroman im *Stern*, in dem es um einen schottischen Langstreckenläufer geht. (GER)

413 Illustration pleine page pour une série d'articles dans *Playboy* consacrée aux normes groupales sexuelles: allusion à la sexualité conjugale. (USA)
414 Double page initiale d'un article d'*Omni* où l'on débat des possibilités de téléperception d'événements. (USA)
415 «La course.» Illustration noir-blanc pour un feuilleton publié dans *Stern*. Le roman a pour héros un coureur de fond écossais. (GER)

414

ARTIST / KÜNSTLER / ARTISTE:

413 Kinuko Craft
414 Anne Kinggard
415 Hans Hillmann

DESIGNER / GESTALTER:

413 Kerig Pope
414 Patrick Deffenbaugh

ART DIRECTOR:

413 Tom Staebler
414 Elizabeth G. Woodson
415 Wolfgang Behnken

PUBLISHER / VERLEGER / EDITEUR:

413 Playboy Enterprises, Inc.
414 Omni Publications International
415 Gruner & Jahr AG & Co.

415

FOOD

Comics 54, 55
TV & Radio 56

ILLUSTRATION BY RANDALL ENOS

Fashions may change, but the fallacies linger on

The unsavory facts about fad dieting

By Gail Perrin
Globe Staff

Every year, especially this time of year, millions of people look in their mirrors, turn slowly and face the fact that they are fat. Maybe only a few pounds, maybe several pounds, but overweight nonetheless.

Most of these millions want the easy way out. Instead of developing appropriate eating behaviors to fit their particular lifestyles and tastes, behaviors that will help them take off one or two pounds a week (that's 52 to 104 pounds a year), the impatient majority want to shed those unwanted pounds as quickly as possible.

How?

A fad diet.

Every year there is a new one to try, and a new one at which to fail. Nutrition professionals agree that 95 percent of the people who lose weight on a fad diet gain it back within a year. But they also point out that one of the pluses of fad diets —

many of which are seriously deficient nutritionally — is that they are so restrictive or so boring that people cannot stay on them long enough to really harm themselves.

However, according to Johanna Dwyer, director of the Frances Stern Nutrition Center at New England Medical Center Hospital, any fad diet can be dangerous to anyone who is taking powerful medication or who has a health problem. Specifically, she says, one should not go on a fad diet if one has any cardiac or digestive problems, high blood pressure, diabetes or serious emotional problem. Fad diets are also out for pregnant or lactating women and for anyone under age 15.

"Fad diets are based on hope," says Alexis Beck, clinical nutritionist with River Bridge Psychological Associates in Wellesley. "Our emotions have no IQs. If you hear someone say, 'Drink this stuff three times a day and you'll be gorgeous,' you'll drink it!"

The Cambridge Diet, for instance, is a liquid diet of 330 calories a day.

"How can you get proper nutrition on 330 calories a day?" asks Beck, noting that to get it even on 900 calories a day would take conscientious planning. "What do you learn by dieting? The diet has you looking away from food. You're going to lose lean body mass and fluids.

"Remember, a fad is a style that many people are interested in for a short time, a passing fashion, a craze. There is no magic in weight management. And people should consider exercise. Exercise is a good 50 percent of weight management.

"Honestly," she continues, "I can't support any one diet, as I feel everybody needs to develop his or her own eating style, an eating style that works for that person. The person should eat responsibly and enjoy food. For some people, that may mean six small meals a day; for others only two. The principle is balance."

A good, working diet should include a selection

of foods from the so-called basic four food groups — plant and animal proteins such as meat, fish, poultry, nuts, dried beans and peas; dairy products such as milk and cheese; fruits and vegetables; and bread, cereal and grain products.

Specialists generally agree that, for any weight loss treatment plan to be effective it must address the following issues: behavior modification, nutrition education, cue control (learning how not to respond to stimuli that normally produce a reaction to want to eat), relaxation, exercise training, assertiveness and substitution behavior training (either going for what you really want or substituting a diversionary activity for eating).

Depending upon one's height, weight and level of physical activity, most professionals recommend a weight-reduction program calling for a variety of foods providing anywhere from 900 to 1500 calories a day. (After the goal is achieved, a

FAD DIETS, Page 42

R·A·P·O·S·A

escolhia uma das mocinhas intelectuais presentes e ia dormir o sono dos justos no colchão de seu quarto, único resquício pequeno-burguês permitido na casa.

— Quando saírem, deixem a porta aberta. Despejado de dois apartamentos. Alegações: falta de pagamento, desordem, atentado ao pudor, cantadas nas empregadinhas da vizinhança. Resolveu voltar à natureza e comprou uma casa num bairro, adquirida com a venda do carro e seis meses de trabalho insano numa agência de publicidade.

— Este dinheiro é minha liberdade. Não escrevo para o mercado.

As notícias corriam desencontradas. O livro já estava concluído, havendo apenas dificuldades de edição. O livro era escrito palavra após palavra, artesanato interminável. O livro já alcançava mil e duzentas páginas — sendo que a última remetia à primeira, num moto-perpétuo.

— Tem nada de novo — um hereje.

— Jamais foi tentado ao nível do significante! Definitivo como sempre. Chegou a Lacan numa manhã de domingo, após uma noitada de cachaça, violão e terço às mil. Alarmado, anunciou que isso exigia a integral reformulação do texto. Outros cinco anos, no mínimo. Os seguidores caíram em desespero, já sem paciência na espera do alimento há tanto desejado. Cinco anos, repetia, superior — os olhos adquirindo uma placidez inesperada, adocicando-se. Surgiu com obras de especulações metapsíquicas, ressuscitou Louis Pauwels e escreveu uma carta para a secção dos leitores da revista Planeta.

Os cabelos voltaram a crescer — não mais encaracolados. Lisos, angélicos, limpos — deu o macacão lee e a camiseta, segundo dizia, para dois inimigos. E passou a usar uma bata longa, amarela, guardando apenas as sandálias de couro cru e a barba.

— A pergunta. . .

E fica parado diante dos seguidores, as mãos soltas sobre as pernas cruzadas, minutos sem fim.

— . . . a resposta. . .

O trabalho com o livro tornava-se mais lento, qualquer progresso extraído gota a gota de seu coração. Tudo seria reformulado. A recuperar uma certa dimensão mística, um alheamento total das malhas do sistema.

— Fazer o contrário é fazer o mesmo. É preciso fazer o duplo metafísico, o reverso ontológico.

Alguns seguidores, nesta altura, foram se retirando. Mas os restantes eram muitos — e mais fervorosos. Viviam em comunidade. Sem sentido o colchão, afinal queimado nos fundos do quintal, um vizinho ameaçando chamar a polícia.

— Desvendar o ser é desvendar o sexo?

Dormiam todos na mesma sala,

as meninas dos cursinhos saíam na madrugada. Escrevia ali mesmo, rodeado por todos, na maior confusão — eram páginas e páginas enegrecidas com rubiscos incompreensíveis, que dizia passar à máquina todas as manhãs, agora trabalhando num jornal apenas no período da tarde.

— Dois meses, e peço demissão. Concluo o livro.

Quinze dias depois foi demitido.

— Tanto melhor.

Trancou-se em casa, anunciou que não receberia visita alguma, urgência de trabalhar sem interrupção. Uma tabuleta dependurada na porta:

"Não estou em casa. Estou na palavra, caso do ser. Não caceteie".

Os amigos cuidaram de garantir a paz. Desaconselhavam vistas, ameaçavam contra crime de lesa-criação. Só uma entrevista foi concedida. As duas estagiárias voltaram espantadas com a palidez do escritor, os olhos afundados em roxo, os cabelos esbranquecidos — nada lembrando o porte atlético do antigo lutador de judô. Prendeu o olhar numa mancha na parede e falou duas horas sem atender a qualquer pergunta. Quando insistiram, murmurou:

— Não sabem fazer perguntas. Respondo ao que deveriam perguntar.

E tornou a falar sobre alquimia, Jung, cristianismo primitivo, as catacumbas, duplos ontológicos e universos paralelos. Sobre a transubstanciação da nova geração numa raça metafísica. Das possibilidades de vida extra-terrena e a respeito de comunicações telepáticas. Sabiam das experiências dos russos? Um último desejo: conhecer o Tibet, talvez abraçar a carreira de monge — pressentia poderes de levitação, a primeira experiência surpreendendo-o no banheiro. Quando deu por encerrada a entrevista, não se despediu. Virou as costas, caminhou para a escada e subiu ao sótão da casa — recolhendo a escada em seguida. Lá foi encontrado dias depois, morto. Entre os dedos, o único papel escrito encontrado na casa:

"LEXIKON: é possível, pelo poder da mente, suspender as batidas do coração".

416 "The Unsavoury Facts about Fad Dieting"; black-and-white illustration for an article in the *Boston Globe*'s Food Section questioning the efficacy of certain well-known diets. (USA)
417 Black-and-white illustration for a feature on youth in the *Raposa* magazine. (BRA)
418, 419 Two illustrations in black and white for reports by Enzo Biagi; Fig. 418: "The Time Around 1935"; portrayed is President Roosevelt; Fig. 419: "The Time Around 1943". (ITA)
420 Complete double spread with full-colour illustrations for a feature on prehistoric animals; taken from the *Texas Monthly* magazine. (USA)

416 «Die äusserst unschmackhaften Tatsachen über Mode-Diäten.» Illustration in Schwarzweiss zu einem Artikel im *Boston Globe* innerhalb der wöchentlichen Serie über Nahrung. (USA)
417 Schwarzweiss-Illustration zu einem Artikel über die Jugend im Magazin *Raposa*. (BRA)
418, 419 Illustrationen in Schwarzweiss für zwei Berichte von Enzo Biagi. Abb. 418: «Die Zeit um 1935»; porträtiert ist Präsident F. D. Roosevelt; Abb. 419: «Die Zeit um 1943». (ITA)
420 Vollständige Doppelseite mit mehrfarbigen Illustrationen für einen Beitrag über Tiere der Urzeit, in der Zeitschrift *Texas Monthly*. (USA)

416 «Les faits peu ragoûtants sur les régimes à la mode.» Illustration noir et blanc pour un article du *Boston Globe* publié dans une série hebdomadaire consacrée à l'alimentation. (USA)
417 Illustration noir et blanc pour un rapport sur la jeunesse paru dans le magazine *Raposa*. (BRA)
418, 419 Deux illustrations noir et blanc pour des récits d'Enzo Biagi. Fig. 418: «Le milieu des années 30.», avec un portrait du Président F. D. Roosevelt; fig. 419: «La vie en 1943». (ITA)
420 Double page complète illustrée en polychromie: étude sur les animaux de la préhistoire parue dans le magazine *Texas Monthly*. (USA)

Magazine Illustrations

420

421

421 Illustration for *The New York Times Magazine* accompanying an article about conductors. (USA)
422, 423 Complete double spreads from *Zeit Magazin* about the physical and psychological development of the unborn child. Fig. 422: At twelve weeks its sense of balance begins to develop and it has started moving; Fig. 423: The seventeen-week-old foetus already closely resembles a newborn child with all five senses well developed, and it starts a sleep-wake rhythm. (GER)
424, 425 Complete cover and illustration for *The New York Times Magazine* referring to an article on the case for missile deployment in Europe. (USA)

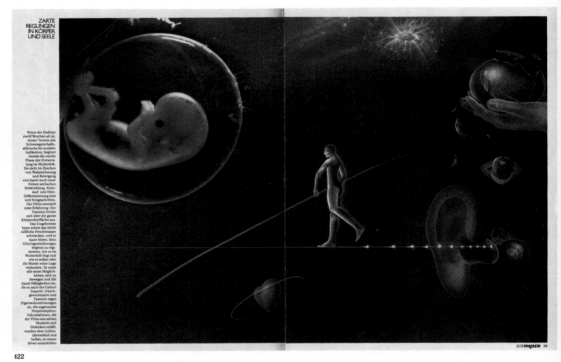

422

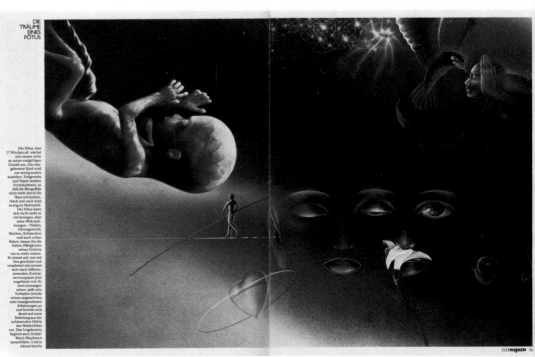

423

ARTIST / KÜNSTLER / ARTISTE:

421 Jean-Claude Suarès
422, 423 Ute Osterwalder
424, 425 Rafal Olbinski

DESIGNER / GESTALTER:

421 Ken Kendrick

ART DIRECTOR:

421, 424, 425 Roger Black
422, 423 Christian Diener

PUBLISHER / VERLEGER / EDITEUR:

421, 424, 425 The New York Times
422, 423 Zeitverlag Gerd Bucerius KG

**Weekend Supplements
Wochenendbeilagen
Suppléments dominicaux**

421 Illustration für das *New York Times Magazine* zu einem Artikel über Dirigenten. (USA)
422, 423 Vollständige Doppelseiten mit blauem Hintergrund aus einer Serie des *Zeit Magazins* über die psychische und physische Entfaltung des Kindes im Mutterleib. Abb. 422: Mit 12 Wochen entwickelt sich u. a. der Gleichgewichtssinn; Abb. 423: Beim 17 Wochen alten Fötus nehmen alle Sinneswahrnehmungen zu. Das Ungeborene träumt, und es beginnen Schlaf-Wach-Rhythmen. (GER)
424, 425 Vollständiger Umschlag und Illustration für eine Ausgabe des *New York Times Magazine* mit einem Artikel über die Stationierung von amerikanischen Raketen in Europa. (USA)

421 Illustration pour le *New York Times Magazine*: article sur les chefs d'orchestres. (USA)
422, 423 Doubles pages complètes au fond bleu tirées d'une série du *Zeit Magazin* qui passe en revue le développement prénatal (psychisme et physiologie). Fig. 422: à 12 semaines, l'organe de l'équilibration se met en place; fig. 423: le fœtus âgé de 17 semaines affine sa perception. L'enfant commence à rêver, et le cycle sommeil-éveil s'installe. (GER)
424, 425 Couverture complète et illustration pour un numéro du *New York Times Magazine* où l'on débat du stationnement des fusées américaines en Europe. (USA)

424

425

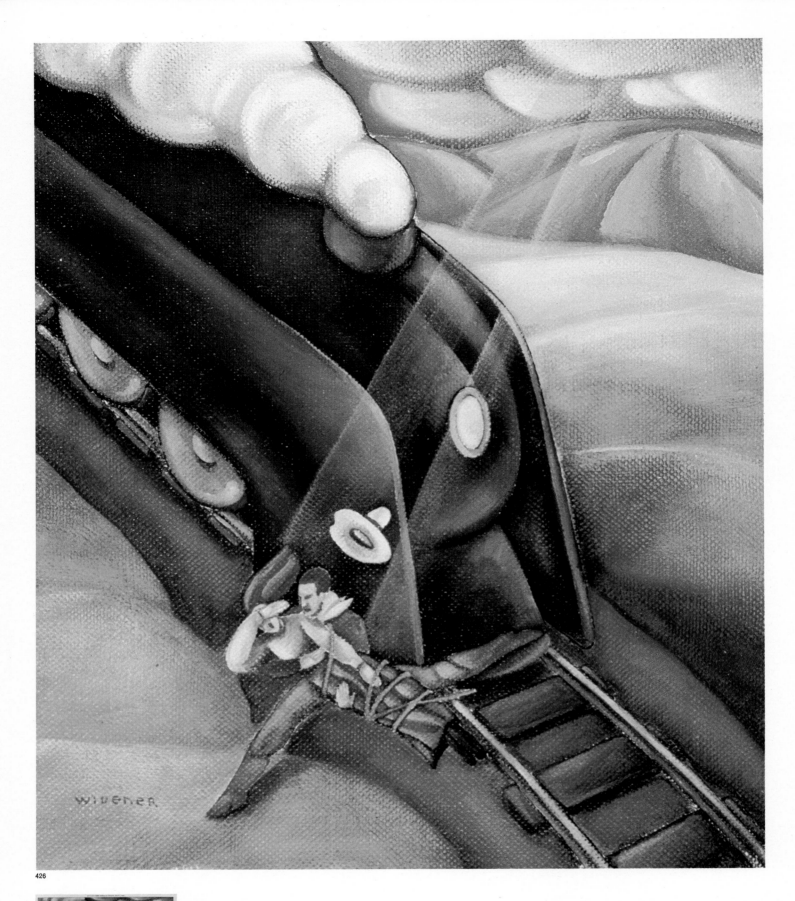

426

427

ARTIST / KÜNSTLER / ARTISTE:

426, 427 Terry Widener
428, 429 Elwood Smith
430 Chris Payne
431 Bonnie Timmons

DESIGNER / GESTALTER / MAQUETTISTE:

426, 427 Ramiro Ramirez
428–431 James Noel Smith

ART DIRECTOR / DIRECTEUR ARTISTIQUE:

426, 427 Ramiro Ramirez
428–431 James Noel Smith

PUBLISHER / VERLEGER / EDITEUR:

426–431 Dallas Times Herald

426, 427 Illustration and complete cover for an article about "Texas Heroes" in the Sunday magazine *Westward* published by the *Dallas Times Herald*. (USA)
428–431 Three more *Westward* covers in full colour and also an illustration (Fig. 431) for an article about nude dancing girls who were engaged in the 1930's, much to the concern of the Texan Baptist ministers who saw the work of the devil in such an enterprise. (USA)

426, 427 Illustration und vollständiger Umschlag zu einem Artikel über «Texas-Helden» im Sonntags-Magazin *Westward*, herausgegeben vom *Dallas Times Herald*. (USA)
428–431 Drei weitere mehrfarbige *Westward*-Umschläge sowie eine Illustration (Abb. 431) für einen Artikel über Nackttänzerinnen, die anno 1936 engagiert wurden, zum grossen Ärger der Geistlichen, die in diesem Akt den Teufel sehen wollten. (USA)

426, 427 Illustration et couverture complète du magazine dominical *Westward* du *Dallas Times Herald*. On y trouve un article sur les «héros du Texas». (USA)
428–431 Trois autres couvertures polychromes de *Westward*, ainsi qu'une illustration (fig. 431) pour un article sur les premières danseuses nues en 1936, à une époque où les prêtres y voyaient les cornes du diable. (USA)

428

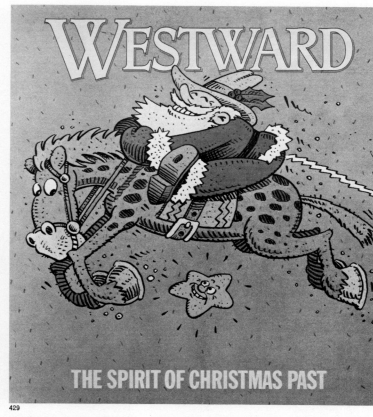

429

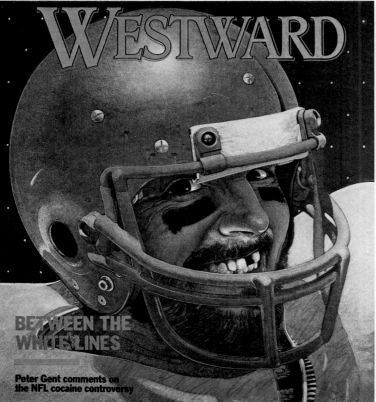

430

431

432

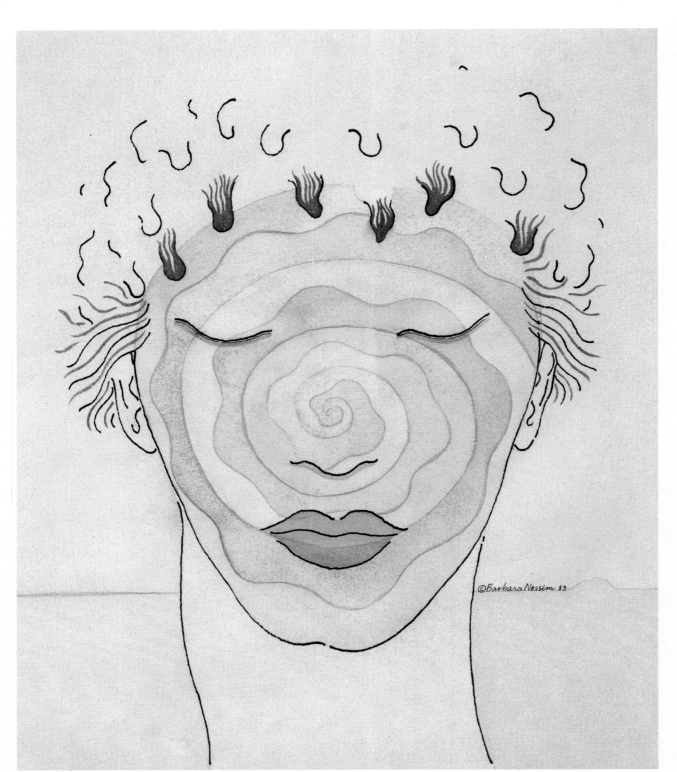

433

ARTIST / KÜNSTLER / ARTISTE:

432, 433 Barbara Nessim
434 Terry Allen
435 Devis Grebu
436 Anthony Russo
437 Steve Guarnaccia

DESIGNER / GESTALTER:

432–437 Ronn Campisi

ART DIRECTOR:

432–437 Ronn Campisi

PUBLISHER / VERLEGER / EDITEUR:

432–437 The Boston Globe

434

435

436

437

432, 433 Full-colour cover and illustration for an article in the *Boston Globe Magazine* about the effectiveness of meditation on mind and body. (USA)
434–437 Full-colour cover (Fig. 434) referring to an article about tax losses in Boston, and also three illustrations from the *Boston Globe Magazine* to illustrate various stories. (USA)

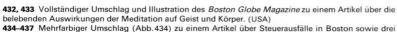

432, 433 Vollständiger Umschlag und Illustration des *Boston Globe Magazine* zu einem Artikel über die belebenden Auswirkungen der Meditation auf Geist und Körper. (USA)
434–437 Mehrfarbiger Umschlag (Abb. 434) zu einem Artikel über Steuerausfälle in Boston sowie drei Illustrationen aus dem *Boston Globe Magazine* für verschiedene Erzählungen. (USA)

432, 433 Couverture complète et illustration du *Boston Globe Magazine* sur le sujet des effets bienfaisants de la méditation pour l'équilibre du corps et de l'esprit. (USA)
434–437 Couverture polychrome (fig. 434) du *Boston Globe Magazine* sur le thème de la diminution de la rentrée d'impôts à Boston et trois illustrations de divers récits. (USA)

438

ARTIST / KÜNSTLER / ARTISTE:

438 Cathie Bleck
439 Bart Forbes
440 George F. Kocar
441 Geoffrey Moss
442 Gary Viskupic
443 Todd Grande

DESIGNER / GESTALTER / MAQUETTISTE:

438, 439 James Noel Smith
440 Sam Capuano
441 Diane Green
442 Lee Hill

ART DIRECTOR:

438, 439 James Noel Smith
440 Greg Paul
441 Tom Ruis
442 Miriam Smith
443 Michael Carroll

PUBLISHER / VERLEGER / EDITEUR:

438, 439 Dallas Times Herald
440 The Plain Dealer Publishing Co.
441 The New York Daily News
442 Newsday Inc.
443 Minneapolis Star and Tribune

439

440

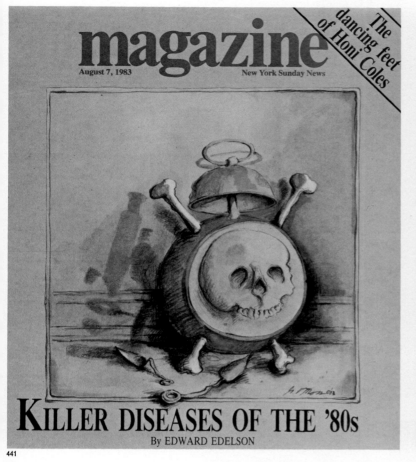

441

442

443

438 Black-and-white illustration for a humorous article in the *Dallas Times Herald* about cats. (USA)
439 Full-page illustration in blue and green tones in the *Dallas Times Herald* for an article about an attempt to interview the elusive authoress of the book *To Kill a Mockingbird*. (USA)
440 For an article about baseball in *The Plain Dealer Magazine*. In bright colours. (USA)
441 Complete cover of the *New York Daily News* Sunday magazine. The illustration refers to the leading article. In shades of yellow with red. (USA)
442 Full-page black-and-white illustration for an article in *Newsday Magazine* about the increase in emotional and physical exhaustion in teachers, known as "Teacher Burnout Syndrome". (USA)
443 For a story in the *Minneapolis Star* and *Tribune* about a middle-aged businessman who tries to hide the fact from his family that he has lost his job. In soft, pale watercolours. (USA)

438 Schwarzweiss-Illustration für einen Beitrag im *Dallas Times Herald* über Katzen. (USA)
439 Ganzseitige Illustration in Blau- und Grüntönen für einen Beitrag über Harper Lee, die Autorin des Romans *Wer die Nachtigall stört*. Aus *Dallas Times Herald*. (USA)
440 Für einen Beitrag über Baseball, in *The Plain Dealer Magazine*. In bunten Farben. (USA)
441 Umschlag für das Sonntagsmagazin der *New York Daily News*. Die Illustration bezieht sich auf den Leitartikel über tödliche Krankheiten in den 80er Jahren. Gelbtöne mit Rot. (USA)
442 Ganzseitige Illustration in Schwarzweiss für einen Artikel im *Newsday Magazine* über die physische und psychische Überbeanspruchung von Lehrern, das «Ausbrenn-Syndrom». (USA)
443 Für eine Geschichte im *Minneapolis Star* und *Tribune*. Das Thema ist ein älterer Mann, der vor seiner Familie verbirgt, dass er seine Stelle verloren hat. In zarten Aquarellfarben. (USA)

438 Illustration noir et blanc pour un article du *Dallas Times Herald* sur les chats. (USA)
439 «Trouver un merle moqueur», allusion au livre populaire d'Harper Lee. Illustration pleine page, tons bleus et verts, pour un rapport du *Dallas Times Herald* sur la romancière. (USA)
440 Pour un article du *Plain Dealer Magazine* sur le base-ball. Couleurs vives. (USA)
441 Couverture du magazine dominical du *New York Daily News*. L'illustration se rapporte à l'article de fond sur les maladies mortelles des années 80. Divers jaunes, avec du rouge. (USA)
442 Illustration pleine page, en noir et blanc, pour un article du *Newsday Magazine* sur le stress qui frappe les enseignants et provoque un véritable syndrome de l'épuisement total. (USA)
443 Pour un récit paru dans le *Minneapolis Star* et la *Tribune*. Il y est question d'un vieil homme qui n'ose révéler à sa famille qu'il a perdu son job. Teintes délicates d'aquarelle. (USA)

444

445

446

ARTIST / KÜNSTLER / ARTISTE:

444 Patrick Blackwell
445 Andrzej Dudzinski
446, 447 Randall Enos

DESIGNER / GESTALTER / MAQUETTISTE:

444–447 Ronn Campisi

ART DIRECTOR / DIRECTEUR ARTISTIQUE:

444–447 Ronn Campisi

PUBLISHER / VERLEGER / EDITEUR:

444–447 The Boston Globe

444 For the Christmas edition of the *Boston Globe Magazine*. Red with green. (USA)
445 Full-page illustration for a feature in the *Boston Globe Magazine* entitled "Commanding Presence—the Anatomy of Military Power". (USA)
446 For a feature in the *Boston Globe Magazine* with light-hearted advice on how to cheat on dieting. Pigs' heads in red and pink on a green background. (USA)
447 Illustration for the *Boston Globe Magazine* accompanying an article about a novelist's experience in an attempt to become a film extra. (USA)

444 Für die Weihnachtsausgabe des *Boston Globe Magazine*. Rot mit Grün. (USA)
445 Ganzseitige Illustration für einen Beitrag im *Boston Globe Magazine* mit dem Titel «Imponierendes Gehabe – die Anatomie militärischer Macht». (USA)
446 Für einen Beitrag im *Boston Globe Magazine* mit Ratschlägen, wie man bei Diätkuren am besten mogelt. Schweinsköpfe in Rosa bzw. Rot vor grünem Hintergrund. (USA)
447 Illustration für den im *Boston Globe Magazine* erschienenen Erlebnisbericht eines Statisten beim Film. (USA)

444 Pour le numéro de Noël du *Boston Globe Magazine*. Rouge, avec du vert. (USA)
445 Illustration pleine page pour un article du *Boston Globe Magazine* intitulé «Affirmation de soi imposante – anatomie de la puissance militaire». (USA)
446 Pour un article du *Boston Globe Magazine* qui donne des tuyaux pour tricher quand on fait du régime. Têtes de porcs rose respectivement rouge sur fond vert. (USA)
447 Illustration pour le récit des expériences d'un figurant au cinéma, paru dans le *Boston Globe Magazine*. (USA)

448

449

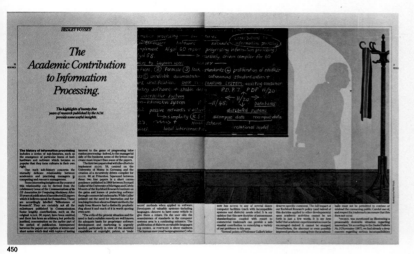

450

452

451

ARTIST / KÜNSTLER / ARTISTE:

448 Brad Holland
449 Donna Muir/Su Huntley
450 Peter Knock
451 Barbara Buchwald
452 Robert Hunt

DESIGNER / GESTALTER / MAQUETTISTE:

449, 450 David Hillman/Bruce Mau
451 Barbara Buchwald
452 David Broom

ART DIRECTOR / DIRECTEUR ARTISTIQUE:

448 Mick Wiggins
449, 450 David Hillman
451 Hans Kuh
452 David Broom

AGENCY / AGENTUR / AGENCE – STUDIO:

449, 450 Pentagram
452 Broom & Broom, Inc.

PUBLISHER / VERLEGER / EDITEUR:

448 PC World Magazine
449, 450 Ericsson Information Systems
451 Vogel Verlag
452 Miller Freeman Publications

448 Illustration accompanying the review of a book entitled *The Fifth Generation: Artificial Intelligence and Japan's Computer Challenge*. From *PC World*. (USA)
449, 450 Double spreads from the automated-communications journal *Information Resource Management*. Fig. 449: the user's behaviour in the new environment of the computer systems. Fig. 450 relates to the academic research papers published on the various aspects of information processing. Both illustrations in full-colour. (GBR)
451 Full-page illustration in blue and pink tones from the computer publication *Chip*. (GER)
452 For the introductory double spread accompanying an article in *Micro Communications*. (USA)

448 Illustration für die Besprechung eines Buches mit dem Titel «Die fünfte Generation». Das Thema ist künstliche Intelligenz und die japanische Herausforderung auf dem Gebiet der Computertechnik. Aus *PC World*. (USA)
449, 450 Doppelseiten aus der Computer-Fachzeitschrift *Information Resource Management* mit Artikeln über (Abb. 449) Verhalten der Computer-Benutzer und (Abb. 450) akademische Forschungsbeiträge auf dem Gebiet der Informatik. Beide Illustrationen mehrfarbig. (GBR)
451 Ganzseitige Illustration in Blau- und Rosatönen aus der Computer-Fachzeitschrift *Chip*. (GER)
452 Für die einleitende Doppelseite zu einem Artikel in *Micro Communications*. (USA)

448 Illustration pour le compte rendu d'un livre intitulé «La Cinquième Génération». Il s'agit de la 5ᵉ génération des ordinateurs et de l'effort japonais pour mettre au point une intelligence artificielle. Paru dans *PC World*. (USA)
449, 450 Doubles pages de la revue d'informatique *Information Resource Management*: les réactions des utilisateurs d'ordinateurs (fig. 449); communications scientifiques dans le domaine de l'informatique (fig. 450). Les deux illustrations en polychromie. (GBR)
451 Illustration pleine page, divers bleus et roses, pour la revue d'informatique *Chip*. (GER)
452 Pour la double page initiale d'un article publié dans *Micro Communications*. (USA)

ARTIST / KÜNSTLER / ARTISTE:

453, 454 Linda Gottfried
455 Sandra Filipucci
456 Dagmar Frinta
457–459 Donna Muir/Su Huntley
460 Chris Spollen

DESIGNER / GESTALTER / MAQUETTISTE:

457–459 David Hillman/Bruce Mau

ART DIRECTOR:

453–456 Tina Adamek
457–459 David Hillman
460 Jae Medila

AGENCY / AGENTUR / AGENCE – STUDIO:

457–459 Pentagram

PUBLISHER / VERLEGER / EDITEUR:

453–456 McGraw Hill Publishing Co.
457–459 Ericsson Information Systems
460 Ziff-Davis Publishing

453

454

Trade Magazines
Fachzeitschriften
Revues professionnelles

453, 454 Computer-generated illustration in original size and the cover of the medical journal *Postgraduate Medicine*. It concerns the application of computer technology in medicine. (USA)
455, 456 Illustrations from the medical journal *Postgraduate Medicine*. Fig. 455: for an article about the mechanisms and possible causes of Alzheimer's disease; in brown and pink shades. Fig. 456 illustrates an article on the Western view of acupuncture; brown tones with blue. (USA)
457–459 Illustrations and complete double spread from the automated-communications journal *Information Resource Management*. Figs. 457, 458 refer to farmland being put to other uses with the advancement of technology. Fig. 459 asks if computer professionals should have more responsibilities. (GBR)
460 For an article about "AIDS" in the magazine *Psychology Today*. Predominantly red. (USA)

457

455

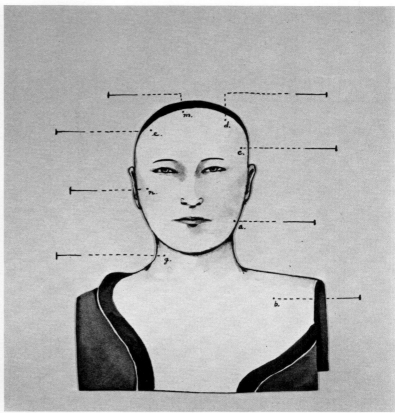

456

453, 454 Mit dem Computer hergestellte Illustration in Originalgrösse und Umschlag der medizinischen Fachzeitschrift *Postgraduate Medicine*. Thema ist der Computer-Einsatz in der Medizin. (USA)
455, 456 Illustrationen aus der medizinischen Fachzeitschrift *Postgraduate Medicine*. Abb. 455: für einen Artikel über Mechanismen und Ursachen der Alzheimer-Krankheit; in Brauntönen mit Rosa. Abb. 456: zum Thema Akupunktur; in Brauntönen mit Blau. (USA)
457–459 Illustration und vollständige Doppelseite aus der Computer-Fachzeitschrift *Information Resource Management*. Abb. 457, 458 beziehen sich auf die durch Computer ermöglichten Landeinsparungen, in Abb. 459 geht es um die soziale Verantwortung der Computer-Techniker. (GBR)
460 Für einen Beitrag über «AIDS» in der Fachzeitschrift *Psychology Today*. Vorwiegend rot. (USA)

453, 454 Illustration au format original réalisée avec l'assistance de l'ordinateur, et couverture de la revue médicale *Postgraduate Medicine*: l'informatique médicale. (USA)
455, 456 Illustrations tirées de la revue médicale *Postgraduate Medicine*. Fig. 455: pour un article sur les mécanismes et l'étiologie de la maladie d'Alzheimer, divers bruns, avec du rose; fig. 456: l'acupuncture, divers bruns, avec du bleu. (USA)
457–459 Illustration et double page complète de la revue d'informatique *Information Resource Management*. Les fig. 457, 458 concernent les économies de terrains réalisées grâce à l'ordinateur, la fig. 459 la responsabilité sociale de l'informaticien. (GBR)
460 Pour un article intitulé «SIDAS» de la revue *Psychology Today*. Rouge prédominant. (USA)

458

459

460

461

462

463

Trade Magazines
Fachzeitschriften
Revues professionnelles

ARTIST / KÜNSTLER / ARTISTE:

461 Earl Keleny
462 Jeffrey Schrier
463 Erich Maas
464, 465 Dagmar Frinta

DESIGNER / GESTALTER / MAQUETTISTE:

463 Karl W. Henschel
464 Wayne Fitzpatrick
465 Mary Challinor

ART DIRECTOR / DIRECTEUR ARTISTIQUE:

461, 462 Tina Adamek
463 Karl W. Henschel
464 Wayne Fitzpatrick
465 Joyce Black/Rodney Williams

AGENCY / AGENTUR / AGENCE – STUDIO:

463 Studio Sign

PUBLISHER / VERLEGER / EDITEUR:

461, 462 McGraw Hill Publishing Co.
463 Beltz Verlag
464, 465 American Association for the
Advancement of Science

464

461, 462 Illustrations in *The Physician and Sportsmedicine*.
Fig. 461: "Haematological Variations after Endurance Running with Hard and Soft-soled Running Shoes." Green, grey, blue-pink; Fig. 462: "How I Manage Infectious Mononucleosis." Green, violet and yellow. (USA)
463 "Less Work for Everyone"—from an article in *Psychologie heute*; Karl Marx is the leisure-time windsurfer. In full colour. (GER)
464, 465 Full-colour illustrations for an article in the *Science* magazine stating that a chemical found to be present in the spinal fluid may help to identify potential suicides. (USA)

461, 462 Illustrationen im Magazin *The Physician and Sportsmedicine*. Abb. 461: Für einen Test über Blutveränderungen bei Langstrecken-Läufern mit hart- und weichbesohlten Rennschuhen. Grün, grau, blau-rosa; Abb. 462: «Wie infektiöse Mononukleosis behandelt werden kann.» Grün, violett und dunkelgelb. (USA)
463 «Weniger Arbeit für alle.» Aus einem Artikel in der Zeitschrift *Psychologie heute*; Karl Marx als aktiver Freizeit-Surfer. In Farbe. (GER)
464, 465 Mehrfarbige Illustrationen für einen Artikel im *Science*-Magazin über im Gehirn feststellbare Selbstmordanzeichen. (USA)

461, 462 Illustrations du magazine *The Physician and Sportsmedicine*. Fig. 461: pour un test déterminant les variations de la composition du sang chez des coureurs de fond équipés de semelles rigides ou souples; vert, gris, bleu-rose; fig. 462: «Comment traiter la mononucléose infectieuse»; vert, violet, jaune. (USA)
463 «Moins de travail pour tous.» Article dans *Psychologie heute*. Karl Marx en tant que surfeur sur l'eau des loisirs. Couleur. (GER)
464, 465 Illustrations polychromes pour un article du magazine professionnel *Science* sur les signaux suicidaires au niveau cérébral. (USA)

465

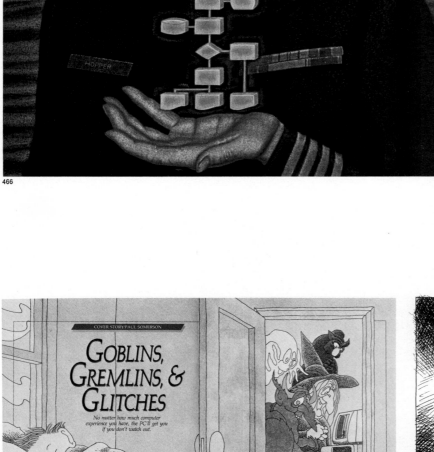

INTERVIEW/COREY SANDLER

Captain Grace Hopper is a co-author of COBOL and a foremother of the computer revolution. As the oldest officer on active duty in the United States Navy, she can still rock the boat.

Keeping Up With
GRACE

On the wall of her small corner of a small office in the Washington, D.C., Navy Yard hangs a framed antique copy of the Articles of the Government of the United States Navy. Navy personnel, from swabbies to admirals, refer to them as the "rocks and shoals." But for Captain Grace Murray Hopper, special adviser to the commander of the Naval Data Automation Command, and the oldest (and perhaps most famous) active-duty officer in the U.S. Navy, their framed presence points up a great irony lost on no one who meets her.

Captain Hopper loves to rock the boat.

"Somebody has to! There will always have to be a few people who will stick their necks out. Otherwise we'd never get anywhere," she said in a recent interview with PC.

PC MAGAZINE *199* DECEMBER 1983

466

467

468

466–468 Complete double spreads from the computer magazine *PC Magazine*. Fig. 466: Full-colour illustration for an interview with Grace Hopper, oldest active officer in the US navy and co-author of COBOL computer language; Fig. 467: A pastel-toned illustration for the cover story about "gremlins" causing havoc in personal computers; Fig. 468: A black-and-white illustration for a report on a TV series in which a group of boys' homemade computer is able to tap databases. (USA)
469–471 Covers of the monthly *Industrial Launderer* magazine, aimed at the industrial cleaning and laundering business. Fig. 469: Brown and blue floor tiles, white dust mop. (USA)

466–468 Vollständige Doppelseiten aus der Computer-Fachzeitschrift *PC Magazine*. Abb. 466: Mehrfarbige Illustration für ein Interview mit Grace Hopper, einem Pionier der Computerbranche und aktiven Marine-Kapitän; Abb. 467: Illustration in Pastelltönen zur Titelgeschichte über aufkommende Personal-Computer-«Kobolde»; Abb. 468: Schwarzweiss-Illustration für einen Bericht über eine TV-Reihe mit Computern: «Warum die ‹Guten› keine Personal-Computer verwenden.» (USA)
469–471 Umschläge der Monats-Fachzeitschrift *Industrial Launderer*, welche sich an Wäschereien und Reinigungsinstitute wendet. Abb. 469: Braun-blauer Bodenbelag, weisser Mop. (USA)

466–468 Doubles pages complètes de la revue d'informatique *PC Magazine*. Fig. 466: illustration polychrome pour une interview de Grace Hopper, pionnier de l'informatique et officier de marine actif; fig. 467: illustration en tons pastel pour le récit annoncé en couvertures des lutins qui envahissent les ordinateurs personnels; fig. 468: illustration noir et blanc pour un rapport sur une série TV où les ordinateurs jouent un rôle important. (USA)
469–471 Couvertures du mensuel *Industrial Launderer* lu par les employeurs de la branche nettoyage et blanchisserie industriels. Fig. 469: revêtement de sol bleu brun, balai de coton blanc. (USA)

ARTIST / KÜNSTLER / ARTISTE:

466 Ed Soyka
467 Gahan Wilson
468 Brad Holland
469 Jack Lefkowitz
470 Pam Lefkowitz
471 M. V. Strnad

DESIGNER / GESTALTER / MAQUETTISTE:

466–468 Mitch Shostak
469–471 Jack Lefkowitz

ART DIRECTOR / DIRECTEUR ARTISTIQUE:

466–468 Mitch Shostak
469–471 Jack Lefkowitz

AGENCY / AGENTUR / AGENCE – STUDIO:

469–471 Jack Lefkowitz Inc.

PUBLISHER / VERLEGER / EDITEUR:

466–468 Ziff-Davis Publishing
468–471 Institute of Industrial Launderers

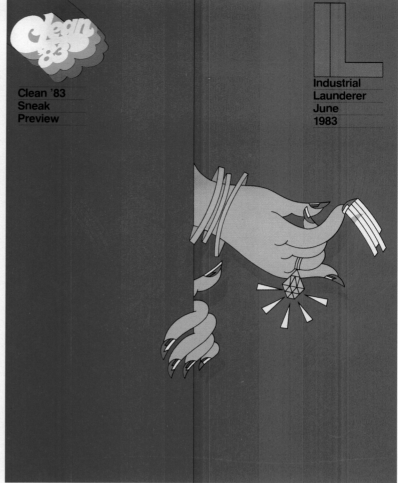

Clean '83
Sneak
Preview

Industrial
Launderer
June
1983

470

Industrial
Launderer
August
1983

Dust Mop
Flammability:
A Sweeping
Problem?

469

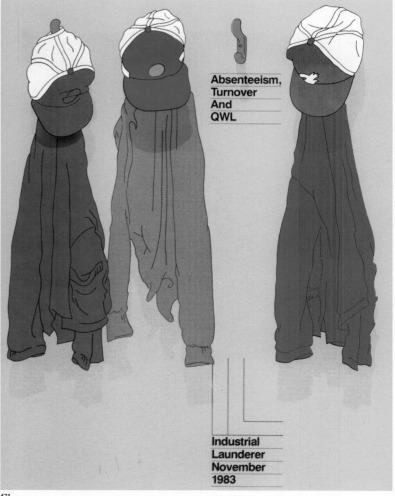

Absenteeism,
Turnover
And
QWL

Industrial
Launderer
November
1983

471

472

474

Trade Magazines

473

ARTIST / KÜNSTLER / ARTISTE:

472 Randall Enos
473 James Tughan
474, 475 Jerzy Kolacz

DESIGNER / GESTALTER / MAQUETTISTE:

473 James Tughan

ART DIRECTOR / DIRECTEUR ARTISTIQUE:

472 Bett McLean
473 Jackie Young
474, 475 Steve Manley

AGENCY / AGENTUR / AGENCE – STUDIO:

473 Ink
474, 475 Reactor Art & Design

PUBLISHER / VERLEGER / EDITEUR:

472 13–30 Corporation
473 Financial Post Magazine
474, 475 Canadian Business Magazine

472 Illustration in *Best of Business* for an article about free trade. (USA)
473 To illustrate a report entitled "Financial Planning Untangling the Maze" in the *Financial Post Magazine*. In green, blue and yellow. (CAN)
474 For a feature in *Canadian Business* on the talent waiting for top jobs in the big banks. (CAN)
475 Full-page illustration in *Information Technology* for an article entitled "The Problem with Backing Brains" relating to the taxman's attitude to investment in high technology. (CAN)

472 Illustration im *Best of Business* für einen Artikel über den freien Handel. (USA)
473 Finanzielle Labyrinthe sollen durch sorgfältige Planung entwirrt werden. Illustration für einen Bericht im *Financial Post Magazine*, in Grün, Blau und Gelb. (CAN)
474 Vorwiegend in Braun-Beige-Tönen gehaltene Illustration für einen Artikel im *Canadian Business Magazine* über Talente, die auf Top-Jobs in Grossbanken warten. (CAN)
475 Ganzseitige Illustration in der Fachzeitschrift *Information Technology* für einen Artikel über neue Wege und Möglichkeiten in der Unternehmensfinanzierung. (CAN)

472 Illustration pour *Best of Business*: article sur le libre échange. (USA)
473 Les labyrinthes financiers et leur antidote: une planification judicieuse. Illustration d'un rapport paru dans le *Financial Post Magazine*. Vert, bleu, jaune. (CAN)
474 Illustration aux tons brun et beige prédominants pour un article du *Canadian Business Magazine* consacré aux candidats de talent aux postes directeurs des grandes banques. (CAN)
475 Illustration pleine page pour la revue spécialisée *Information Technology*: article sur les voies nouvelles qui s'ouvrent au financement des entreprises. (CAN)

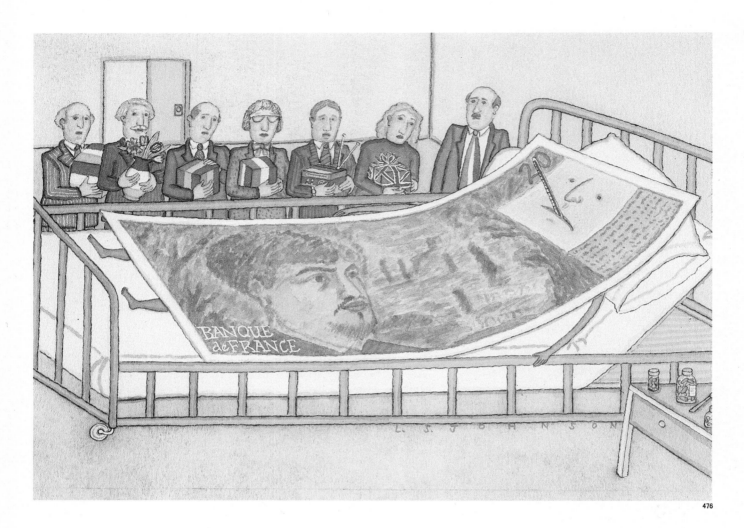

476

Winning The Thyroid Game

BY DAVID H. SOLOMON, M.D.

Common, insidious, and elusive in people over age 60, thyroid disease is both under- and overdiagnosed. Not only the clinical but also the laboratory findings of thyroid disease may be imitated by other conditions and the reverse is even commoner. In an elderly person with underlying cardiac disease, for example, increases in the level of thyroid hormone too slight to produce typical symptoms of hyperthyroidism may produce increased angina, /continued

TRANSITION
SEPTEMBER 1983

20

21

477

ARTIST / KÜNSTLER / ARTISTE:

476 Lonni Sue Johnson
477 E.T. Steadman
478 Shelley Browning
479, 480 Blair Drawson

DESIGNER / GESTALTER / MAQUETTISTE:

476 Judi Adel
477 Lisa Walfish
478–480 Shari Spier

ART DIRECTOR / DIRECTEUR ARTISTIQUE:

476 Judi Adel
477 James T. Walsh
478–480 Louis Fishauf

AGENCY / AGENTUR / AGENCE – STUDIO:

478–480 Reactor Art & Design

PUBLISHER / VERLEGER / EDITEUR:

476 Business Week
477 Fischer Medical Publications
478–480 Executive Magazine

476 The ailing French franc is the subject of this illustration in *Businessweek*. (USA)
477 Complete double spread from *Transition* magazine for an article about thyroid disease. (USA)
478–480 Illustrations in full colour from the magazine *Executive*. Fig. 478: "Turn Problems into Profits by Selling the Solutions." Fig. 479 relates to the relationship between unions and management, "Learning to Deal with an Arranged Marriage". Fig. 480 illustrates an article entitled "Ruling the Home Roost: Some Globetrotting Presidents Prefer it". The story refers to the choice some executives have to make between working for a national or multi-national company. (CAN)

476 Der kränkliche französische Franc ist Gegenstand dieser Illustration in *Businessweek*. (USA)
477 Vollständige Doppelseite aus der Fachzeitschrift *Transition* zu einem Artikel über Schilddrüsenfunktionen. «Das Schilddrüsenspiel gewinnen.» (USA)
478–480 Mehrfarbige Illustrationen aus dem Magazin *Executive*. Abb. 478: Problemlösungen können für den Finder zu einer Quelle des Profits werden. Abb. 479: Die Gewerkschaft als Partner in einer «Vernunftsehe». Abb. 480: Illustration zur Titelgeschichte über Vor- und Nachteile multinationaler und nationaler Arbeitgeber für Manager. (CAN)

476 Le franc français alité constitue le sujet de cette illustration de *Businessweek*. (USA)
477 Double page complète de la revue professionnelle *Transition*, pour un article sur la thyroïde et ses fonctions. «Gagner le jeu de la thyroïde.» (USA)
478–480 Illustrations polychromes pour le magazine *Executive*. Fig. 478: La solution de problèmes peut valoir des profits à son découvreur. Fig. 479: Les syndicats partenaires d'un mariage de raison. Fig. 480: Illustration du rapport annoncé en couverture sur les avantages et les inconvénients d'un job de dirigeant de société multinationale ou nationale. (CAN)

478

479

480

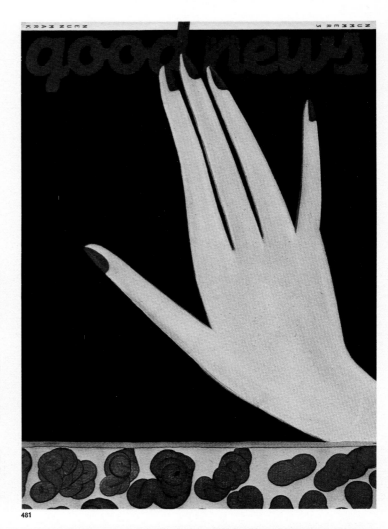

481

481–485 *Good News*, a newspaper in large format is aimed at readers with a special feeling for illustration, text and photos which stimulate interchange of thought. Issued once yearly, each number is devoted to a particular topic. Fig. 481: Cover for No. 3 on "Love". Fig. 482: Complete double spread to a text by W. B. Yeats; bottle-green clothes and instruments. Fig. 483: Full-page black-and-white illustration for "Intown manœuvres with robot invaders". Fig. 484: Cover for No. 2 on the topic "Man and Machine", in full colour. Fig. 485: Illustration for No. 3 on "Love"; predominately in shades of blue. (GER)

481–485 *Good News*, eine grossformatige Zeitschrift für Illustration, Text und Photo, erscheint einmal jährlich und will zum Gedankenaustausch anregen. Jede Nummer ist einem bestimmten Thema gewidmet. Abb. 481: Umschlag für Nr. 3, zum Thema «Liebe». Abb. 482: Vollständige Doppelseite zu einem Text von W. B. Yeats; flaschengrüne Kleidung und Geräte. Abb. 483: Ganzseitige Schwarzweiss-Illustration zu «innerstädtischen Manöverübungen mit Roboterinvasoren». Abb. 484: Umschlagillustration von Ausgabe Nr. 2, zum Thema «Mensch und Maschine». Abb. 485: Vorwiegend in Blautönen gehaltene Illustration. (GER)

481–485 *Good News*, un magazine annuel au grand format traitant de l'illustration, du texte et de la photo, entend favoriser l'échange des idées. Chaque numéro est consacré à un sujet déterminé. Fig. 481: couverture du n° 3 («L'Amour»). Fig. 482: double page complète accompagnant un texte de W. B. Yeats; vêtements et appareils vert bouteille. Fig. 483: illustration noir et blanc, «manœuvres urbaines avec des robots envahisseurs». Fig. 484: illustration de couverture du n° 2 («L'Homme et la Machine»). Fig. 485: illustration aux tons bleus prédominants. (GER)

482

483

484

485

ARTIST / KÜNSTLER / ARTISTE:
481–485 Hartwig Jung

ART DIRECTOR / DIRECTEUR ARTISTIQUE:
481–485 Hartwig Jung

PUBLISHER / VERLEGER / EDITEUR:
481–485 Good News

197

486

ARTIST / KÜNSTLER / ARTISTE:

486 Milton Glaser
487, 488 Dagmar Frinta
489 Lonni Sue Johnson

DESIGNER / GESTALTER / MAQUETTISTE:

486 Don Nelson
487, 488 Marcia Wright

ART DIRECTOR / DIRECTEUR ARTISTIQUE:

486 Don Nelson
487, 488 Marcia Wright
489 Bob Eichinger

AGENCY / AGENTUR / AGENCE – STUDIO:

486 Milton Glaser, Inc.
487, 488 Ambassador Magazine
489 Eichinger Inc.

PUBLISHER / VERLEGER / EDITEUR:

486 Notre Dame Magazine
487, 488 TWA
489 AT&T

486 Martin Luther on the cover of the *Notre Dame Magazine*. Robe and hat in dark green with blue, pale yellow ray of light with coloured particles. (USA)
487, 488 Illustrations in mainly blue and green from the *Ambassador Magazine*, the house organ of the American airline TWA. (USA)
489 "Some Unfinished Business." Illustration for a feature about changes in the telecommunications market in *Quest*, the house organ of AT&T. (USA)

486 Martin Luther auf dem Umschlag des *Notre Dame Magazine*. Kleidung und Hut in Dunkelgrün mit Blau, heller Lichtstrahl mit Farbpartikeln. (USA)
487, 488 Vorwiegend in Blau und Grün gehaltene Illustrationen aus der Hauszeitschrift *Ambassador* der amerikanischen Fluggesellschaft TWA. (USA)
489 «Einige unerledigte Geschäfte.» Illustration für einen Artikel über Änderungen auf dem Telekommunikationsmarkt in *Quest*, der Hauszeitschrift von AT&T. (USA)

486 «Ce que Martin Luther signifie pour nous»: couverture du *Notre Dame Magazine*. Vêtements et couvre-chef vert foncé, avec du bleu, rayon lumineux coloré. (USA)
487, 488 Illustrations (où dominent le bleu et le vert) pour la revue d'entreprise *Ambassador* de la compagnie aérienne américaine TWA. (USA)
489 «Quelques affaires pas encore terminées.» Illustration pour un article concernant les transformations intervenant sur le marché des télécommunications, dans *Quest* de AT&T. (USA)

487

488

490

ARTIST / KÜNSTLER / ARTISTE:

490 Diane Teske Harris
491 Scott Reynolds
492, 493 Geoffrey Moss

ART DIRECTOR:

490–492 Tina Adamek
493 Jim Walsh

PUBLISHER / VERLEGER / EDITEUR:

490–492 McGraw Hill Publications Co.
493 Fischer Medical Publications

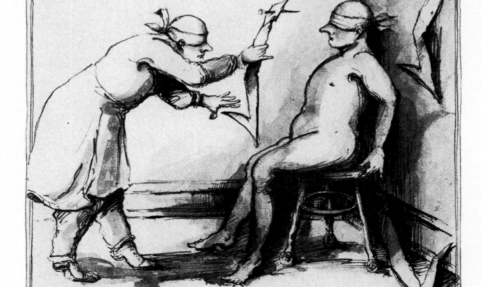

492

491

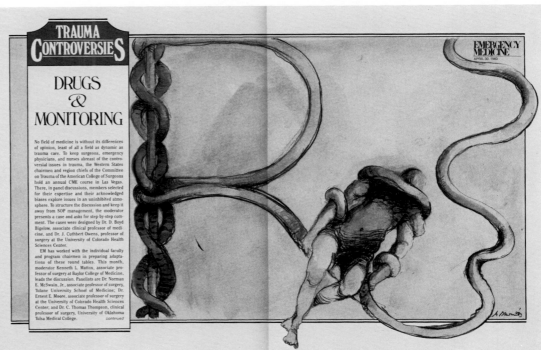

493

490, 491 Illustrations from the magazine *Postgraduate Medicine*. Fig. 490 on the physical, psychological and sociological problems for patients suffering from vulvar disease; Fig. 491 for a feature on AIDS. (USA)
492 Black-and-white illustration for a feature on the changing attitudes towards the annual medical checkup. Taken from *Postgraduate Medicine*. (USA)
493 Soft watercolours to illustrate an article on the controversial issues facing medical experts on the treatment of trauma. In *Emergency Medicine* magazine. (USA)

490, 491 Aus der Fachzeitschrift *Postgraduate Medicine*. Abb. 490 für einen Artikel über Erkrankungen der Vulva; Abb. 491 für einen Artikel über die «AIDS-Epidemie». (USA)
492 Schwarzweiss-Illustration für einen Artikel mit neuen Ansichten über die jährliche, gründliche Untersuchung beim Arzt. Aus *Postgraduate Medicine*. (USA)
493 Illustration in der Fachzeitschrift *Emergency Medicine* für einen Artikel über eine Fachdiskussion zum Thema «Trauma-Behandlung». In Pastelltönen. (USA)

490, 491 Pour la revue spécialisée *Postgraduate Medicine*. Fig. 490: pour un article sur les maladies de la vulve; fig. 491: pour un article sur l'épidémie du SIDAS. (USA)
492 Illustration noir et blanc pour un article de *Postgraduate Medicine* qui présente des vues nouvelles sur le check-up médical annuel. (USA)
493 Illustration pour la revue spécialisée *Emergency Medicine*: discussion des méthodes de traitement de traumatismes, pour spécialistes. Tons pastel. (USA)

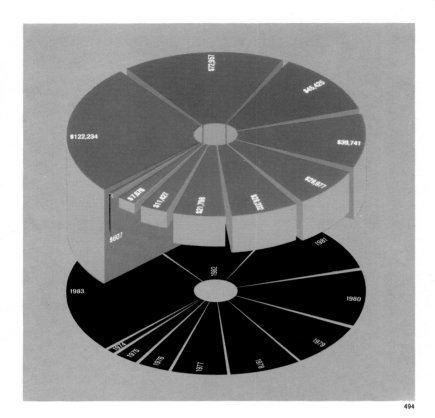

494

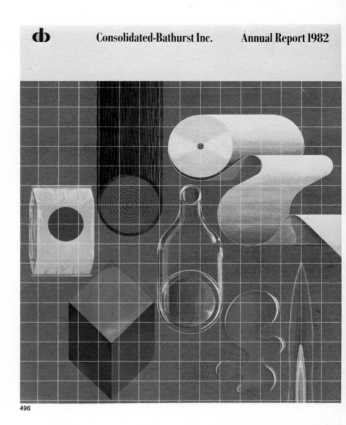

496

497

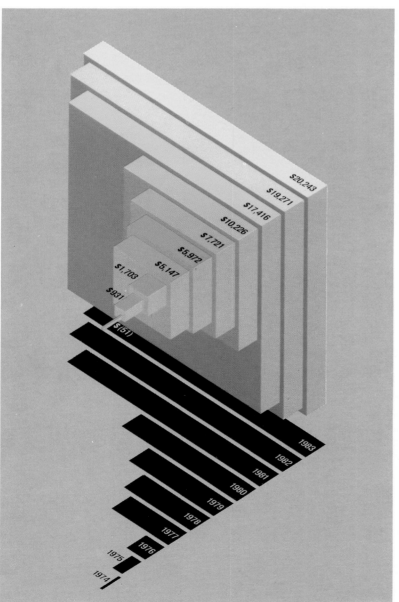

495

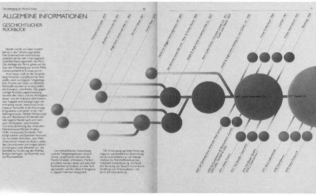

494, 495 Pages presenting total assets and stockholders' equity in three-dimensional form, from the 1983 annual report of the Clabir Corporation. (USA)
496 Cover of an annual report from Consolidated-Bathurst Inc. (CAN)
497 Graph from an annual report; historical review of the *Nestlé* group. (SWI)
498–500 Full-page illustrations and front cover (with flap) from the annual report of the advertising agency Geers Gross with domicile in London and New York. Figs. 498 and 499 relate to the chapters "Advertising" and "Finance". (GBR)

494, 495 Seiten aus einem Jahresbericht der Clabir Corporation mit dreidimensionaler Darstellung des Vermögensstandes und des Aktienkapitals. (USA)
496 Umschlag eines Jahresberichtes der Consolidated-Bathurst Inc. (CAN)
497 Darstellung aus einem Jahresbericht: Geschichte der *Nestlé*-Gruppe. (SWI)
498–500 Ganzseitige Illustrationen und Vorderseite (mit Klappe) des Umschlags eines Jahresberichtes der Werbeagentur Geers Gross mit Sitz in London und New York. Abb. 498 und 499 betreffen die Kapitel «Werbung» und «Finanzen». (GBR)

494, 495 Pages tirées d'un rapport annuel de la Clabir Corporation: représentation tridimensionnelle des actifs et du capital social. (USA)
496 Couverture d'un rapport annuel de Consolidated-Bathurst Inc. (CAN)
497 Graphique d'un rapport annuel: historique de *Nestlé*. Polychromie. (SWI)
498–500 Illustrations pleine page et première page et rabat de couverture pour un rapport annuel de l'agence de publicité Geers Gross (Londres et New York). Fig. 498 et 499 concernent les chapitres «publicité» et «finances». (GBR)

Advertising Portfolio

498

Accounts & Finance

499

Annual Reports
Jahresberichte
Rapports annuels

ARTIST / KÜNSTLER / ARTISTE:

494, 495 Tom Morin/Henry Georgke/
          Jerry Hablitzel
496 Rolf Harder
497 Freddy Huguenin
498–500 Seymour Chwast

DESIGNER / GESTALTER / MAQUETTISTE:

494, 495 Tom Morin
496 Rolf Harder
497 Otto Allgöwer
498–500 Alan Fletcher/Lisa de Francis

ART DIRECTOR:

494, 495 Jack Hough/Tom Morin
496 Rolf Harder
497 Otto Allgöwer
498–500 Alain Fletcher

AGENCY / AGENTUR:

494, 495 Jack Hough Associates
496 Rolf Harder & Associates
497 Nestec, Abt. Grafik und Druck
498–500 Pentagram

Annual Report & Accounts 1982   Geers Gross

500

ARTIST / KÜNSTLER / ARTISTE:

501, 502 Alan E. Cober
503, 504 Geoffrey Moss
505, 506 Tadashi Ohashi
507 David Montiel

DESIGNER / GESTALTER / MAQUETTISTE:

501, 502 Linda Grimm
503, 504 Bennett Robinson/Paula Zographos
505, 506 Tadashi Ohashi
507 Linda Hinrichs/Sandra McHenry

ART DIRECTOR / DIRECTEUR ARTISTIQUE:

501, 502 John Waters
503, 504 Bennett Robinson
505, 506 Tadashi Ohashi
507 Linda Hinrichs

501

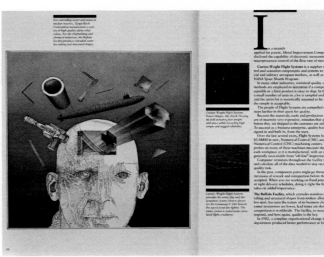

502

501, 502 Cover and double spread from an annual report of the Curtiss-Wright Corporation; here relating to the manufacture of nuclear reactor safety-relief valves and seamless tubing for ship-building and chemical industries. Both illustrations with white head, coloured elements on blue. (USA)
503, 504 "New Opportunities in a Changing World." Cover and full-page illustration from an annual report of the American Can Company. Fig. 503 globe in greenish-yellow, orange clouds on pale yellow background; Fig. 504 in dark brown on cream-tinted stock. (USA)
505, 506 Complete covers from a house organ issued by the seasoning and sauce manufacturers *Kikkoman*. Fig. 505 in modest colours, Fig. 506 in bright green with red and yellow. (JPN)
507 Double spread with full-colour illustrations from the chapter "New Therapeutic and Diagnostic Areas" taken from the annual report 1983 of the Syntex Corporation. (USA)

501, 502 Umschlag und Doppelseite aus einem Jahresbericht der Curtiss-Wright Corporation, hier mit Bezug auf die Röhren- und Ventilherstellung für Kraftwerke, Raketen, Schiffe und Flugzeuge. Beide Illustrationen mit hellem Kopf und verschiedenfarbigen Elementen auf grünblauem Grund. (USA)
503, 504 Umschlag und ganzseitige Illustration aus einem Jahresbericht der American Can Company unter dem Titel «Neue Möglichkeiten in einer sich verändernden Welt». Abb. 503 mehrfarbig, Abb. 504 braun, beide auf hellgelbem Papier. (USA)
505, 506 Vollständige Umschläge einer Hauszeitschrift des Gewürz- und Saucenherstellers *Kikkoman*. Abb. 505 in zurückhaltenden Farben, Abb. 506 in Grüntönen mit Rot und Gelb. (JPN)
507 Doppelseite mit mehrfarbigen Illustrationen aus dem Kapitel «neue therapeutische und diagnostische Gebiete» des Jahresberichtes 1983 für die Syntex Corporation. (USA)

American Can
Company
Annual Report
1982

New
Opportunities
in a
Changing
World

503

504

●特集・コールド クッキング
505

●特集
ニューサラダ
クッキング
506

501, 502 Couverture et double page d'un rapport annuel de la Curtiss-Wright Corporation: gamme de tuyaux et soupapes pour centrales, fusées, navires et avions. Dans les deux illustrations, la tête est claire, les éléments de diverses couleurs se profilent sur fond bleu vert. (USA)
503, 504 Couverture et illustration pleine page d'un rapport annuel de l'American Can Company intitulé «De nouvelles opportunités dans un monde en transformation constante». La fig. 503 est en polychromie, la fig. 504 en brun, les deux sur papier jaune clair. (USA)
505, 506 Couvertures complètes d'une revue d'entreprise du fabricant de sauces et condiments *Kikkoman*. Fig. 505: tons discrets; fig. 506: divers verts, avec du rouge et du jaune. (JPN)
507 Double page illustrée en polychromie, dans le rapport annuel pour 1983 de la Syntex Corporation, intitulée «Nouveaux domaines ouverts à la thérapeutique et au diagnostic». (USA)

AGENCY / AGENTUR / AGENCE – STUDIO:

501, 502　John Waters Associates
503, 504　Corporate Graphics Inc.
507　Jonson Pedersen Hinrichs & Shakery

in the treatment of patients who are at high risk of having a severe stroke or heart attack. Other important indications may include the treatment of coronary artery disease, peripheral arterial disease, and sickle cell disease. A study of ticlopidine for the prevention of diabetic retinopathy is being conducted in France and Belgium by Sanofi.

Since large numbers of patients must be studied for a number of years before Syntex and regulatory agencies are able to evaluate the safety and efficacy of such a potent compound for very serious cardiovascular and other circulatory diseases, the development of ticlopidine for therapeutic indications will be a long-term project. More than 3,500 patients in the United States and Canada are expected to be enrolled in just the two major stroke studies during the next three to four

Circulating platelets in blood play a role in a number of disease processes. Ticlopidine, a potent platelet aggregation inhibitor, is being studied for a number of indications including the treatment of stroke, high risk coronary disease, peripheral arterial disease, sickle cell disease, and diabetic retinopathy.

The discovery and development of important compounds to treat serious cardiovascular diseases represent the largest research effort ever undertaken at Syntex in a single therapeutic area.

years. Results of the trials in stroke are expected to be available in 1987–1988. Syntex has rights to market ticlopidine in the United States, Canada and Mexico.

In addition to its major product development programs, Syntex is pursuing a significant basic research program aimed at finding important new cardiovascular medicines. Of particular interest are research programs directed at the discovery and development of agents which reduce damage following myocardial infarction or stroke, and new therapeutic agents for the treatment of heart failure.

Syntex will increase its contacts with scientists in the academic community through the recently established Syntex Scholars Program. This program is designed to provide financial support to cardiovascular investigators in the formative stages of their careers. Key academic institutions are invited to nominate candidates for the award. Each year, a non-Syntex scientific advisory committee will recommend an individual to be named a Syntex Scholar. The selected scientist will receive a grant of up to $50,000 a year for three years to conduct research in the cardiovascular field at the college or university where the Scholar holds a faculty appointment.

ANTI-ULCER

An extensive research effort at Syntex to find more effective ways to treat patients suffering from gastrointestinal disease has resulted in the discovery of a new compound which is effective in treating ulcer disease.

Clinical studies with the highly potent compound, called enprostil, have demonstrated a three-fold mechanism of action: it reduces stomach acid levels, increases the resistance of stomach tissue to damage, and reduces serum gastrin. It is a prostaglandin analog, and as such, differs from histamine receptor antagonists, which are

the major prescription drugs widely used to treat ulcer disease.

These provide relief by a single mechanism of action: reduced acid secretion. Enprostil has proven to be long-acting and highly effective in patients, suggesting that it may represent an important therapeutic advance over existing products which are not effective in all patients, which allow a relatively high rate of recurrence, and which may produce undesirable side effects.

Assuming that additional clinical studies with patients confirm the safety and efficacy of enprostil for the

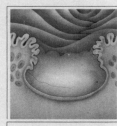

Syntex Research's enprostil, a prostaglandin analog, is being studied for use in treating ulcer disease (such as the disease represented above).

20　　　21

507

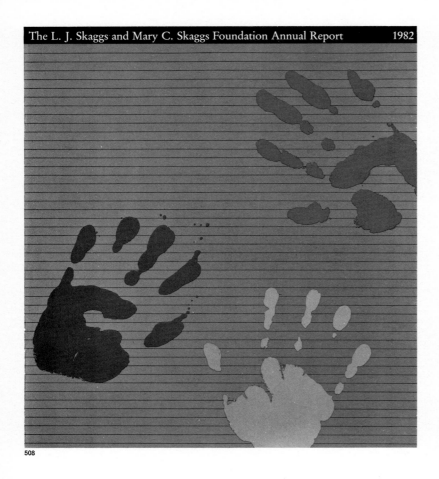

508

Annual Reports
Jahresberichte
Rapports annuels

ARTIST / KÜNSTLER / ARTISTE:

509 Rik Besser/Paul Bice
510 Tadanori Yokoo
511 Eugene Mihaesco

DESIGNER / GESTALTER / MAQUETTISTE:

508 Michael Vanderbyl
509 Rik Besser
510 Tadanori Yokoo
511 Colin Forbes/Kasper Schmid

ART DIRECTOR / DIRECTEUR ARTISTIQUE:

508 Michael Vanderbyl
509 Robert Miles Runyan
510 Tadanori Yokoo
511 Colin Forbes

AGENCY / AGENTUR / AGENCE – STUDIO:

508 Vanderbyl Design
509 Robert Miles Runyan & Associates
511 Pentagram USA

508 Cover of an annual report of Skaggs Foundation. Red, blue, yellow on beige. (USA)
509 The Electro Rent Corporation specializes in leasing electronic equipment. Shown on the cover of their annual report 1983 is the universal "keypad". (USA)
510 Cover of an annual report for Amnesty International Japan. (JPN)
511 Illustration from an annual report of the finance company Drexel Burnham Lambert, concerning a report on curbing inflation in America by the Federal Reserve. (USA)

508 Für den Jahresbericht der Skaggs-Stiftung. Rot, Blau und Gelb auf Beige. (USA)
509 Mehrfarbiger Umschlag für den Jahresbericht 1983 der Electro Rent Corporation, die elektrische und elektronische Geräte vermietet. (USA)
510 Vorderseite des Jahresberichtes von Amnesty International Japan. (JPN)
511 Illustration aus dem Jahresbericht eines Finanzierungsunternehmens, hier für einen Beitrag über Kontrolle der Inflation durch die US Nationalbank. (USA)

508 Pour un rapport annuel de la Fondation Skaggs. Rouge, bleu, jaune sur beige. (USA)
509 Couverture polychrome du rapport annuel pour 1983 de l'Electro Rent Corporation, spécialisée dans la location d'appareils électriques et électroniques. (USA)
510 Première page de couverture d'un rapport annuel d'Amnesty International. (JPN)
511 Illustration pour un rapport annuel de la société financière Drexel Burnham Lambert. Elle a trait à un article sur le contrôle de l'inflation par la Banque nationale. (USA)

509

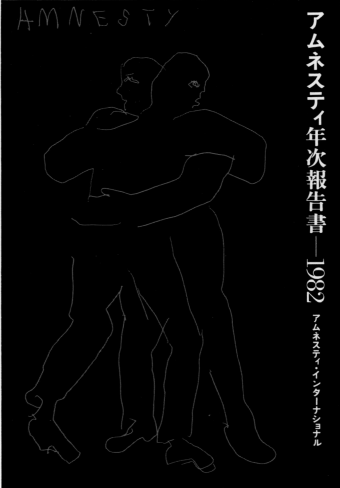

510

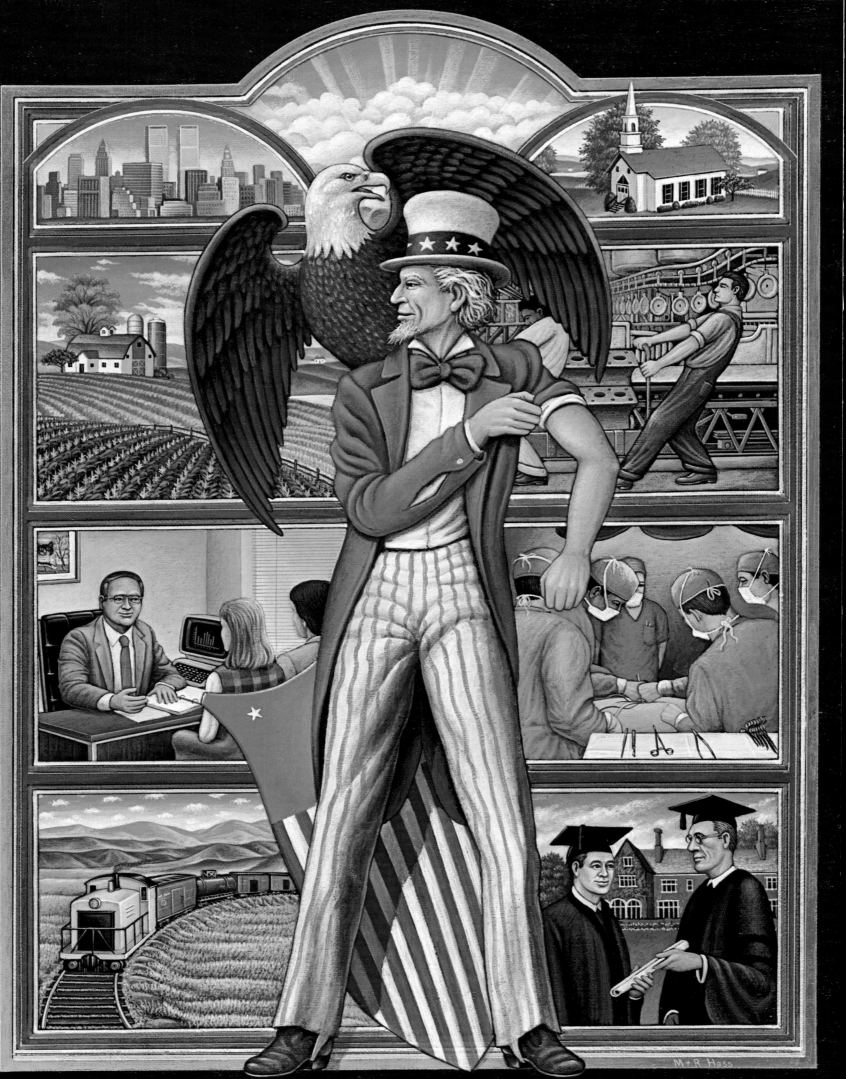

513

514

ARTIST / KÜNSTLER / ARTISTE:

512, 513 Mark & Richard Hess
514 Pierre Praquin
515 A. Nguyen / D. Botti (Photo)

DESIGNER / GESTALTER / MAQUETTISTE:

512, 513 Colin Forbes
514, 515 Any Dubois

ART DIRECTOR / DIRECTEUR ARTISTIQUE:

512, 513 Colin Forbes
514, 515 Jacques Tribondeau

AGENCY / AGENTUR / AGENCE – STUDIO:

512, 513 Pentagram USA

512, 513 Illustration and complete double spread from an annual report of the finance company Drexel Burnham Lambert. The article concerns the social, political and ethical factors forming the American economy. (USA)
514 Cover of *Pétrole Progrès*, house organ of *Esso*, France. Topic is the one hundred years of scientific and technological development. (FRA)
515 Double spread from an issue of *Pétrole Progrès*, the house organ of *Esso*, France (see Fig.514). The accompanying article is about solvents and their application in the manufacture of various products. In full colour. (FRA)

512, 513 Illustration und vollständige Doppelseite aus einem Jahresbericht des Finanzierungsunternehmens Drexel Burnham Lambert. Der dazugehörige Artikel befasst sich mit dem Staatshaushalt und den Sozialprogrammen. (USA)
514 Umschlag von *Pétrole Progrès*, Hauszeitschrift von *Esso*, Frankreich. Thema ist die 100jährige wissenschaftliche und technische Erfahrung. (FRA)
515 Doppelseite einer Ausgabe von *Pétrole Progrès*, Hauszeitschrift von *Esso*, Frankreich (s. Abb.514). Hier geht es um die Verwendung von Lösungsstoffen in der Herstellung verschiedener Produkte. In Farbe. (FRA)

512, 513 Illustration et double page complète d'un rapport annuel de la société financière Drexel Burnham Lambert. L'article correspondant a trait au budget de l'Etat et aux programmes de solidarité sociale. (USA)
514 Couverture de *Pétrole Progrès*, la revue d'entreprise d'*Esso* France: l'expérience centenaire acquise aux plans scientifique et technologique. (FRA)
515 Double page d'un numéro de *Pétrole Progrès*, revue d'entreprise d'*Esso* France (cf. la fig.514). On y discute l'application de divers solvants au processus de fabrication de toute une série de produits. En couleur. (FRA)

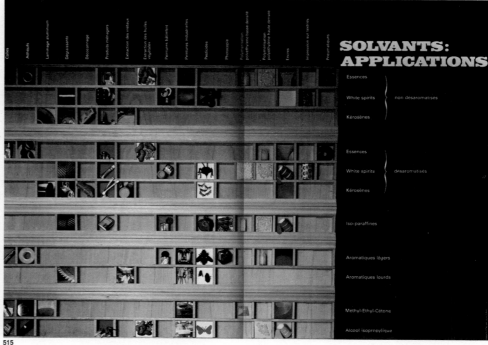
515

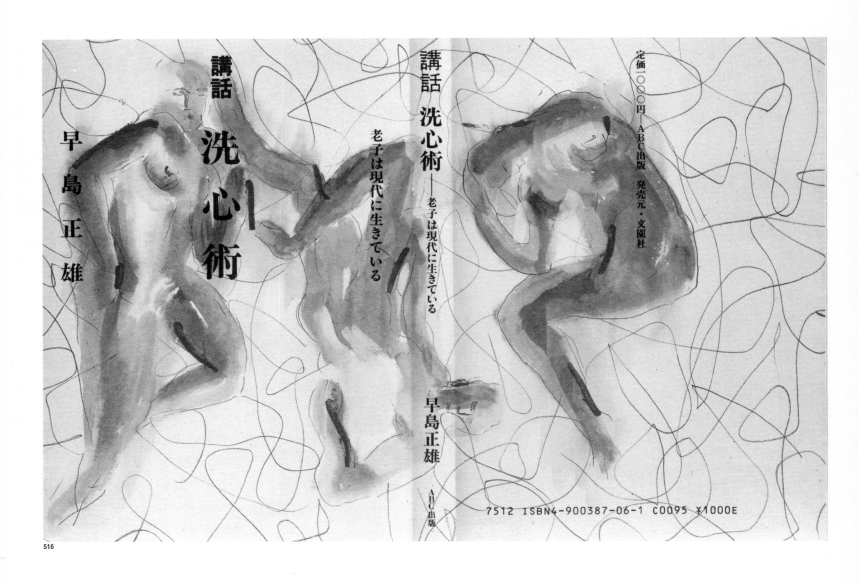

講話 洗心術

早島正雄

講話 洗心術 ——老子は現代に生きている

老子は現代に生きている

早島正雄

ABC出版

定価一〇〇〇円 ——ABC出版 発売元・文園社

7512 ISBN4-900387-06-1 C0095 ¥1000E

Book Covers
Buchumschläge
Couvertures de livres

516 Complete cover for a Japanese book. Human figures in a red wash, black writing on beige stock. (JPN)
517, 518 Illustrations in original size for book covers from a series of contemporary world literature issued by *Aventura* Press. Fig. 517: for a novel by the Czech author Jiří Gruša; fig. 518: for a book by the Brazilian anthropologist Darcy Ribeiro on the conflict between the Amazon Indians and Western modes of living. (USA)
519 Front and spine of the dust jacket for an Iranian book. The story is set in the 19th century. Blue, brown and yellow. (IRA)
520 Complete cover for the Iranian version of Orwell's *1984.* (IRA)

516 Vollständiger Umschlag für ein japanisches Buch. Gestalten in warmem Rot, Schrift schwarz auf beigefarbenem Papier. (JPN)
517, 518 Illustrationen in Originalgrösse für Buchumschläge aus einer Reihe zeitgenössischer Weltliteratur, die vom *Aventura*-Verlag herausgegeben wird. Abb. 517: für eine Erzählung des tschechischen Autors Jiří Gruša, Abb. 518: für ein Buch des brasilianischen Anthropologen Darcy Ribeiro. (USA)
519 Vorderseite und Rücken eines Buchumschlags für eine iranische Erzählung, die im 19. Jh. spielt. Blau, braun, gelb. (IRA)
520 Vollständiger Umschlag für die iranische Ausgabe von George Orwells *1984.* Mehrfarbig auf schwarzem Grund. (IRA)

516 Couverture complète pour un livre japonais. Personnages rouge chaud, texte noir sur papier beige. (JPN)
517, 518 Illustrations au format original pour des couvertures d'ouvrages de la littérature mondiale contemporaine réunis en collection par les Editions *Aventura.* Fig. 517: pour une nouvelle du Tchèque Jiří Gruša; fig. 518: pour un livre de l'anthropologue brésilien Darcy Ribeiro. (USA)
519 Recto et dos de la jaquette d'un livre iranien dont l'action se situe au XIXe siècle. Bleu, brun, jaune. (IRA)
520 Couverture complète de l'édition iranienne de *1984,* par George Orwell. Polychromie sur fond noir. (IRA)

519

520

ARTIST / KÜNSTLER / ARTISTE:

516 Tadanori Yokoo
517 Dagmar Frinta
518 Melanie Marder Parks
519, 520 Ebrahim Haghighi

DESIGNER / GESTALTER / MAQUETTISTE:

516 Tadanori Yokoo
517, 518 Keith Sheridan
519, 520 Ebrahim Haghighi

ART DIRECTOR / DIRECTEUR ARTISTIQUE:

516 Tadanori Yokoo
517, 518 Judy Loeser
519, 520 Ebrahim Haghighi

AGENCY / AGENTUR / AGENCE – STUDIO:

517, 518 Keith Sheridan Associates Inc.

PUBLISHER / VERLEGER / EDITEUR:

516 ABC Shuppan Publishing Co.
517, 518 Random House, Inc.
519 Nashr Now Publishing Co.
520 Morvarid Publishing Co.

ARTIST / KÜNSTLER / ARTISTE:

521 Bascove
522 Martha Sedgwick
523 Jan Buchholz / Reni Hinsch
524 Adam Korpak
525, 526 Ralph Steadman

DESIGNER / GESTALTER:

521 Neil Stuart
522 Martha Sedgwick
523 Jan Buchholz / Reni Hinsch
524 Adam Korpak
525, 526 Ian Craig

ART DIRECTOR:

521 Neil Stuart
522 Matt Tepper
524 Adam Korpak

PUBLISHER / VERLEGER / EDITEUR:

521 Viking / Penguin
522 Avon Books
523 Fischer Taschenbuch Verlag
524 Söderströms & Co.
525, 526 Jonathan Cape

521

522

523

524

Book Covers
Buchumschläge
Couvertures de livres

521 Cover of a paperback issued by *Viking/Penguin*. In bright colours. (USA)
522 For an *Avon* paperback; the eternal triangle theme. White cycles on soft green ground. (USA)
523 Cover of a *Fischer* paperback, "The Wittiest Medical Jokes". Skin tones, blue, violet, on white. (GER)
524 Book cover for a story of a man abandoned by his family and living alone. (FIN)
525, 526 Illustrative detail and complete cover of a book by English cartoonist Ralph Steadman. Leonardo is pictured here as Christ in the artist's own rendering of "The Last Supper". (GBR)

521 Umschlag für ein Taschenbuch mit dem Titel «Die rebellierenden Engel». In Farbe. (USA)
522 Für ein *Avon*-Taschenbuch mit einer Dreiecksgeschichte. Weiss auf sanftem Grün. (USA)
523 Umschlag für ein *Fischer*-Taschenbuch. Hautton, Blautöne und Violett auf weissem Grund. (GER)
524 Für ein Buch über einen Mann, der, von seiner Familie verlassen, allein leben muss. (FIN)
525, 526 Leonardo als Christusfigur im «Abendmahl». Detail der Illustration und vollständiger Umschlag eines Buches des englischen Karikaturisten und Illustrators Ralph Steadman, der auf Leonardos Spuren wandelte. Erschienen bei *Jonathan Cape*, London. (GBR)

521 Couverture d'un livre de poche intitulé «Les Anges rebelles». En couleur. (USA)
522 Couverture pour un livre de poche *Avon* (une histoire triangulaire). Blanc sur vert tendre. (USA)
523 Couverture d'un livre de poche *Fischer*. Chair, divers bleus, violet sur blanc. (GER)
524 Pour un livre dont le héros, abandonné par sa famille, vit en solitaire. (FIN)
525, 526 Léonard en Christ de la «Cène». Détail de l'illustration et couverture complète d'un livre du caricaturiste et illustrateur anglais Ralph Steadman en pèlerinage chez Léonard. L'ouvrage a été publié aux Editions *Jonathan Cape* de Londres. (GBR)

526

525

527

ARTIST / KÜNSTLER / ARTISTE:

527–529 Friso Henstra
531 Wendell Minor

DESIGNER / GESTALTER / MAQUETTISTE:

527–529 Friso Henstra
530 Gilbert Lesser
531 Wendell Minor

ART DIRECTOR / DIRECTEUR ARTISTIQUE:

530 Gilbert Lesser
531 Lidia Ferrara / Sara Eisenman

AGENCY / AGENTUR / AGENCE – STUDIO:

531 W. Minor Design

PUBLISHER / VERLEGER / EDITEUR:

527–529 J. B. Lippincott
530 Theatre Communications Group, Inc.
531 Alfred A. Knopf, Inc.

529

530

527–529 Illustrations from the back and front of the dust jacket, as well as the complete dust jacket of a children's picture-story book of a cat and mouse chase in which the mouse, wearing sneakers, outwits the cat. (USA)
530 Complete cover in red, white and black for a guide to the nonprofit professional theatres in America, offering photographs of their productions and playtitles index. (USA)
531 Complete cover of a book entitled A Gathering of Old Men, issued by Knopf. Black lettering for the book title on yellow and orange. Figures in muted colours. (USA)

527–529 Illustrationen für die Rück- und Vorderseite sowie der vollständige Schutzumschlag für ein Bilderbuch, dessen Held eine Maus in Turnschuhen ist. (USA)
530 Vollständiger Umschlag in Rot, Weiss und Schwarz für einen Führer, der über die nicht-kommerziellen, professionellen Theater der USA Auskunft gibt. (USA)
531 Vollständiger Umschlag für ein Buch mit dem Titel «Die Versammlung der alten Männer», das bei Knopf erschienen ist. In zurückhaltenden, dumpfen Farben, Titel in Schwarz und Gelb, mit Orange und Olivgrün. (USA)

527–529 Illustrations pour le recto et le verso de la jaquette, et la jaquette complète d'un livre d'images, qui met en scène une souris chaussée de chaussures de gym, dont les aventures commencent lors de la rencontre d'un chat. (USA)
530 Couverture complète, rouge, blanc, noir, d'un guide des théâtres professionnels non commerciaux existant aux Etats-Unis. (USA)
531 Couverture complète d'un ouvrage intitulé «La réunion des vieux», publié chez Knopf. Les couleurs sont discrètes et mates. Le titre apparaît en noir et en jaune, avec des adjonctions d'orange et d'olive. (USA)

528

531

394-51468-8   KNOPF

Book Covers
Buchumschläge
Couvertures de livres

ARTIST / KÜNSTLER / ARTISTE:

532 Shin Matsunaga
533, 534 John McConnell / Lisa De Francis / John Rushworth
535 Brad Holland
536 Tadanori Yokoo

DESIGNER / GESTALTER / MAQUETTISTE:

532 Shin Matsunaga
533, 534 John McConnell / Lisa De Francis / John Rushworth
535 Louise Fili
536 Tadanori Yokoo

ART DIRECTOR / DIRECTEUR ARTISTIQUE:

532 Shin Matsunaga
533, 534 John McConnell
535 Louise Fili
536 Tadanori Yokoo

AGENCY / AGENTUR / AGENCE – STUDIO:

533, 534 Pentagram

PUBLISHER / VERLEGER / EDITEUR:

532 Tojusha
533, 534 Faber & Faber Ltd.
535 American Illustration
536 Kobe Shimbun Shuppan Center

532

532 Cover of a Japanese art book. The oval shapes of the red and green outer pages are punched out in different sizes allowing the blue and black underlying pages to show through. (JPN)
533, 534 Series of book covers for the publishers *Faber & Faber.* Fig. 533: volume 1 and 2 about Kandinsky's writings on art; Fig. 534: for two volumes in the literature series. (GBR)
535 Complete dust jacket for the second volume of *American Illustration.* Black "tortoise-pens" on blue-toned background, lettering in light beige and red. (USA)
536 For a book about the Japanese artist Tadanori Yokoo, a large format (78½×46 cm) complete dust jacket. (JPN)

535

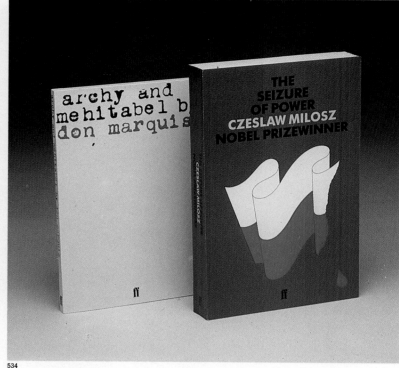

533

534

532 Umschlag eines japanischen Kunstbuches. Die Ovale des roten und grünen Deckblattes sind unterschiedlich gross ausgestanzt. (JPN)
533, 534 Buchumschläge des Verlags *Faber & Faber*. Abb. 533: Band 1 und 2 über Kandinskys Schriften zur Kunst; Abb. 534: für zwei Bände der Literaturreihe. (GBR)
535 Vollständiger Schutzumschlag für den 2. Band von *American Illustration*. Blau-Schwarz-Töne, Schrift in Beige und Rot. (USA)
536 Grossformatiger, vollständiger Schutzumschlag für ein Buch über den japanischen Künstler Tadanori Yokoo. (JPN)

532 Couverture d'un livre d'art japonais. Les ovales découpés dans le cache rouge et vert sont de dimensions différentes. (JPN)
533, 534 Couvertures de titres des Editions *Faber & Faber*. Fig. 533: deux volumes des écrits de Kandinsky sur l'art; fig. 534: deux titres de la collection littéraire. (GBR)
535 Jaquette complète du 2ᵉ volume d'*American Illustration*. Tons noir bleu, texte figurant en beige et en rouge. (USA)
536 Jaquette complète, au grand format (78½ × 46 cm), pour un ouvrage consacré à l'artiste japonais Tadanori Yokoo. (JPN)

536

537

538

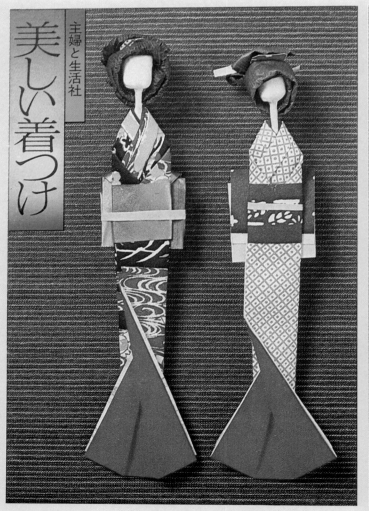

539

537 Cover of *The Cow Book*; a black-and-white cow, light beige shell, green water, pale pink roses and blue sky. (GBR)
538 Illustration for the cover of a book with the title *Tales for Jung Folk*; short "Jungian" (Carl Jung) stories. Mainly blue and gold. (GBR)
539 Complete cover for a book about the kimono. (JPN)
540, 541 Cover illustrations for two Agatha Christie novels. Fig. 540 with red rose and blood splashes, yellow tapemeasure in white maze. (USA)

537 Umschlag für ein «Kuh-Buch», mit schwarzweisser Kuh, hellbrauner Muschel, grünem Wasser, hellroten Rosen und blauem Himmel. (GBR)
538 Illustration für den Umschlag eines Buches mit dem Titel «Geschichten für Jung (C. G. Jung)-Volk». Vorwiegend in Blau und Gold. (GBR)
539 Vollständiger Umschlag für ein Buch über Kimonos. (JPN)
540, 541 Umschlagillustration für zwei Krimis von Agatha Christie. Abb. 540 mit gelbem Bandmass, roter Rose und roten Blutstropfen. (USA)

537 Couverture d'un «Livre de la vache»: vache noire et blanche, coquillage brun clair, eau verte, roses rouge clair, ciel bleu. (GBR)
538 Illustration pour la couverture d'un livre intitulé «Histoires pour le peuple (C. G.) Jung». Bleu et or prédominants. (GBR)
539 Couverture complète d'un ouvrage sur l'art des kimonos. (JPN)
540, 541 Illustrations de couverture pour deux romans d'Agatha Christie. Fig. 540 avec mètre jaune, rose rouge et gouttes de sang rouges. (USA)

ARTIST / KÜNSTLER / ARTISTE:

537, 538 James Marsh
539 Yutaka Hasegawa
540, 541 Marvin Mattelson

DESIGNER / GESTALTER / MAQUETTISTE:

537, 538 James Marsh
539 Yutaka Hasegawa
540, 541 Marvin Mattelson

ART DIRECTOR / DIRECTEUR ARTISTIQUE:

537 Marc Gallant
538 Richard Roberts
539 Yutaka Hasegawa
540, 541 Patty Pecararo

PUBLISHER / VERLEGER / EDITEUR:

537 Alfred A. Knopf
538 Vemar Equinox
539 Shufu to Seikatsu sha
540, 541 Dell Books

542

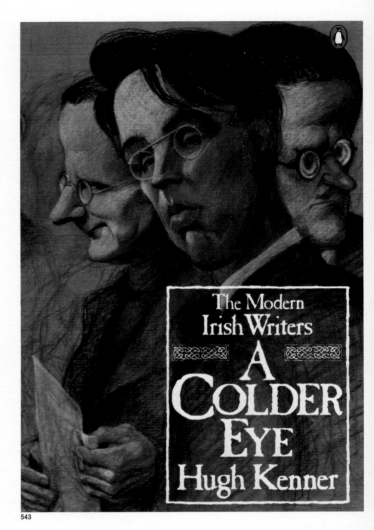

543

Book Covers
Buchumschläge
Couvertures de livres

542 Front cover of the dust jacket for a book aimed at expectant parents. (JPN)
543 Cover in brown and beige tones for a book about Irish writers. Lettering in white. (USA)
544 Dust jacket of a book. The sub-title is "A Slightly Wicked View of the Holy See". (USA)
545 Cover of a Polish children's book; predominantly in shades of brown, beige and white. (POL)
546 Full-colour cover of a pop-up book on the mechanisms of the human body, in which the illustrations are scale models that can be operated to make the heart beat, the lungs breathe etc. (GBR)
547 Cover illustration of a historical book dealing with hierarchic institutions. (USA)
548 Cover of a book on North-American wild flowers and their nomenclature. Leaves in bright green colours, flowers in brown, pink and white. (USA)

542 Schutzumschlag-Vorderseite eines Buches für werdende Eltern. (JPN)
543 Umschlag in Braun-Beige-Tönen für ein Buch über irische Schriftsteller. Weisse Schrift. (USA)
544 Buchumschlag mit dem Untertitel «Eine leicht boshafte Sicht auf den päpstlichen Stuhl». (USA)
545 Umschlag eines polnischen Kinderbuches; überwiegend in Braun, Beige und Weiss. (POL)
546 Mehrfarbiger Buchumschlag für ein Anschauungswerk über den menschlichen Körper, mit dreidimensionalen Illustrationen im Innenteil. Schwarze Schrift. (GBR)
547 Umschlag-Illustration eines Buches über das Leben am Hof aus historischer Sicht. (USA)
548 Mehrfarbiger Umschlag für ein Buch über nordamerikanische Wildpflanzen und die Entstehung ihrer Namen. (USA)

542 Recto de la jaquette d'un ouvrage d'instruction pour futurs parents. (JPN)
543 Couverture en tons beige brun d'un livre sur les écrivains irlandais. Texte blanc. (USA)
544 Couverture d'un livre sous-titré «Vue malicieuse du siège papal». (USA)
545 Couverture d'un livre d'enfants polonais; brun, beige, blanc prédominants. (POL)
546 Couverture polychrome d'un guide illustré du corps humain. Les illustrations dans le corps de l'ouvrage sont tridimensionnelles. Texte noir. (GBR)
547 Illustration de couverture pour un livre traitant des mœurs des cours royales d'antan. (USA)
548 Couverture polychrome d'un ouvrage descriptif des plantes sauvages d'Amérique du Nord comportant également un essai onomastique. (USA)

544

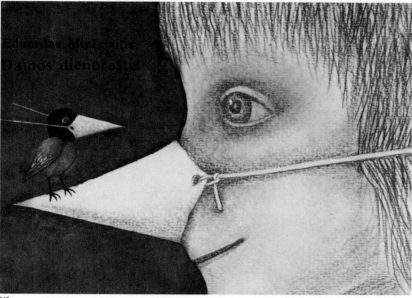

545

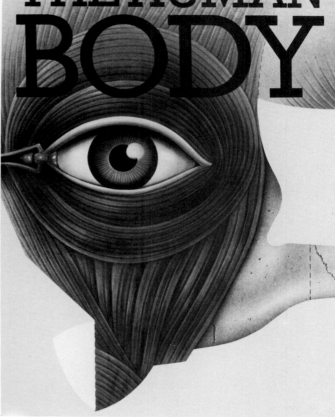

A three-dimensional study by Jonathan Miller and David Pelham

THE HUMAN BODY

546

547

Who Named the Daisy?
Who Named the Rose?
A ROVING DICTIONARY
of
NORTH AMERICAN
WILD FLOWERS
Mary Durant

548

4

Trademarks
Schutzmarken
Marques et emblèmes

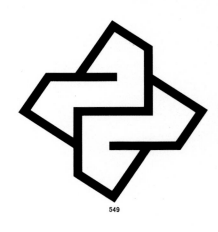

549

550

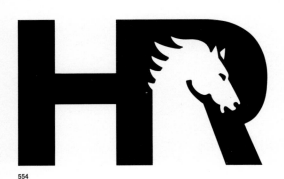

554

555

PinarCuatro

556

549 Symbol for the South Hill Park Arts Centre, Berkshire, England. (GBR)
550 Symbol for a road-testing company (Wegmeetdienst) in Holland. (NLD)
551 Symbol for *Interlink*, a joint venture credit-card system for five banks. (USA)
552 Logotype for Canadian tourist promotion. (CAN)
553 Logotype for *Security Trust*, an insurance organization. (USA)
554 Symbol for Hedlund Ranch, breeders and trainers of thoroughbred horses. (USA)
555 Symbol for the Otsuki Gallery. (JPN)
556 Symbol for a Spanish building company. (SPA)
557 Symbol for the Canada Israel Cultural Foundation. (CAN)
558 Logo for the petroleum company *Ferrante Petroli*. (ITA)
559 Trademark for Fleming H. Revell Company, book publishers. (USA)
560 Logotype for the *Diconix* Corporation. (USA)
561 Symbol for the architectural design firm Myers, Johnson & Jones. (USA)

549 Symbol für ein Kulturzentrum in Berkshire, England. (GBR)
550 Symbol für einen Strassenprüfdienst (Wegmeetdienst) in Holland. (NLD)
551 Symbol für *Interlink*, ein gemeinsames Kreditkartensystem von fünf Banken. (USA)
552 Schriftzug für kanadische Touristenwerbung. (CAN)
553 Schriftzug für *Security Trust*, ein Versicherungsunternehmen. (USA)
554 Signet für die Hedlund Ranch, Züchter und Trainer von Rennpferden. (USA)
555 Symbol für die Otsuki-Galerie. (JPN)
556 Symbol für ein spanisches Bauunternehmen. (SPA)
557 Symbol für eine kanadisch-israelische Kulturstiftung. (CAN)
558 Logo für die Erdölgesellschaft *Ferrante Petroli*. (ITA)
559 Schutzmarke für den Fleming-H.-Revell-Verlag. (USA)
560 Schriftzug für ein Unternehmen mit dem Namen *Diconix*. (USA)
561 Signet für das Architektur-Büro Myers, Johnson & Jones. (USA)

549 Emblème d'un centre culturel du Berkshire, en Angleterre. (GBR)
550 Emblème d'un service de contrôle des routes (Wegmeetdienst) aux Pays-Bas. (NLD)
551 Emblème d'*Interlink*, système de cartes de crédit commun à 5 banques. (USA)
552 Logo de l'Office national canadien du tourisme. (CAN)
553 Logo de *Security Trust*, une compagnie d'assurances. (USA)
554 Emblème de Hedlund Ranch, éleveur et entraîneur de chevaux de course. (USA)
555 Emblème de la galerie Otsuki. (JPN)
556 Emblème d'une entreprise de construction espagnole. (SPA)
557 Emblème d'une fondation culturelle canado-israélienne. (CAN)
558 Logo de la société pétrolière *Ferrante Petroli*. (ITA)
559 Marque déposée pour les Editions Fleming-H.-Revell. (USA)
560 Logo de l'entreprise *Diconix*. (USA)
561 Emblème du bureau d'architectes Myers, Johnson & Jones. (USA)

559

551

552

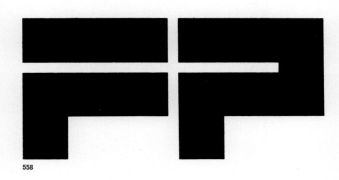

553

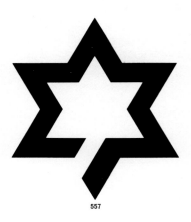

557

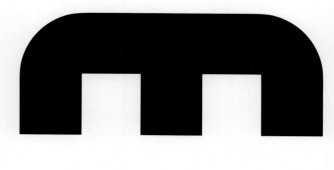

558

561

560

562

566

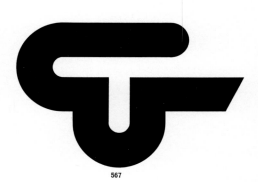

567

568

572

573

574

563

564

565

569

570

571

575

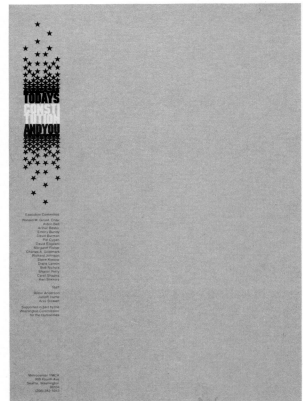

576

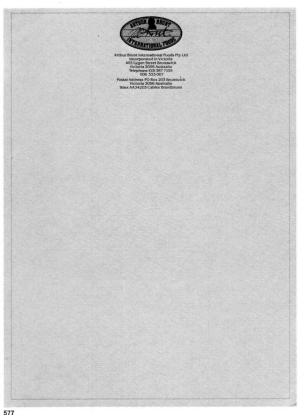

577

578

DESIGNER / GESTALTER / MAQUETTISTE:

575 Ilde Ianigro
576 Jack Anderson
577 Ken Cato
578 Russel Halfhide
579 Sharon Dowson / Clive Gay / Dirk Voorneveld
581, 582 Robert Cipriani

ART DIRECTOR / DIRECTEUR ARTISTIQUE:

575 Ilde Ianigro
576 Jack Anderson
577 Ken Cato
578 Russel Halfhide
579 Clive Gay
581, 582 Robert Cipriani

AGENCY / AGENTUR / AGENCE – STUDIO:

575 Coopstudio
576 John Hornall Design Works
577 Ken Cato Design Company Pty Ltd
578 Russel Halfhide
579 Pentragraph (Pty) Ltd
580 Miran Estudio
581, 582 Robert Cipriani Associates

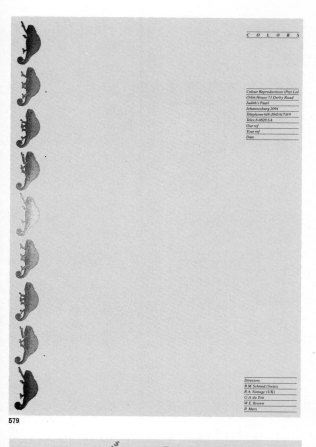

579

580

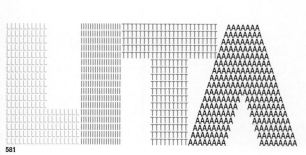

581

575 Special letterhead to mark the 7th national congress of an agricultural co-operative association. (ITA)
576 "Today's Constitution and You"; letterhead title in red, white and blue for an American YMCA performance. (USA)
577 For an international foodstuffs corporation. Brown, with red signature on yellow stock. (AUS)
578 Letterhead with black hand and red stroke of brush for the graphic design studio of Russel Halfhide. (WIN)
579 A chameleon as symbol for colour printing of Colour Reproductions (Pty) Ltd., on stationery and advertising material for the firm. Shown here is the letterhead. (SAF)
580 Reader's correction marks in red on a black-printed letterhead for a lady editor and proof-reader. (BRA)
581, 582 Visiting card, letterhead with letters in various colours and a sheet of the blind-embossed version, as well as the envelope, for Lita Cipriani. Pale yellow stock. (USA)

575 Anlässlich des 7. internationalen Kongresses einer landwirtschaftlichen Kooperative verwendeter Briefbogen. (ITA)
576 Briefbogen für eine Veranstaltung des christlichen Vereins junger Männer in den USA (YMCA) zu dem Thema «Die Verfassung heute und Du». Titel in Rot-Weiss-Blau. (USA)
577 Für ein Unternehmen der Lebensmittelbranche. Brauntöne mit roter Signatur auf gelb getöntem Papier. (AUS)
578 Briefbogen mit schwarzer Hand und rotem Pinselstrich für den Graphiker Russel Halfhide. (WIN)
579 Ein Chamäleon als Symbol für die Farbreproduktionen von Colour Reproductions (Pty) Ltd. auf dem Geschäftspapier und Werbematerial der Firma, hier der Briefbogen. (SAF)
580 Mit Korrekturzeichen versehenes Briefpapier für eine Redakteurin und Korrektorin. (BRA)
581, 582 Visitenkarte, Briefbogen mit verschiedenfarbigen Buchstaben und Bogen mit blindgeprägter Version, sowie das Couvert, für Lita Cipriani. Gelb getöntes Papier. (USA)

575 En-tête utilisé pour le 7ᵉ congrès national d'un mouvement coopératif agricole. (ITA)
576 En-tête pour une manifestation de l'YMCA, l'association chrétienne des jeunes gens des Etats-Unis, sur le thème de «La Constitution d'aujourd'hui et toi». Titre rouge, blanc, bleu. (USA)
577 Pour une entreprise de la branche alimentaire. Divers bruns, signature rouge, papier jaunâtre. (AUS)
578 En-tête orné d'une main noire et d'un coup de pinceau rouge pour un studio de design. (WIN)
579 Le caméléon sert ici d'emblème pour l'en-tête, mais aussi pour les autres imprimés et le matériel publicitaire de Colour Reproductions (Pty) Ltd., entreprise spécialisée dans l'impression couleur. (SAF)
580 En-tête illustré de signes de correction, pour une rédactrice-correctrice. (BRA)
581, 582 Carte de visite, en-tête aux lettres de diverses couleurs, feuille agrémentée d'une version gaufrée à sec, enveloppe, pour Lita Cipriani. Papier jaunâtre. (USA)

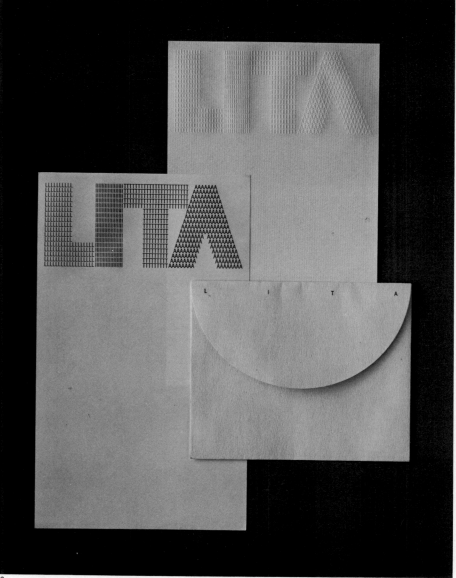

582

583 Red and black printed letterhead for a magazine of visual communication. (BRA)
584 Stationery and promotional matter for *Kroin*, suppliers of architectural complements. (USA)
585 Letterhead for a graphic magazine. Title lettering in brick red. (BRA)
586 Letterhead with the trademark for eyeglasses by *Highlander*. (USA)
587 For a team of calligraphers with names Quay and Gray. In grey, pale blue and white. (GBR)
588 Letterhead for a graphic designer. The complete heading is perforated. (USA)
589 For Jack Morton Productions, Inc. Printed in yellow and grey on white stock. (USA)
590 Letterhead for the graphic designer Oswaldo Miranda. Black and red on white. (BRA)

583 Rot und schwarz bedruckter Briefbogen für eine Zeitschrift für visuelle Kommunikation. (BRA)
584 Briefpapier und Drucksachen für *Kroin*, Lieferanten von architektonischem Zubehör. (USA)
585 Briefbogen für eine Graphik-Zeitschrift. Schriftzug in Ziegelrot. (BRA)
586 Briefkopf mit der Schutzmarke für Augengläser von *Highlander*. (USA)
587 Für ein Kalligraphen-Team. Grau (einem der Namen entsprechend), Hellblau und Weiss. (GBR)
588 Briefbogen für einen Graphik-Designer. Der Briefkopf ist abtrennbar. (USA)
589 Für Jack Morton Productions, Inc. Aufdruck in Gelb und Grau auf weissem Papier. (USA)
590 Briefbogen für den Graphik-Designer Oswaldo Miranda. Schwarz und Rot auf Weiss. (BRA)

583 En-tête pour un magazine de communication visuelle. Impression rouge et noir. (BRA)
584 Papier à lettres et imprimés pour *Kroin*, fournisseur de matériaux d'installation. (USA)
585 En-tête pour un magazine d'art graphique. Titre rouge brique. (BRA)
586 En-tête orné de la marque déposée des verres de lunettes *Highlander*. (USA)
587 Pour une équipe de calligraphes. Gris (selon l'un des noms), bleu clair, blanc. (GBR)
588 Papier à lettres d'un artiste graphique. L'en-tête est détachable. (USA)
589 Pour Jack Morton Productions, Inc. Impression en jaune et gris sur papier blanc. (USA)
590 En-tête pour le graphiste Oswaldo Miranda. Noir et rouge sur blanc. (BRA)

583

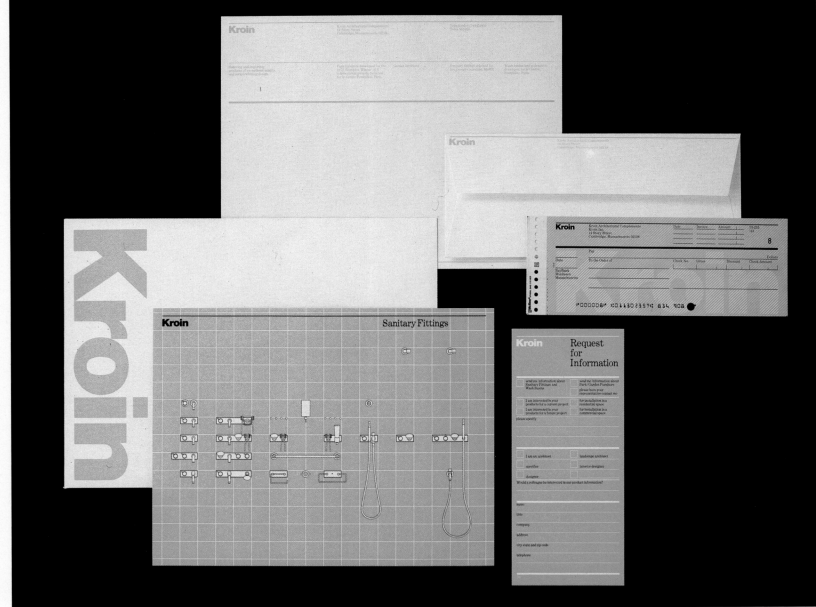

584

585

586

587

588

589

590

DESIGNER / GESTALTER / MAQUETTISTE:

583, 585, 590 Oswaldo Miranda (Miran)
584 Peter Laundy
586 McCaffery & Ratner, Inc.
587 David Quay
588 Art Chantry
589 Steff Geissbuhler

ART DIRECTOR / DIRECTEUR ARTISTIQUE:

583, 585, 590 Oswaldo Miranda
584 Massimo Vignelli
586 Sheila McCaffery
587 David Quay/Paul Gray
588 Art Chantry
589 Steff Geissbuhler

AGENCY / AGENTUR / AGENCE – STUDIO:

583, 585, 590 Miran Estudio
584 Vignelli Associates
586 McCaffery & Ratner, Inc.
587 Quay & Gray Lettering Designers
588 Art Chantry Design
589 Chermayeff & Geismar Associates

DESIGNER / GESTALTER / MAQUETTISTE:

591–593, 597 Yusaku Kamekura
594, 595 Michael Herold
596 James Cross
598 Jun Yoshida / Toshinori Nozaki
599 Kazumasa Nagai

ART DIRECTOR / DIRECTEUR ARTISTIQUE:

591–593, 597 Yusaku Kamekura
594, 595 Michael Herold
598 Shozo Murase
599 Kazumasa Nagai

AGENCY / AGENTUR / AGENCE – STUDIO:

598 Pure Planning Design Office
599 Nippon Design Center

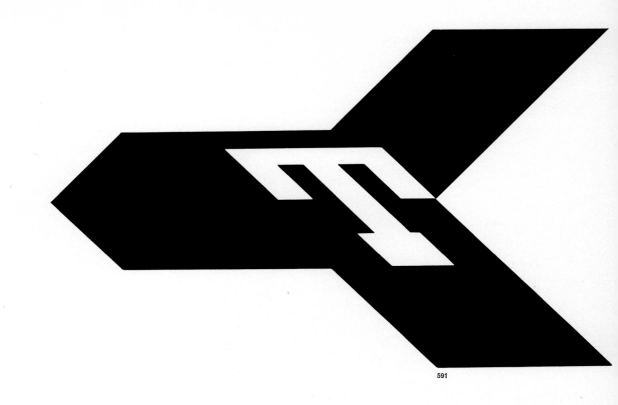

591

594

595

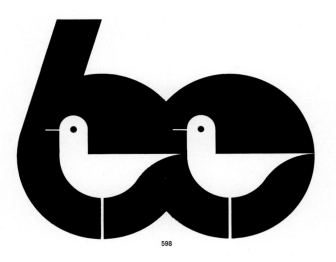

598

599

591 Trademark for Tokyu Air Cargo Co. Ltd., now no longer in use. (JPN)
592 Symbol for the Japan Industrial Designers' Association. (JPN)
593 Symbol for the East-West Culture Communication Association. (JPN)
594 Symbol for the Stuttgart Trade Fair. (GER)
595 Symbol for the Theissen Building Centre, a do-it-yourself retail outlet. (GER)
596 Symbol for an orthopaedic hospital in Los Angeles. (USA)
597 Trademark for the papermakers Toho Shigyo and Toho Kako Co. Ltd. (JPN)
598 Symbol for the 60th anniversary of the Toho Gakuen Junior College and High School. (JPN)
599 Symbol for the Japanese Broadcasting Corporation MBC, Kagoshima. (JPN)

591 Signet für Tokyu Air Cargo, jetzt nicht mehr in Gebrauch. (JPN)
592 Symbol für die japanische Vereinigung der Industrie Designer. (JPN)
593 Symbol für die Ost-West-Kulturaustausch-Vereinigung. (JPN)
594 Signet für die «Messe Stuttgart». (GER)
595 Signet für die «Theissen Bauzentrale», ein Baumarkt für Heimwerkerbedarf. (GER)
596 Symbol für ein orthopädisches Spital in Los Angeles. (USA)
597 Handelsmarke für die Papierhersteller Toho Shigyo und Toho Kako Co. (JPN)
598 Signet zum 60. Geburtstag von Toho Gakuen Junior College & High School. (JPN)
599 Symbol für die japanische Radiogesellschaft MBC, Kagoshima. (JPN)

591 Emblème de Tokyu Air Cargo; n'est plus utilisé. (JPN)
592 Emblème de l'association japonaise des esthéticiens industriels. (JPN)
593 Emblème de l'association des échanges culturels Est–Ouest. (JPN)
594 Emblème de la Foire de Stuttgart. (GER)
595 Emblème de la «centrale de construction Theissen». (GER)
596 Emblème d'un hôpital orthopédique de Los Angeles. (USA)
597 Marque de commerce des papetiers Toho Shigyo et Toho Kako Co. (JPN)
598 Emblème créé pour le 60ᵉ anniversaire du Toho Gakuen Junior College & High School. (JPN)
599 Emblème de la société de radiodiffusion japonaise MBC à Kagoshima. (JPN)

600

601

ARTIST / KÜNSTLER / ARTISTE:

601–604 Milton Glaser

DESIGNER / GESTALTER / MAQUETTISTE:

601–604 Milton Glaser/Wolfgang Heuwinkel (Zanders)

ART DIRECTOR / DIRECTEUR ARTISTIQUE:

601–604 Milton Glaser/Wolfgang Heuwinkel (Zanders)

600–604 «Meister der Farbe», ein von *Zanders Feinpapiere* für 1984 herausgegebener Kalender, geschaffen von Milton Glaser, als «Hommage» an von ihm verehrte Künstler. Die Idee war, für jeden Monat eine geniale Künstlerpersönlichkeit inmitten der für sie charakteristischen Stilmerkmale zu porträtieren. Abb. 600: Schwarzes Deckblatt mit mehrfarbigen «Zeichen»; Abb. 601: Vollständiges Blatt mit separatem Monatskalendarium. Die Zeichnung basiert auf einem frühen Holzschnitt von Utamaro und zeigt ihn bei der Arbeit; Abb. 602: Sonia Delaunays Porträt reflektiert ihr charakteristisches Vokabular von Kreisformen und leuchtenden Farben; Abb. 603: Giorgio de Chirico, umgeben von surrealistischen Elementen; Abb. 604: Paul Klee, eingerahmt von verschieden grossen Farbgittern, mit denen er experimentiert hat. (GER)

600–604 "Masters of Colour", a 1984 calendar published by *Zanders Feinpapiere*, created by Milton Glaser as homage to some of his favourite artists. For each month there is an artist portrayed against a background characteristic of his own particular style. Fig. 600: Black cover with brush-strokes in full colour and punched-out irregular holes showing the silver undersheet through; Fig. 601: Complete page with single monthly calendar. The drawing is based on an early woodcut by Utamaro and shows him at work; Fig. 602: Sonia Delaunay's portrait reflects her characteristic inclination for circular forms and brilliant colours; Fig. 603: Giorgio de Chirico seated, surrounded by surrealistic elements; Fig. 604: Paul Klee, profiled within stylistically abstract elements. Size of the calendar: 81×55 cm. (GER)

600–604 «Maîtres de la couleur», le calendrier des *Papiers Fins Zanders* pour 1984 réalisé par Milton Glaser en hommage aux artistes qu'il vénère. L'idée de base: placer pour chaque mois l'une de ces personnalités géniales dans un cadre stylistique approprié. Fig. 600: feuillet de garde aux «signes» polychromes. Fig. 601: feuillet complet avec, séparément, le calendrier mensuel. Le dessin s'inspire de l'une des premières gravures sur bois d'Utamaro et le montre en plein travail. Fig. 602: le portrait de Sonia Delaunay reflète son vocabulaire caractéristique fait de formes circulaires et de couleurs lumineuses. Fig. 603: Giorgio de Chirico assis, entouré d'éléments surréalistes. Fig. 604: Paul Klee, encadré des trames couleur de dimensions variables qui lui servirent de structures expérimentales. (GER)

602

603

ZANDERS

604

235

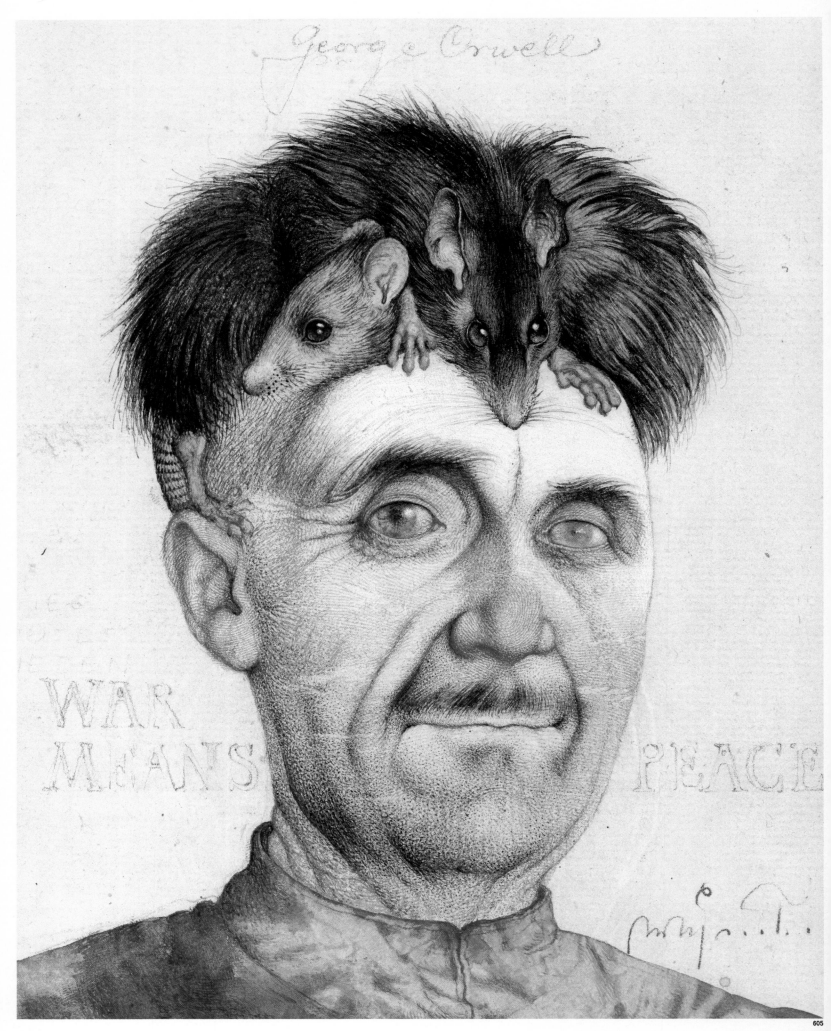

George Orwell

WAR MEANS PEACE

605

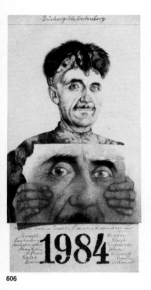

606

ARTIST / KÜNSTLER / ARTISTE:
605–610 Michael Mathias Prechtl

DESIGNER / GESTALTER:
605–610 Michael Mathias Prechtl

605–610 Michael Mathias Prechtl's Literature Calendar for 1984 shows thirteen famous personalities. After each full-colour illustration follows a text by the relevant person, together with the month's calendar. Fig. 605: George Orwell; Fig. 606: Complete title page; Fig. 607: J. I. Samjatin; Fig. 608: Rosa Luxemburg; Fig. 609: Jakob van Hoddis; Fig. 610: Jaroslav Hašek. The size of the calendar is 63×31,5 cm. (GER)

605–610 Michael Mathias Prechtls Literaturkalender für 1984 zeigt dreizehn bekannte Persönlichkeiten. Nach jeder Farbillustration ist auf dem nächsten Blatt ein Text der betreffenden Person und das Monatskalendarium gedruckt. Abb. 605: George Orwell; Abb. 606: Vollständiges Titelblatt; Abb. 607: J. I. Samjatin; Abb. 608: Rosa Luxemburg; Abb. 609: Jakob van Hoddis; Abb. 610: Jaroslav Hašek. Format: 63 × 31,5 cm. (GER)

605–610 Le calendrier littéraire de Michael Mathias Prechtl pour 1984 présente treize célébrités. Le feuillet suivant chaque illustration couleur comporte un texte du personnage et le calendrier mensuel. Fig. 605: George Orwell; fig. 606: feuillet de titre complet; fig. 607: J. I. Samjatin; fig. 608: Rosa Luxemburg; fig. 609: Jakob van Hoddis; fig. 610: Jaroslav Hašek. Le format du calendrier est de 63×31,5 cm. (GER)

Calendars

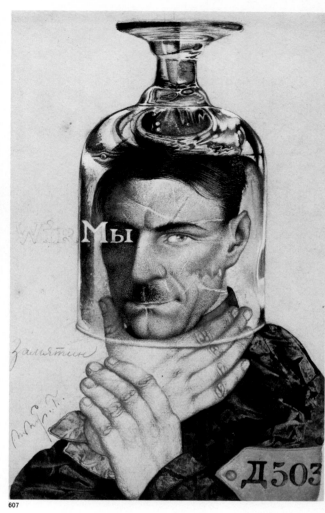

607

608

609

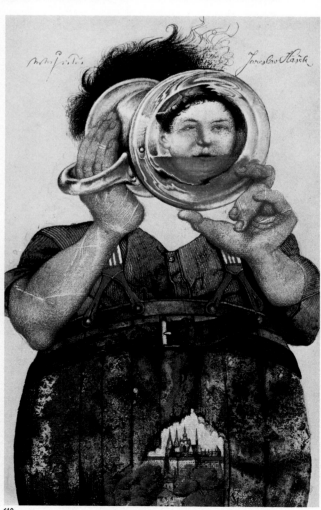

610

611

612

611 Tube styling for a medicinal hair-care product. Violet shades, grey and black on white. (AUS)
612 Bottle styling for the red wine *Dolcetto d'Alba*. (ITA)
613 Packaging for *Grès Monsieur*, here for the Eau de Toilette in blue and silver on dark blue and in blue and white for shower gel and deodorant stick of the *Grès Monsieur Sport* range. (FRA)
614 Shipping carton, size 29×41×9,5 cm, for a small portable computer. Colours are anthracite with white, yellow and green lettering, light blue display screen. (USA)
615 Cassette, shown closed and half open, with a quartz watch, *Muratti Time*, destined for the Italian market. (SWI)

611 Tubengestaltung für ein medizinisches Haarpflegemittel. Violett-Töne, Grau und Schwarz auf Weiss. (AUS)
612 Flaschenausstattung für Rotwein *Dolcetto d'Alba*. (ITA)
613 Packungsfamilie für *Grès Monsieur*. Eau de Toilette in Blautönen mit Silber. Blau-weisse Verpackung für Dusch-Gel und Deodorantstift der Linie *Grès Monsieur Sport*. (FRA)
614 Versandkarton im Format 29×41×9,5 cm für einen tragbaren Kleincomputer. Anthrazit, Weiss, Gelb und Grün. (USA)
615 Geschlossene und halbgeöffnete Kassette mit einer für den italienischen Markt bestimmten Quarzuhr, *Muratti Time*. (SWI)

611 Tube plastique pour des cosmétiques médicaux pour cheveux. Divers violets, gris, noir sur blanc. (AUS)
612 Etude de bouteille pour le vin rouge *Dolcetto d'Alba*. (ITA)
613 Gamme de conditionnements pour les produits *Grès Monsieur*. Ici le carton pour l'eau de toilette en divers bleus, avec de l'argent. Emballage bleu blanc pour le gel de douche et le déodorant de la ligne spéciale *Grès Monsieur Sport*. (FRA)
614 Carton d'emballage au format 29×41×9,5 cm pour un microprocesseur portable. Anthracite, blanc, jaune, vert. (USA)
615 Caissette fermée et mi-ouverte contenant une montre à quartz *Muratti Time* destinée au marché italien. (SWI)

613

ARTIST / KÜNSTLER / ARTISTE:

613 Alain de Mourgues
615 Jacques Saxod

DESIGNER / GESTALTER / MAQUETTISTE:

611 Heinz Grunwald
612 Silvio Coppola
613 Pierre Dinand
614 Myland McRevey
615 Maurice Progin

ART DIRECTOR / DIRECTEUR ARTISTIQUE:

611 Heinz Grunwald
612 Silvio Coppola
614 Barry Deutsch
615 Maurice Progin

AGENCY / AGENTUR / AGENCE:

611 The Grunwald Design Group
612 Studio Coppola
614 Steinhilber, Deutsch & Gard
615 Maurice Progin

614

615

616

617

ARTIST / KÜNSTLER / ARTISTE:

616, 617 Shozo Kakutani
619 Angelo Sganzerla

DESIGNER / GESTALTER / MAQUETTISTE:

616, 617 Shozo Kakutani
618 Kenji Asano
619 Angelo Sganzerla
620 Kenji Maezawa

ART DIRECTOR / DIRECTEUR ARTISTIQUE:

616, 617 Shozo Kakutani
618 Atsuo Aoyama / Yasutoshi Imaeda
619 Angelo Sganzerla
620 Kenji Maezawa

AGENCY / AGENTUR / AGENCE – STUDIO:

618 Dai Nippon Printing Co. Ltd.
619 Angelo Sganzerla

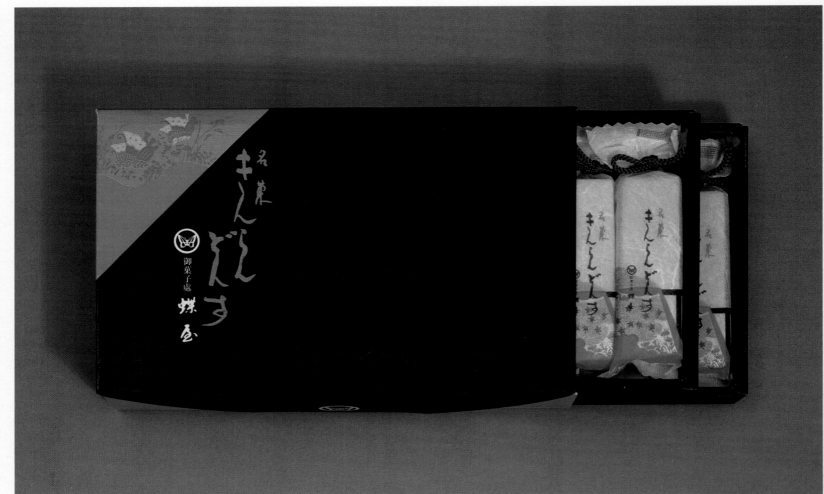

618

619

620

616 Gift packaging for Japanese noodles and soup. The illustration, in brick red, represents the noodle paste and the rolling pin. Calligraphy in black on white ground. (JPN)
617 Folding cardboard boxes for Japanese specialities. Brown, greyish green, black and white. (JPN)
618 Box with two sliding elements as gift packaging for Japanese confectionery. (JPN)
619 Label styling for various kinds of natural-fruit jams. (ITA)
620 Metal boxes for food products of the *Seibu* store. Brown tones, red, white and black. (JPN)

616 Geschenkpackung für japanische Nudeln und Suppe. Die Zeichnung, in Ziegelrot, stellt den Nudelteig und das Rollholz dar. Schriftzeichen schwarz auf weissem Grund. (JPN)
617 Karton-Faltschachteln für japanische Spezialitäten. Braun, Graugrün, Schwarz und Weiss. (JPN)
618 Schachtel mit zwei Schiebeelementen als Geschenkverpackung für japanisches Gebäck. (JPN)
619 Etikettgestaltung für verschiedene Sorten natürlicher Fruchtkonfitüre. (ITA)
620 Metalldosen für Esswaren des Kaufhauses *Seibu*. Brauntöne, Rot, Weiss und Schwarz. (JPN)

616 Emballage-cadeau de nouilles et potage japonais. Le dessin rouge brique représente la pâte à nouilles et le rouleau. Caractères en noir sur fond blanc. (JPN)
617 Cartons pliants pour spécialités japonaises. Brun, vert gris, noir, blanc. (JPN)
618 Boîte-cadeau pour gâteaux secs japonais, pourvue de deux éléments coulissants. (JPN)
619 Conception d'étiquettes pour une gamme de confiture de fruits naturelles du *Centro Botanico*. (ITA)
620 Boîtes métalliques pour aliments des grands magasins *Seibu*. Divers bruns, rouge, blanc, noir. (JPN)

621

Packaging / Packungen / Emballages

ARTIST / KÜNSTLER / ARTISTE:

621 Flett Henderson & Arnold
622 Osterwalder Office
623 Lena Gan

DESIGNER / GESTALTER / MAQUETTISTE:

621 Flett Henderson & Arnold
622 Ernst Friedel Maischein
623 Ken Cato
624 Dawn Fogler
625 Joep Bergmans / Rob van den Berg

621 Front and back of a carton and desk-promotion item for doctors, for the introduction of a new heart drug. (AUS)
622 Glass jar and cork lid; an advertising-campaign item for BASF Vitamins. (GER)
623 Packaging design for an air-freshener. In warm yellow tones. (AUS)
624 A real starfish on blue tissue paper inside a cardboard box sent to travel agencies to promote a resort on the coast of Florida. (USA)
625 Packaging for the Dutch *Willem-II* cigars. Reddish-brown with gold. (NLD)

621 Vorder- und Rückseite eines Kartons und Werbegeschenk für Ärzte, im Zusammenhang mit der Einführung eines neuen Herzmedikaments. (AUS)
622 Glas mit Korkdeckel; Teil einer Werbesendung für BASF-Vitamine. (GER)
623 Packungsgestaltung für einen Lufterfrischer. In warmen Gelbtönen. (AUS)
624 Seestern auf blauem Seidenpapier, in einer Kartonschachtel an Reisebüros versandt, als Werbung für ein Seebad an Floridas Küste. (USA)
625 Packungsfamilie für *Willem-II*-Zigarren. Braunrot mit Gold. (NLD)

621 Recto et verso d'un carton et cadeau publicitaire pour le corps médical, lors du lancement d'un nouveau médicament cardiaque. (AUS)
622 Bocal au couvercle de liège; publicité des vitamines BASF. (GER)
623 Etude d'emballage pour un désodorisant. Teintes jaunes chaudes. (AUS)
624 Etoile de mer sur papier de soie bleu, expédiée dans un carton aux agences de voyages; publicité pour une station balnéaire en Floride. (USA)
625 Gamme d'emballage des cigares *Willem II.* Roux, avec de l'or. (NLD)

622

623

624

625

626

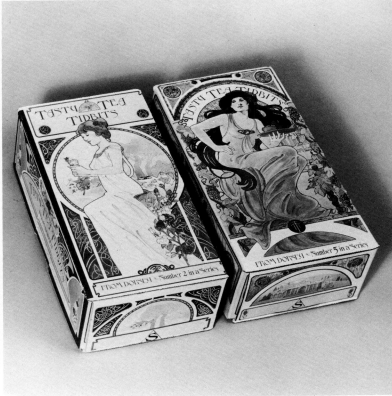

627

ARTIST / KÜNSTLER / ARTISTE:

627 Judith Friedman
628 Erhard Schürer
629–631 Armando Yslas

DESIGNER / GESTALTER / MAQUETTISTE:

626 Tibor Kalman
627 Steve Voorhees
628 Erhard Schürer / Roland Mehler
629–631 Nancy Stock / Scott Bolestridge

Packaging
Packungen
Emballages

626 A yellow paperweight with blue lines; hardened plastic, resembling crumpled paper. (USA)
627 Examples from a mailing series of five sorts of biscuits sent to doctors. Each of the five mailings contains biscuits typical for a certain country (here England and Italy). Also enclosed is a matching letter and business reply card to order samples of tablets. The letter "T" plays a key role in this advertising campaign (Tablet, Tested, Tolerated etc.). (USA)
628 Packaging range for *Scholl* foot-care products. Consistent use of three sections; blue-and-white trademark at top, text in the middle, and illustration in the bottom section. (GER)
629–631 Variants of a packaging programme for agricultural chemicals. As these chemicals are dangerous, great emphasis is placed on easily-understood pictograms and clear type. (USA)

626 Briefbeschwerer, verpackt in gelbe, gehärtete Plastikfolie mit blauen Streifen. (USA)
627 Beispiele aus einer Serie von fünf Biskuit-Versand-Schachteln, die für Werbesendungen an Ärzte verwendet wurden. Neben der für ein bestimmtes Land typisches Gebäck (hier England und Italien) ist eine Bestellkarte für ein Medikament beigelegt. Der Buchstabe «T» von «Tee» und «Tablette» dient als Beziehungspunkt. (USA)
628 Für Fusspflegeprodukte von *Scholl*. Konsequente Dreiteilung mit blau-weissem Markenzeichen im oberen gelben Feld, Text im mittleren gelben und Illustration im unteren weissen Feld. (GER)
629–631 Aus einem Verpackungsprogramm für Chemikalien zur Unkraut- und Insektenvertilgung im landwirtschaftlichen Bereich. Da es sich um giftige Produkte handelt, ist auf eine leicht verständliche Packungsgestaltung Wert gelegt worden. (USA)

626 Presse-papiers emballé dans une feuille de plastique durci jaune; raies bleues. (USA)
627 Exemples d'une série de cinq boîtes d'expédition de biscuits utilisées pour des envois publicitaires au corps médical. On y trouve des biscuits représentatifs d'un pays déterminé (ici, l'Angleterre et l'Italie) et une carte de commande pour un médicament. Le «T» renvoie à «thé» (biscuits pour le thé) et à «tablet» (mot anglais pour «comprimé»). (USA)
628 Pour les produits *Scholl* pour les soins des pieds. Impression tripartite: marque blanc bleu en haut (fond jaune), texte au milieu (fond jaune), illustration en bas (sur blanc). (GER)
629–631 Exemples d'emballages dans une ligne de produits herbicides et insecticides pour l'agriculture. Comme il s'agit de substances toxiques, la présentation des emballages a été simplifiée au maximum pour en faciliter l'identification. (USA)

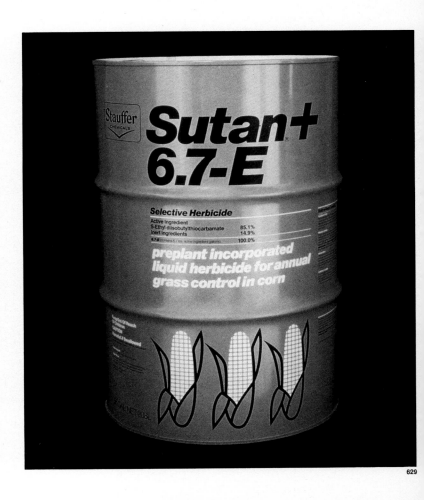

629

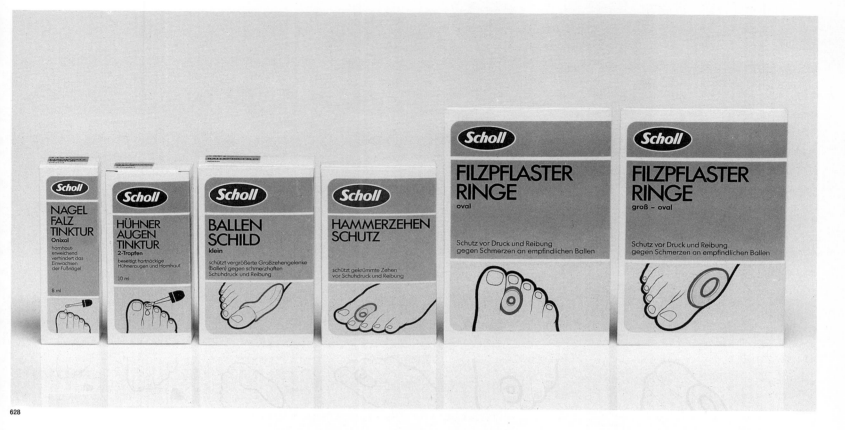

628

ART DIRECTOR / DIRECTEUR ARTISTIQUE:

626 Tibor Kalman
627 Steve Voorhees
628 Knut Hartmann / Roland Mehler
629–631 Robert P. Gersin

AGENCY / AGENTUR / AGENCE – STUDIO:

626 M & Co.
627 Sieber & McIntyre
628 Knut Hartmann Design
629–631 Robert P. Gersin Associates

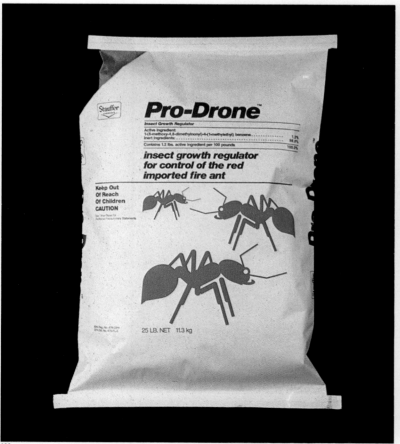

630

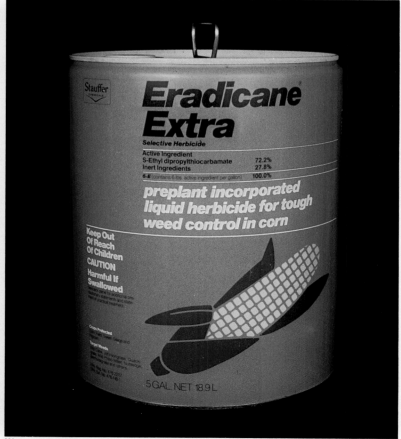

631

ARTIST / KÜNSTLER / ARTISTE:

632 Tony Hurley
633 Shigeru Akizuki
634 Shozo Kakutani

DESIGNER / GESTALTER / MAQUETTISTE:

632 Gail Sharp / Mark Wickens
633 Shigeru Akizuki
634 Shozo Kakutani
635 Pierre Mendell
636 Peter Adam
637 Fernando Medina

ART DIRECTOR / DIRECTEUR ARTISTIQUE:

632 Michael Peters
633 Shigeru Akizuki
634 Shozo Kakutani
635 Pierrre Mendell
636 Gottshalk & Ash Int'l
637 Fernando Medina

AGENCY / AGENTUR / AGENCE – STUDIO:

632 Michael Peters & Partners Ltd.
635 Mendell & Oberer
637 Fernando Medina

632

633

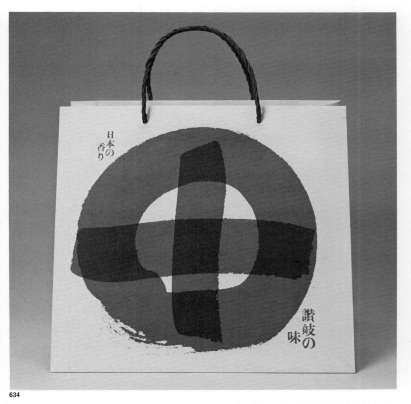

634

635

636

637

Packaging
Packungen
Emballages

632 Range of jars for various relishes of the brand *Fine Fare*. The identification is through colour coding of the labels and clear illustration of the contents. (GBR)
633 Bottle with paper label and cylindrical cardboard container for *Hascup* syrup. (JPN)
634 Grey and blue printed carrier-bag for traditional Japanese confectionery. (JPN)
635 Carrier-bag as part of the graphic identity for *Harry's* ladies fashions. (GER)
636 Carton with punched-out display windows for three bottles of wine. Black, red, white. (CAN)
637 Can styling for soft beverages of the brand *Clipper*. (SPA)

632 Serie von Gläsern für verschiedene Gewürzsaucen der Marke *Fine Fare*. Sortendifferenzierung durch Farbkodierung der Etiketts und Darstellung der Geschmacksrichtung. (GBR)
633 Flasche mit Papieretikett und zylindrischer Kartonbehälter für *Hascup*-Sirup. (JPN)
634 Graublau bedruckte Tragtasche für traditionelles japanisches Gebäck. (JPN)
635 Tragtasche mit Kordelgriff als Teil der Ausstattung für *Harry's* Damenmoden. (GER)
636 Karton mit ausgestanzten Sichtfenstern für drei Flaschen Wein. Schwarz, Rot, Weiss. (CAN)
637 Dosenausstattung für Erfrischungsgetränke der Marke *Clipper*. (SPA)

632 Série de bocaux pour diverses sauces épicées *Fine Fare*, différenciées par le code couleur des étiquettes et la représentation illustré de la saveur en question. (GBR)
633 Bouteille, étiquette papier et emballage carton cylindrique pour le sirop *Hascup*. (JPN)
634 Cabas servant à transporter des biscuits japonais traditionnels. Impression gris bleu. (JPN)
635 Cabas en papier à poignée en cordelette pour le magasin de modes féminines *Harry's*. (GER)
636 Carton de transport pour trois bouteilles de vin montrées en découpe. Noir, rouge, blanc. (CAN)
637 Etude de boîtes pour des boissons rafraîchissantes de la marque *Clipper*. (SPA)

638–643

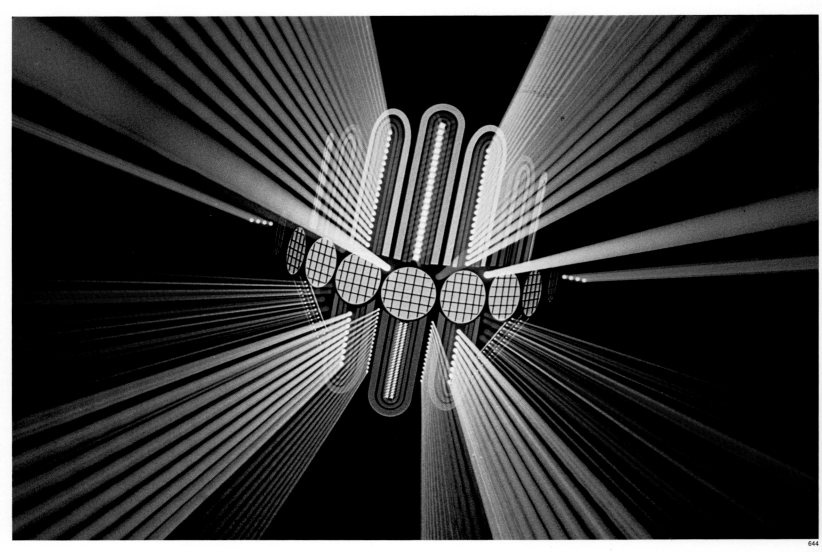

644

Film / Television / Fernsehen

ARTIST / KÜNSTLER / ARTISTE:

638–643 Otto David Sherman
644–648 Bill Baker (Photo)

DESIGNER / GESTALTER / MAQUETTISTE:

638–643 Julene Gliko
644–648 Otto David Shermann

ART DIRECTOR / DIRECTEUR ARTISTIQUE:

638–643 Julene Gliko
644–648 Otto David Sherman

AGENCY / AGENTUR / AGENCE – STUDIO:

638–648 Otto David Sherman, Inc.

638–643 Examples from a series of slides used for demonstration purposes at business presentations and business lectures. The subjects shown here deal with communication in business life in general, the variety of ideas and requirements and the communication between the client, the creator and the user, for instance in architecture. (USA)
644–648 Special-effect experiments used in the creation of modules for multi-projection business slide presentations. (USA)

638–643 Beispiele aus einer Reihe von Dias, die für die Veranschaulichung von Wirtschaftsreferaten und -präsentationen verwendet werden. Die Themen sind hier Kommunikation im allgemeinen Geschäfts-leben, die Unterschiedlichkeit von Vorstellungen und Bedürfnissen und die Kommunikation zwischen Auftraggeber, Ausführenden und Benutzern, am Beispiel der Architektur. (USA)
644–648 Experimente mit Spezialeffekten als Beispiele von Darstellungsformen für Dia-Präsentationen im Zusammenhang mit Wirtschaftsreferaten. (USA)

638–643 Exemples d'une série de diapos servant à visualiser des communications et présentations dans le domaine des affaires. Les sujets: la communication dans la vie économique en général, les différences affectant les concepts et les besoins, la communication entre client, exécutants et utilisateurs appliquée à l'exemple de l'architecture. (USA)
644–648 L'expérimentation d'effets spéciaux est exemplaire des formes que peuvent affecter les diapos présentant des faits économiques dans des meetings d'affaires. (USA)

645–648

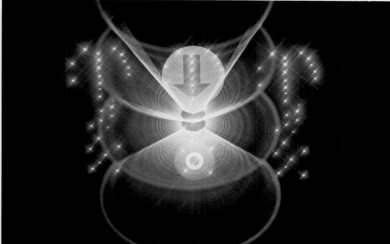
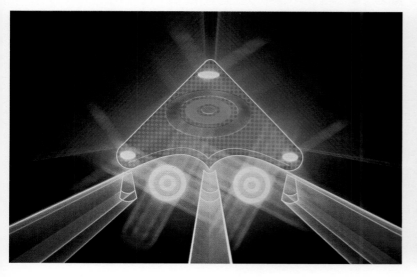

649

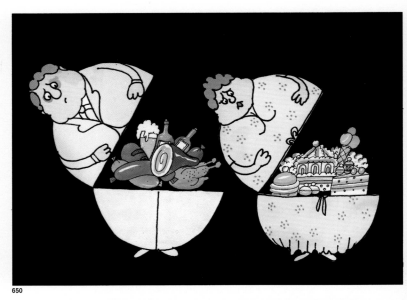

650

651

652

Film / Television / Fernsehen

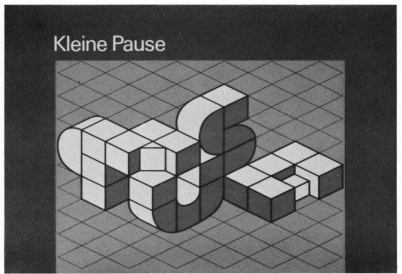

Kleine Pause

653

649–656 Television graphics from the productions of the television authority of German and Romansh speaking Switzerland (DRS). Figs. 649–652: cartoon-film sequence showing the effectiveness of various slimming methods, from a critical consumer programme; Fig. 653: slide announcing a short interval; Figs. 654–656: frames from a partly animated TV series in 13 seven-minute instalments for pre-school age viewers. It is based on the children's story "The Witch Liquorice" by Eveline Hasler, published by Benziger Verlag, Zurich, and illustrated by the Prague artist Peter Sis, who also undertook the creation of the TV series. Here the German title (Fig. 654), the witch's kitchen (Fig. 655) and a forest clearing with the witch's house (Fig. 656). (SWI)

649–656 Fernseh-Graphik des Fernsehens der Deutschen und Rätoromanischen Schweiz (DRS). Abb. 649–652: Trickfilmsequenz, welche die Wirksamkeit verschiedener Schlankheitskuren kritisch beleuchtet. Ein Beitrag aus dem Konsumentenmagazin «Kassensturz»; Abb. 653: Beispiel eines Einschalt-dias für kurze Pausen; Abb. 654–656: Bilder aus einer teilweise animierten Fernsehserie, für das Vorschul-programm des Ressorts Jugend realisiert. Es handelt sich um die von Eveline Hasler geschriebene Geschichte *Die Hexe Lakritze*, die vom Benziger Verlag, Zürich, veröffentlicht und vom Prager Künstler Peter Sis illustriert wurde, der auch die Ausführung der Fernsehserie (13×7 Minuten) übernommen hat. Hier der Titel (Abb. 654), die Küche der Hexe (Abb. 655) und eine Waldlichtung mit Hexenhaus und Kräutergarten (Abb. 656). (SWI)

649–656 Créations graphiques pour la Télévision de Suisse alémanique et romanche DRS. Fig. 649–652: séquence animée où diverses cures d'amaigrissement sont analysées d'un œil critique, dans le cadre du magazine des consommateurs «Kassensturz»; fig. 653: exemple d'annonce graphique d'une petite pause; fig. 654–656: images tirées d'une émission télévisée partiellement animée, pour le programme préscolaire du département Jeunesse. Il s'agit du conte d'Eveline Hasler, *Die Hexe Lakritze* (La Sorcière Réglisse), paru aux Editions Benziger de Zurich, avec les illustrations du Pragois Peter Sis, qui s'est également chargé des dessins pour la série télévisée (13 épisodes de 7 minutes chacun). Ici le titre allemand (fig. 654), la cuisine de la sorcière (fig. 655) et sa maison dans une clairière (fig. 656). (SWI)

654

655

ARTIST / KÜNSTLER / ARTISTE:

649–652 Doris Peter
654–656 Peter Sis

DESIGNER / GESTALTER / MAQUETTISTE:

649–652 Hanspeter Wyss
653 Rosmarie Tissi

ART DIRECTOR / DIRECTEUR ARTISTIQUE:

653 Charlotte Guidi

CAMERA:

654–656 Daniel Hummel / C-Trick Basel

PRODUCER / PRODUZENT / PRODUCTION:

649–656 DRS Television

656

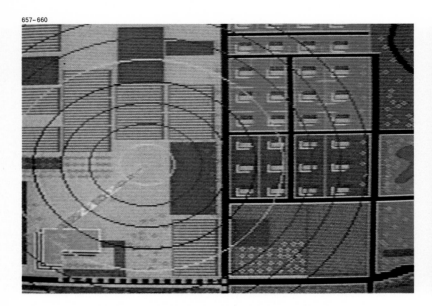 

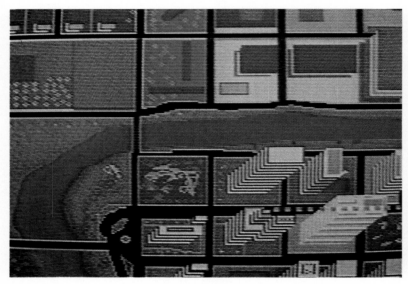 

Film / Television / Fernsehen

657–660 Sequence from a science programme shown on TV and explaining the systems of bringing television into the home. It was produced with puppets and computer-animator techniques. (USA)
661–664 Frames from a sixty-second television commercial for Shell (UK) Ltd. (GBR)
665–672 Frames from a television commercial for the Swiss Cheese Union advertising Swiss Fondue. The initials "FIGUGEGL" stand for "Fondue is good and puts you in a good mood" (in German). (SWI)

657–660 Sequenz aus einer wissenschaftlichen Fernsehreihe, in welcher Fernsehübertragungssysteme erklärt werden. Produziert wurden die Bilder mit Hilfe von Computer-Animationstechniken. (USA)
661–664 Bilder aus einem Sechzig-Sekunden-Fernsehwerbespot für Shell (UK) Ltd. (GBR)
665–672 Bilder aus einem TV-Werbefilm für die Schweizerische Käseunion, innerhalb einer Kampagne für Käse-Fondue unter dem Kennwort «FIGUGEGL» (Fondue ist gut und gibt eine gute Laune). (SWI)

657–660 Séquence télévisée figurant dans une émission scientifique consacrée aux systèmes de transmission d'images TV. Dessins créés avec l'assistance de l'ordinateur. (USA)
661–664 Images d'un spot télévisé de soixante secondes réalisé pour Shell (UK) Ltd. (GBR)
665–672 Images d'un film publicitaire TV de l'Union suisse du fromage dans le cadre d'une campagne «FIGUGEGL» (sigle de «la fondue, c'est bon, et ça vous ragaillardit») pour la fondue. (SWI)

ARTIST / KÜNSTLER / ARTISTE:

657–660 Mark Fisher / Paul Souza
661–664 John Leatherbarrow / Peter Wood
665–672 Adelchi Galloni

DESIGNER / GESTALTER / MAQUETTISTE:

657–660 Paul Souza
661–664 Allen Forster
665–672 Jerko Tognola

ART DIRECTOR / DIRECTEUR ARTISTIQUE:

657–660 Paul Souza
661–664 Gary Horner
665–672 Adelchi Galloni

AGENCY / AGENTUR / AGENCE – STUDIO:

657–660 WGBH Design
661–664 Ogilvy & Mather
665–672 Gisler & Gisler

PRODUCER / PRODUZENT / PRODUCTION:

657–660 WGBH Television
661–665 Richard Williams Animation
665–672 Frama Film

673

674

675

Film / Television / Fernsehen

ARTIST / KÜNSTLER / ARTISTE:
680–688 Tony Munzlinger

DESIGNER / GESTALTER / MAQUETTISTE:
673–679 Marcela Halousková
680–688 Tony Munzlinger

ART DIRECTOR / DIRECTEUR ARTISTIQUE:
673–679 František Mikeš
680–688 Tony Munzlinger

AGENCY / AGENTUR / AGENCE – STUDIO:
673–679 Československá Televize
680–688 Südwestfunk Baden-Baden

PRODUCER / PRODUZENT / PRODUCTION:
673–679 Československá Televize
680–688 Südwestfunk Baden-Baden

676

677

678

679

673–675 "The Painting Class". Sequence from a thirteen-part cartoon-film series for children on the subject of choosing a career. Bright colours in combined techniques on beige ground. (CSR)
676 Frame from a seven-minute cartoon film based on an old miner's song "The Maiden is Crying". Soft colours. (CSR)
677–679 Sequence from a seven-part cartoon film "Seven Times about Honza" which introduced young viewers to the classical Bohemian fairytales. (CSR)
680–688 "Adventure with Herakles" was a German television (ARD) cartoon-film series about the Greek demigod Heracles and his adventures in ancient Greece. A picture-book accompanying the series was published, with verses by Anton Zink, recounting the ancient Greek legends in present-day language. (GER)

673–675 «Die malende Klasse.» Sequenz aus einer dreizehnteiligen Trickfilmserie für Kinder zum Thema Berufswahl. Bunte Farben in Mischtechnik auf beigem Grund. (CSR)
676 Bild aus einem 7-Minuten-Zeichentrickfilm nach dem alten Bergmannslied «Es weinte die Jungfrau». Zarte Farben. (CSR)
677–679 Sequenz aus einem siebenteiligen Zeichentrickfilm «Sieben mal über Honza», der die kleinen Zuschauer mit den klassischen böhmischen Märchen bekannt machen soll. (CSR)
680–688 «Abenteuer mit Herakles» heisst diese vom Deutschen Fernsehen ARD ausgestrahlte Trickfilmserie über die Götter und Helden der Antike. Zu den sechs Folgen ist auch ein Bildband mit Versen von Anton Zink über den griechischen Halbgott Herakles und seine zwölf Heldentaten erschienen. (GER)

673–675 «La classe de peinture.» Séquence d'une série animée en 13 épisodes destinée à guider les enfants dans le choix de leur métier. Couleurs vives, technique mixte, fond beige. (CSR)
676 Image d'un dessin animé de sept minutes tiré d'une vieille chanson de mineurs, «Et la vierge pleura». Couleurs tendres. (CSR)
677–679 Séquence d'un dessin animé en sept épisodes, «Sept fois au-dessus de Honza», qui entend familiariser les enfants avec les contes classiques de Bohème. (CSR)
680–688 «Les Aventures d'Hercule», dessin animé en six épisodes diffusé par la Télévision allemande ARD en même temps que paraissait un album illustré où Anton Zink met en vers les exploits du demi-dieu grec Hercule/Héraclès et ses douze travaux héroïques contés dans l'émission. (GER)

680

681

682

683

684

685

686

687

688

689

690

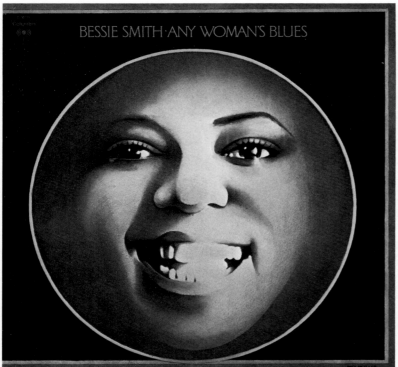

691

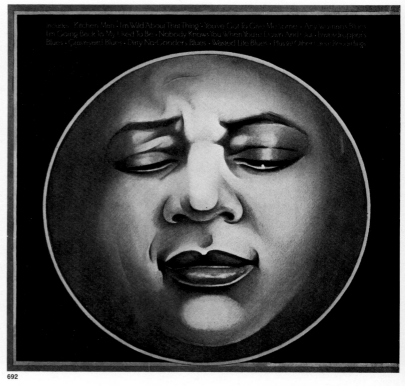

692

Record Covers
Schallplattenhüllen
Pochettes de disques

689 Schallplattenhülle für Aufnahmen des Country-Sängers und Gitarristen Stevie Ray Vaughan. (USA)
690 Vorderseite der Hülle für eine Schallplatte von Muddy Waters. Auf der Rückseite ist ebenfalls ein Porträt des Jazz-Musikers, dieses Mal mit breitem Lächeln. In Brauntönen mit Rosa. (USA)
691, 692 Vorder- und Rückseite einer Schallplattenhülle für Aufnahmen der Blues-Sängerin Bessie Smith. Jeweils schwarzer Hintergrund und gelb umrandeter Kreis; das Gesicht auf der Vorderseite vorwiegend in Violett-, auf der Rückseite in Türkistönen. (USA)
693 Hülle für eine Schallplatte mit einer Auswahl von Aufnahmen verschiedener Interpreten der populären Musikszene der 70er und 80er Jahre. (USA)

689 Record cover for an album by the guitarist and country singer Stevie Ray Vaughan. (USA)
690 Front of the cover of a record by Muddy Waters. On the back there is another portrait of the jazz musician—but with a broad smile. In shades of brown with pink. (USA)
691, 692 Front and back of a record-album cover for the blues singer Bessie Smith. Both illustrations are on a black background encircled with yellow; the face on the front is mainly in violet tones and on the back it is chiefly in turquoise shades. (USA)
693 Cover of an album containing a selection of various recordings by groups which were popular in the music scene of the seventies and eighties. (USA)

689 Pochette d'un disque du chanteur de country music et guitariste Stevie Ray Vaughan. (USA)
690 Recto de la pochette d'un disque de Muddy Waters. Le même portrait du jazzman se retrouve au verso, mais avec un grand sourire. Divers bruns, avec du rose. (USA)
691, 692 Recto et verso d'un disque de la chanteuse de blues Bessie Smith. Dans les deux cas, cercle jaune, fond noir. Le visage du recto de la pochette apparaît surtout en violet, celui du verso en turquoise. (USA)
693 Pochette d'un disque réunissant diverses vedettes de la chanson populaire des années 1970 et 1980, produit par CBS. (USA)

ARTIST / KÜNSTLER / ARTISTE:

689 Brad Holland
690–692 Philip Hays
693 Marshall Arisman

ART DIRECTOR / DIRECTEUR ARTISTIQUE:

689 John Berg / Allen Weinberg
693 Allen Weinberg

PUBLISHER / VERLEGER / EDITEUR:

689, 693 CBS Records
690 Blue Sky Records / CBS Inc.
691, 692 Columbia Records

693

694

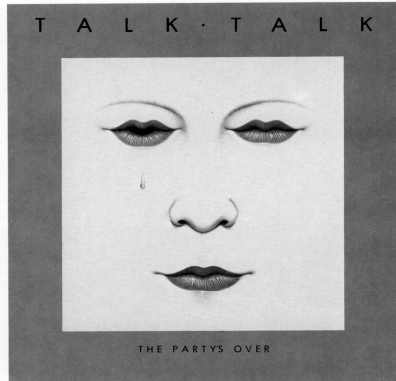

695

698

699

ARTIST / KÜNSTLER / ARTISTE:

694 Andy Post
695 James Marsh
696 Keijiro Ozumi
697 Martin Springett
698 Etienne Delessert
699 Robert Goldstrom
700 Elwood Smith
701 Holger Matthies

DESIGNER / GESTALTER / MAQUETTISTE:

694 Brian Boyd
695 James Marsh
696 Keijiro Ozumi
697 Martin Soldat
700 Paula Scher
701 Holger Matthies

ART DIRECTOR / DIRECTEUR ARTISTIQUE:

694 Brian Boyd
695 Keith Aspden
696 Keijiro Ozumi
697 Martin Soldat / Martin Springett
698 Etienne Delessert
699 Allen Weinberg
700 Paula Scher

AGENCY / AGENTUR / AGENCE – STUDIO:

694 Richards, Sullivan, Brock & Assoc.
698 Carabosse

PUBLISHER / VERLEGER / EDITEUR:

694 KVIL Radio Station
695 EMI Records
696 Spaniel Records
697 Anthem Records
698 Disques Mary-Josée
699, 700 CBS Records
701 Phonogram GmbH

696

697

700

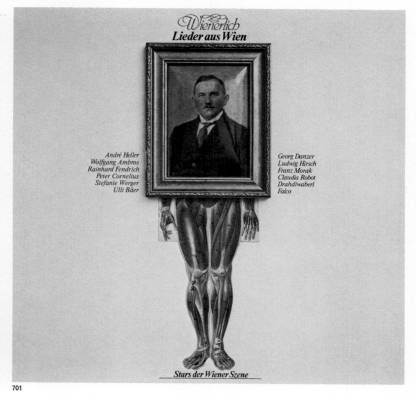

701

694 Cover of a Christmas album with new arrangements of "oldies", published by a radio station. (USA)
695 For the Talk Talk group's album, an allusion to the band's name and importance of lyrics. (GBR)
696 Cover of a *Spaniel* record. Yellow bulldog, blue title on black ground. (JPN)
697 Cover of an album by the group Coney Hatch. Blue and brown tones, yellow lettering. (CAN)
698 "The White Donkey", cover of a record of children's songs by Henri Dès. In full colour. (SWI)
699 Cover of the record by the group Blue Rose. (USA)
700 Full-colour album cover for a medley of previously-released "Beach Music" hits. (USA)
701 Cover of a record with satirical songs on Vienna, by various "Stars of the Vienna Scene". (GER)

694 Pour un disque de chants de Noël produit par une station de radio. (USA)
695 Pour un disque du groupe Talk Talk. Bouche rouge, deux yeux-bouches bleus. (GBR)
696 Pochette d'un disque *Spaniel*. Bouledogue jaune, titre bleu sur noir. (JPN)
697 Pochette d'un disque *Anthem* du groupe Coney Hatch. Divers bleus et bruns, texte en jaune. (CAN)
698 «L'âne blanc.» Pochette d'un disque de chansons enfantines par Henri Dès. Couleur. (SWI)
699 Pochette de disque pour un enregistrement du groupe Blue Rose (Rose bleue). (USA)
700 Pochette polychromie pour un disque réunissant des tubes qui ont trait à la plage. (USA)
701 Pochette d'un disque de chansons satiriques par diverses vedettes de la scène viennoise. (GER)

694 Für eine Schallplatte mit Weihnachtsweisen, herausgegeben von einem Radio-Sender. (USA)
695 Illustration mit Anspielung auf den Namen der Gruppe Talk Talk. Münder rot und blau. (GBR)
696 Hülle für eine *Spaniel*-Schallplatte. Gelbe Bulldogge, blauer Titel auf Schwarz. (JPN)
697 Schallplattenhülle für die Gruppe Coney Hatch. Blau- und Brauntöne, Schrift gelb. (CAN)
698 «Der weisse Esel.» Hülle für eine Platte mit Kinderliedern von Henri Dès. In Farbe. (SWI)
699 Hülle für eine Schallplatte der Gruppe Blue Rose (blaue Rose). (USA)
700 Mehrfarbige Hülle für eine Zusammenstellung von Hits, die sich auf den Strand beziehen. (USA)
701 Hülle für eine Schallplatte mit «wienerlichen» Liedern von Berühmtheiten der Wiener Szene. (GER)

Record Covers
Schallplattenhüllen
Pochettes de disques

Paper / Papier: Papierfabrik Biberist—Biber art paper, super white, glaced, 130 gm² and Biber Offset SK3, pure white, machine-finished, 140 gm² / Biber-Kunstdruck ultra weiss, glaciert, 130 gm² und Biber-Offset SK3, hochweiss, maschinenglatt, 140 gm²

Printed by / gedruckt von: Offset + Buchdruck AG, Staffelstrasse 12, CH-8021 Zürich

Typesetting / Lichtsatz: Sauerländer AG, Aarau (Univers, MONOTYPE-Lasercomp)

Binding / Einband: Buchbinderei Schumacher AG, Bern/Schmitten

Glossy lamination / Glanzfoliierung: Durolit AG, Pfäffikon SZ